EDWARD BURMAN
SUPREMELY ABOMINABLE
CRIMES: THE TRIAL OF THE
KNIGHTS TEMPLAR

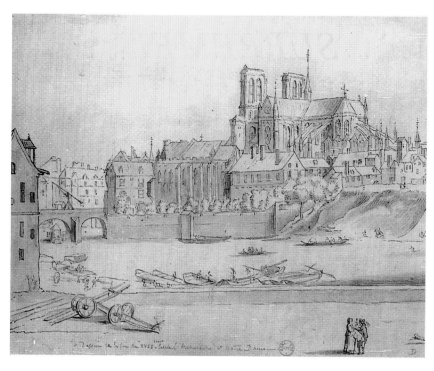

The Bishop's Palace by Notre Dame, showing his private chapel and garden where the Templars were interrogated (*Bibliothèque Nationale*)

SUPREMELY ABOMINABLE CRIMES: THE TRIAL OF THE KNIGHTS TEMPLAR

Edward Burman

ALLISON & BUSBY

First published in 1994 by Allison & Busby
an imprint of Wilson & Day Ltd
5 The Lodge
Richmond Way
London W12 8LW

Copyright © Edward Burman 1994

The moral right of the author has been asserted

ISBN 0 85031 928 5

Typeset by TW Typesetting, Plymouth, Devon
Printed and bound by
Mackays of Chatham Ltd, Lordswood, Chatham, Kent

CONTENTS

ACKNOWLEDGEMENTS

Grateful acknowledgement is made to The Boydell Press for permission to quote from J. M. Upton-Ward's convenient translation of Henri de Curzon's edition of the Templar *Rule: The Rule of the Templars: The French Text of the Rule of the Order of the Knights Templar* (1992). On a more personal level, I should like to thank Professor E. Garuti, Professor Emeritus of Latin Grammar, for help with some difficult passages in the text of the trial transcripts.

Finally, I should like to thank my old and dear Breton friend Jean-François Seguineau for helping me to obtain a copy of Michelet's edition of the transcripts: *Le Procès des Templiers*.

PREFACE

Everyone seems to have heard of the Templars and many have adapted the story to personal exigencies and whims, so much so that it is sometimes difficult to peer through the accretions of myth and legend, or to assess the historical circumstances in which the Order of the Temple flourished. But the trial – or, more correctly, the multiple trials – of the Templars, which may be said to have lasted from the arrest of the members of the Order in France in October 1307 to the death of the Grand Master in March 1314, generated a large quantity of documentary evidence which makes a closer focus possible. The published transcripts of these trials fill around 3,000 pages of often closely printed text, providing, amidst lengthy and often repetitive interrogations, a wealth of information and fascinating detail.

This is particularly true of the records of the two major phases of the trial in Paris. The first phase concerned the interrogation of 138 Templars by the inquisitor-general, Guillaume de Paris, which took place in the Paris Temple from 19 October to 24 November 1307, immediately after the arrest of all Templar brothers within the kingdom of France. The second and most important phase consisted of the hearings of a commission appointed by Pope Clement V, and took place mainly in the bishop's palace between 3 March and 30 May 1310. The records of these crucial proceedings, which consist of third-person transcripts of the court hearings recorded by official scribes, cover the heart of the trial of the Templars. The original confessions which served to bring the Order into disrepute are provided in the transcripts of the former; the most dramatic moment of the whole series of trials is rendered almost tangible by those of the latter. The Latin documents of both these phases of the trial were published by the great French historian Jules Michelet under the title *Le Procès des Templiers* in two now rare volumes in 1841 and 1851, comprising 1,151 pages in all. They were reprinted in an accessible paperback edition in 1987.

The heart of *Supremely Abominable Crimes* is a detailed account and interpretation of the events of the three-month session of the Paris trial which stunned contemporary observers during the spring of 1310. My belief is that a close reading of this brief but dramatic session is the key to understanding the whole affair of the Templars. The Paris trial documents provide the basic material for this reading, while published records of the other trials have been used for reference and elaboration. Major contemporary chronicles which refer to the Templar trial have been used to provide contemporary opinion and eyewitness detail: in particular the Latin chronicle of the monk of St Denis, Guillaume de Nangis, and his unknown continuator; the anonymous semi-official history of the Capetians known as *Les grandes chroniques de France*; the Italian *Croniche* of the Florentine historian Giovanni Villani; the *Excerpta* of the Benedictine monk Jean de Paris, from the Parisian monastery of Saint Victor; and the rhyming chronicle in Old French attributed to a contemporary royal clerk, anonymous but usually referred to as Geoffroi de Paris. The aim has been to create a readable narrative from this often dry and laconic evidence.

The main problem with a controversial, religious and political trial like that of the Templars is to assess the objectivity and truthfulness both of confessions of the accused and of statements by external observers or witnesses. The chroniclers, viewing the Templars from hostile environments such as the royal court or a rival monastic order, necessarily reflect both personal and institutional bias. Witnesses, as we shall see, often appeared in the hope of financial reward. While chroniclers wrote with an often identifiable bias, the Templars themselves spoke – as the trial records clearly show – under the influence of torture, atrocious prison conditions, bribery, fear of God and death, and also peer pressure in prison. But it would be unfeasible nearly 700 years later to examine each witness in terms of possible influence or bias, and then be certain that we were right: in the end, we have only the written records to analyse. In the absence of a perfect solution to this problem, I have attempted to accept the depositions and comments at face value, but never to overlook circumstances surrounding them.

The ghost of the Templars will never be laid. Legends about them continue to proliferate. For the figure of the white mantled knight bearing a red crusading cross – embodying the powerful and often conflicting tropes of monastic purity, blood, holy war, wealth, austerity, and heroic courage – has gathered layers of reference and meaning which make it one of the most potent symbols of European culture. Perhaps the most extraordinary fact about the Templars is that the legends and myths themselves were mainly generated by the trial, a short seven-year episode in their 200-year history. And the trial itself, trawled in continuation for hints and elaborated in the retelling, is cloaked by the aura of myth.

Suddenly, unannounced – so the story runs – on the cold morning of Friday 13 October 1307, the royal officers of King Philip IV of France arrested the members of the Order of the Temple in a simultaneous dawn raid throughout France. Arrests in other countries followed soon afterwards. The proud and heroic knights of the greatest of all crusading orders found themselves charged by the Inquisition with 127 accusations including the denial of Christ, God and the Virgin in secret ceremonies, spitting and urinating on the cross, giving obscene kisses, practising and encouraging sodomy, and indulging in idolatry – in particular, the worship of a mysterious head. Confessions obtained under torture provided evidence of these 'crimes' or 'heresies' and, five years later, the Order of the Temple was formally suppressed by Pope Clement V. This series of events concluded in spectacular fashion with the the burning at the stake of the Grand Master of the Temple, Jacques de Molay, on 18 March 1314. Already enveloped by flames, at the last instant he vehemently denied all charges made against him, asserted the innocence of the Order, and prophesied that God's vengeance would be done. The fact that Pope Clement died in April and Philip the Fair in November of the same year is taken to be the consequence of Jacques de Molay's 'curse' (further vindication was claimed in 1793, when, at the execution of Louis XVI, a French freemason is said to have professed vengeance for Jacques de Molay while dipping his hands in the dead king's blood).

Since the Grand Master's impressive death, the Templars have been drawn into all manner of conspiracy theories and what may be described as *perpetuation myths*, which involve the continuation of Templar rituals or secrets.

One recent version of the legend, *The Temple and the Lodge*, by Michael Baigent and Richard Leigh (1989), develops from the historically plausible fact that some surviving Templars fought against the English under Robert the Bruce at Bannockburn in June 1314 into the thesis that the Order of the Temple survived its formal abolition in clandestine form in Scotland. In thus delineating the origins of freemasonry through Templar survival in Scotland, they follow some masonic theories of the origin of the Hiramic myth, for example that of the Rev. W. W.

Covey-Crump in his book *The Hiramic Tradition* (1934). While an English Templar during the trial stated that English knights had fled to Scotland, here the principal weight is given to the hypothesis that a number of Templar ships sailed out of the Seine and north to Scotland. They are said to have headed first across the English Channel, then to have sailed west of Ireland via Limerick and Galway to avoid the fleet of King Edward II (which was patrolling the east of the Channel and the south of the Irish Sea). Lastly, they sailed from Lough Foyle across the short stretch of the North Channel of the Irish Sea into the Sound of Jura, between Islay and Kintyre.

Such an account is reminiscent of the tradition of a restoration of the Order of the Temple in Scotland maintained by the masonic rite known as the Strict Observance. This tradition holds that some Templars, commanded by a certain Pierre d'Aumont, otherwise unknown but described as the preceptor of Auvergne, escaped to Scotland via Ireland and established a revived order in which Pierre himself succeeded Jacques de Molay as Grand Master – thus creating an unbroken line of masters which continued in later centuries. According to Baigent and Leigh, this line returned to France with the intensely loyal and secretive Scots Guard (the 'Compagnie des Gendarmes Ecossois') formed as a royal bodyguard in 1445 by King Charles VII and thence went back into Scotland in the sixteenth century. It then links up with the academic consensus on the history of freemasonry epitomised by David Stevenson's *The Origins of Freemasonry: Scotland's Century, 1590–1710*.

In fact Baigent and Leigh's theory also splices neatly with the 'official' history of the origins of modern Freemasonry, though the evidence is no more than circumstantial. On this view, medieval elements of craft and legend were enriched by Renaissance ideas and incorporated into an institutional structure of lodges and rituals, and sometime around 1600 melded with the secret recognition procedures known as the Mason Word. It is generally accepted that this took place in Scotland in the 1590s, hence the interest in demonstrating the existence of a link between 1314 and 1590, and the general importance of the Templars in masonic orders, many of whose historians seek to prove a continuity with the medieval order. For instance, the additional masonic order known as the United Religious, Military, and Masonic Orders of the Temple and St John of Jerusalem has a degree known as the Knights Templar organised into preceptories; these knights wear a white tunic emblazoned with a red cross similar to that of the historical Templars. There is yet another masonic degree known as The Knight Templar Priests.

It was also in the late-sixteenth century that connections were made between the Templars, the Rosicrucians and the newly emerging Freemasonry. In the eighteenth century, French authors developed this link into fully fledged Masonic Templarism, in which the Templars were the key figures in a chain of anarchic conspirators which began with Manes, the founder of Manichaeanism, and passed through the Muslim sect of Assassins in medieval Persia and Syria. It was then the Templars who brought these ideas westward, together with the Cathars and Albigensians, where the conspiracy achieved its climax at the Bastille. Charles Louis Cadet de Grassincourt's *Le Tombeau de Jacques Molay ou le secret des conspirateurs, à ceux qui veulent tout savoir* (1796) and Augustin de Barruel's *Mémoires pour servir à l'histoire du Jacobinisme* (1797–8) developed these arguments most fully.

The Assassin link was reinforced and given greater credibility by the German orientalist Joseph von Hammer-Purgstall who, in his *The History of the Assassins* (English translation, 1835), discussed the tendency of secret societies 'to conceal mysteries in the veil of night', and explicitly linked the secret doctrines, dress and hierarchical system of the Templars with the esoterical doctrines of the Assassins. Hammer-Purgstall asserted that the historical founder of the Templars – Hugues de Payens – had established an alliance with the Assassins in Syria, and further confused the issue by referring seven times in the course of his book to the Assassin 'lodge' of Cairo.

Other threads enrich the tapestry. In another recent book, for example, *Born in Blood: The Lost Secrets of Freemasonry* (1989), by John J. Robinson, a fresh twist of the Templar perpetuation myth appears. Starting from the survival of the Templars in Scotland, Robinson goes on to argue that after a period of clandestine existence they emerged again as the organising body of the Peasants' Revolt of 1381. In his view, this body was the 'great society' which several rebel leaders claimed to represent, and also the force behind the Lollards, the English heretics who supported John Wycliff. The particular concern of the men led by Wat Tyler and Jack Straw to destroy Hospitaller properties is taken to be evidence of the Templars' revenge against the rival order which obtained much of their property after the abolition of 1312. In Masonic symbolism the Tyler is the 'sentry, sergeant-at-arms and enforcer' of the Lodge, so Wat Tyler would be a natural pseudonym for the leader of the rebellion. In this way Robinson seeks to demonstrate the origin of Freemasonry in the Knights Templar, for, in his words, the 'Great

Society' of the rebellion 'was the direct descendant of the Templar fugitives and the secret society of Freemasonry'. Then parallel to the Templar–Mason legends is another line of hypotheses which we might label the the 'Baphomet, Idol, and Grail' current.

One of the best-known recent books is Ian Wilson's *The Turin Shroud*, published in 1978 and still in print as a paperback. Departing from references to the idol supposedly worshipped by the Templars which appears in the trial documents, and mentions of the Order in medieval romances as guardians of the Holy Grail, Wilson argues in favour of Templar ownership of the shroud during the crucial 'missing years' between its disappearance during the sack of Constantinople in 1204 to its emergence from secrecy 150 years later in France. The well-known painting of Christ in the ex-Templar church at Templecombe in Somerset is taken to be a copy of the Turin Shroud, and thus presented as evidence that the original was indeed in the possession of the Templars. But the final link is tenuous: the shroud presently held in the cathedral at Turin made its first authenticated appearance in history in the village of Lirey, near Troyes, around 1356, in the possession of a knight called Geoffroi de Charny. This knight in the service of King Philip VI is assumed to be related to the Geoffroi de Charney, preceptor of the Temple in Normandy, who died at the stake in 1314 together with Jacques de Molay. Then, in a move which connects this work in the Grail tradition to the perpetuation myths, Wilson asserts that the second Geoffroi was attempting in the 1350s to revive the Templars under another name.

A more detailed genealogical argument along similar lines, identifying the Turin shroud both with the Holy Grail and with the idol said to have been worshipped by the Templars, appears in Noel Currer-Briggs' fascinating book *The Shroud and the Grail: a Modern Quest for the True Grail* (1987). He begins with two dense chapters in which he seeks to identify the Holy Grail as the lattice-work grill over a shallow casket which was used to contain the shroud, and then goes on to argue that the shroud was in turn identical to the idol which some Templar brothers testified they had seen during secret chapters of the Order. The original part of his complex argument is an attempt to demonstrate that the shroud left Constantinople with the Empress Mary-Margaret, daughter of King Bela III of Hungary and widow of the Byzantine Emperor Isaac II, after the sack in 1204, and then came to Europe after the 1229 crusade of the Emperor Frederick II (1194–1250) and was kept in Germany before being transferred to the Templars in the 1270s. According to Currer-Briggs, the Templars got wind of the imminent arrests and in the General Chapter held in July 1307 a plan was made for Gérard de Villiers, the preceptor for France, to flee Paris with the shroud and hide it in Burgundy – probably in the castle of Monfort – under the protection of Jean de Charny, who he claims was the brother of the Preceptor for Normandy and the father of the Geoffroi de Charny in whose possession the shroud later appeared.

More recently still Graham Hancock, in *The Sign and the Seal: A Quest for the Lost Ark of the Covenant* (1992), seeks to explain the historical enigma of the disappearance of the Ark of the Covenant, which the Israelites worshipped as the incarnation of God on earth, after the reign of King Solomon. Hancock also looks into the etymology of 'grail', but comes to the conclusion that this object may be identified with the Ark of the Covenant. Examining the tradition that King Menelik I of Ethiopia had taken the Ark from Jerusalem to his own country at the time of King Solomon, he suggests that the Templars later discovered information about the Ark or esoteric secrets connected with it – during excavations in their headquarters on the site of the Temple of Solomon – and that they therefore formed the missing link in the chain of transmission of secret architectural knowledge, and were thus the key to the sudden appearance of Gothic architecture around 1130. Then, in 1185, a contingent of knights is said to have travelled to Ethiopia with the exiled Prince Lalibela perhaps with the intention of capturing the Ark of the Covenant. So the Knights Templar are shown to provide the link between the Ark in Ethiopia and the grail tradition, which began around this date with Chrétien de Troyes' *Conte du Graal* and Wolfram von Eschenbach's *Parzival*.

Sooner or later then, as is made evident by this brief review of some books published in the past twenty years, the solution of many historical mysteries is achieved through research into the Templars, as can be seen most sensationally in the argument of such books as Baigent, Leigh and Lincoln's bestselling *The Holy Blood and the Holy Grail* (1982), in the historical survey of the myths presented by Peter Partner in *The Murdered Magicians* (1982), or in fictional terms in the plot of Umberto Eco's novel *Il Pendolo di Foucault* (1988).

Many other books have been written about the Templars (Dessubré's 1928 *Bibliographie* already counted about 1,200 items), and my personal debt should be clear both from references in the text and from the

Bibliography. The aim of this new addition to the list is twofold: first, to provide an accessible but solid narrative of the Parisian trial; and, second, to offer reflection on the provenance of myths and legends associated with the Templars by zooming on to a brief period of their existence. This means focusing on three vital and exciting months of their history out of nearly 200 years. But it is my view that concentrating on the Paris trial in this way, almost as we might read about a contemporary scandal in a news review, brings the tragedy of the Templars into fresh focus.

PART I

SUDDENLY AT DAWN, 13 OCTOBER 1307

1

THE ARREST OF THE TEMPLARS
IN FRANCE

The events of the early morning of Friday 13 October 1307 were such as to rock the delicate equilibrium of the medieval world and place a curse on that date – a superstition which persists to the present time. Contemporaries were well aware that the simultaneous arrest of the Knights Templar throughout France meant that King Philip IV had issued a double challenge to papal authority: first, by arresting members of a wealthy and powerful religious order directly responsible to the pope himself; and second, by imputing to them crimes of heresy which fell within the jurisdiction of the Church. The chronicler and canon regular of the royal abbey of Saint Victor, known as Jean de Paris or Jean de Saint Victor, expresses this sense of profound shock in his entry for that day when he writes that 'something astounding and unheard of since ancient times happened'.

Meticulous plans had been laid to ensure that the arrests would be a total surprise to the Templars. The *Arrest Order* was composed in the form of a letter in King Philip's name by the royal legal counsellor Guillaume de Nogaret and dated 14 September 1307. Although the king claims in the course of the letter to have 'spoken with our most holy father in the Lord, Clement' and to be acting 'at the request of' Guillaume de Paris, the inquisitor-general for France, it seems likely that neither of these men of the Church was party to the document that was drawn up in the seclusion of the monastery of Sainte Marie de Maubuisson, near Pontoise. The initiative came exclusively from the king of France, and the sequence of events demonstrates that Philip was preparing the stage with great care. A few days later, on 22 September, at the nearby abbey of Saint Martin de Pontoise, he appointed de Nogaret to the prestigious office of keeper of the royal seal. This elevation in dignity may be read partly as gratitude for the work already completed, and partly as a move to endow de Nogaret with the powers necessary to

3

influence the course of the rapid trial which the two of them believed
would follow the arrests.

Neither was Pontoise, thirty kilometres north-west of Paris on the road
to Rouen, a casual choice for opening the challenge. For, in 1244, Philip
the Fair's grandfather King Louis IX, better known as St Louis, had fallen
sick whilst staying at the same abbey and had made a solemn vow to God
to go on a crusade to the Holy Land if he survived. He eventually re-
covered, and five years later departed at the head of the Seventh Crusade.
Philip the Fair was devoted to the memory of his grandfather, and
throughout his life he consciously imitated the saintly crusading model.
Yet he himself never went on crusade since the early years of his reign were
devoted to consolidating his throne in France, and also because, after the
fall of Acre, the crusading venture began to lose impetus. As an ambitious
king descended from a great line of crusaders, including Louis VII, Philip
Augustus and his uncles, Count Robert of Artois and Count Charles I of
Anjou, however, he may have conceived the attack against the Order of
the Temple in terms of a personal crusade. To open the attack from a
place so intimately associated in his mind with St Louis was especially apt.

Surprise was all, and in this sense too no point of departure could have
been better than Saint Martin de Pontoise, which stood at a discreet
distance from the eager ears of court gossip. In fact the contemporary
chroniclers who recorded the event all stress the suddenness and unexpectedness of the arrests. The fundamental source, from which most later
versions derive, is the brief account composed by the anonymous continuator of the Latin *Chronicle* of Guillaume de Nangis, a monk at the
royal abbey of St Denis then just outside Paris. He describes the event
in these words:

> On the Friday after the feast of the Blessed Dionysius, the third day
> before the ides of October, all the Templars who were to be found
> within the kingdom of France, towards the same hour, that is when
> the sun began to shine or thereabouts, according to the royal decree
> and order were taken suddenly and sent to the various prisons.

It is this account which times the arrests precisely at dawn, and on Friday
13 October. For the feast day of St Dionysius – better known in his
French form as St Denis, martyr and the first bishop of Paris – falls on
9 October, which in 1307 was a Monday. The ides of October fell on the
Sunday 15. But it is also of particular interest for the emphasis which it
places on the 'suddenness' of the capture (in the Latin *subito capiantur*).

4

Other clerics and the people of Paris were as astounded as Jean de Saint Victor that the brothers of a powerful and honoured order could simply be clapped into irons in such an arbitrary fashion. Their perplexity was increased by the fact that at first there was no hint of the reasons behind the arrest. That secret too had been so well kept that even Bernard Gui, a Dominican like Guillaume de Paris and an experienced inquisitor who we might expect to have had access to more information, remarked in his chronicle *E Floribus Chronicorum* of the events of 13 October that 'the reason for such an unexpected capture was unknown except to a few secretaries and lawyers'.

Thus in a royal swoop unanimously perceived as sudden, unexpected, astounding and unheard of, the knights of a religious order which had come to symbolise in its white mantle and red cross the essence of medieval knighthood, which was said to possess 9,000 manors scattered throughout Europe, and which, owing to their efficiency and capillary structure, facilitated payments and tax collection, managed the royal treasuries of England and France, found themselves quite literally thrown from a position of wealth and power into stinking dungeons. But the charges and explanations of Philip the Fair's *Arrest Order*, which was itself an explosive document that shocked Christendom, were nothing compared to what was to emerge during the seven years of the trial following this arrest.

The *Arrest Order* consists of two distinct parts: the first part, which was written in Latin as though it were intended for the consumption of the clergy and potential critics from the world of scholars of canon law, explains the background in terms of heresy and seeks to justify the arrests. The rhetoric of the opening paragraph of the *Arrest Order* is still impressive today:

A bitter thing, a lamentable thing, a thing horrible to think of and terrible to hear, a detestable crime, an execrable evil deed, an abominable work, a detestable disgrace, a thing wholly inhuman, foreign to all humanity, has, thanks to the reports of several persons worthy of faith, reached our ears, not without striking us with great astonishment and causing us to tremble with violent horror, and, as we consider its gravity an immense pain rises in us, all the more cruelly because there is no doubt that the enormity of the crime overflows to the point of being an offence to the divine majesty, a shame for humanity, a pernicious example of evil and a universal scandal.

5

The Knights Templar are presented as wolves in sheep's clothing who have been guilty of 'astonishing bestiality' and 'supremely abominable crimes', and have had recourse to the 'sensuality of irrational beasts'. After receiving information about the Order from unnamed 'persons worthy of faith', the king claims to have discussed the matter both with Pope Clement V and with the French prelates and his own barons. Then, after an inquiry made by Guillaume de Paris and 'acquiescing in the demands of the said inquisitor' he had decided to arrest the brothers of the Order of the Temple in France: 'We have decreed that all members of the said Order within our realm will be arrested, without any exception, imprisoned and reserved for the judgments of the Church, and that all their moveable and unmoveable property will be seized, placed in our hands and faithfully preserved'.

The second part of the *Arrest Order*, which was written in Old French for the consumption of the less scholarly royal officials, provides practical instructions 'to the *Sénéschals* and *baillis*' of the kingdom of France on how to go about their preparation for the moment of arrest. The royal officials were to choose powerful and honest men 'free of suspicion' within their jurisdiction, in groups proportionate to the number of Templar properties, to assist them on the morning of 13 October. These 'prud'hommes du pays', as the document describes them, were to visit each place established by preliminary enquiries as belonging to the Templars, and to 'arrest the persons, seize their property and mount guard'; then, on the same day, they were to prepare an inventory of goods belonging to the Templar houses or granges where arrests had been made. In these tasks they would be accompanied by royal sergeants, whose duty would be to enforce obedience of the *Arrest Order* in the event of resistance. Once the Templars had been captured, the *sénéschals* and *baillis* were 'to put the persons in isolation under a good and secure guard, make a preliminary inquiry about them, and then call the inquisitor's assistants and examine the truth with care'. The 'truth' in question concerned the first and simplest version of the charges against the Templars, which were soon to be elaborated into the 127 articles of accusation. For the moment, the charges were subsumed in four main points: that the ceremony of reception into the Order of the Temple included a formal denial of Christ, and spitting on the cross; that the ceremony also included the 'obscene kiss'; that the brothers practised sodomy; and that the brothers worshipped an idol in the form of a man's head. The prisoners were to be questioned on the veracity of these practices, and depositions which were taken. These inquiries were to be carried out with due care, and 'with torture if it should be necessary . . .'.

Above all, these pragmatic instructions make it clear how much both secrecy in the weeks of preparation and success in the actual arrests on 13 October were dependent on the loyalty and efficiency of royal administration. For Philip the Fair ruled over a country whose bureaucratic organisation then brooked no rival.

In the first decade of the fourteenth century, the kingdom of France was divided for administrative purposes into twenty-three areas known as *bailliages* or *sénéchausées*. Each of these areas was presided over by a full-time royal official, who was usually known as a *bailli* in the north and a *sénéschal* in the south – although there were exceptions to this rule (the *bailli* was an innovation borrowed from Norman practice, and in England gave rise to the term 'bailiff'). These all-powerful salaried officials, appointed by King Philip himself and therefore the backbone of his administrative system, were responsible for the political, legislative, financial, judicial and military affairs under their jurisdiction. The system had been devised during the long reign of King Philip II, known as Philip Augustus (1180–1223), and was gradually improved until it reached its peak of efficiency with Philip the Fair and his sons.

In France proper, the 'domaine du roi' which represented the traditional heart of the Capetian kingdom, there were nine *bailliages*; in Normandy there were five *bailliages*; and in the lately acquired southern provinces there were seven *sénéchausées* and two *bailliages* (Auvergne and Montagnes d'Auvergne). In the northern French *bailliages* the *bailli* was assisted by a staff of *prévotés* or provosts, and in Normany by *viscomtés* or viscounts; in the southern *sénéchausées*, the *sénéschal* was assisted by a more complex mixture of *baillis*, *vigueries* or senior judges, provosts, and even – in Carcassonne – *châtellenies* or governors. In larger areas, and especially those furthest from Paris, there was a corresponding number of lesser officials. Thus the nearby *bailliage* of Sens had seventeen provosts, while the *sénéchausée* of Toulouse and l'Albigeois counted one *viguerie* and ninety-six *baillis*. Together these officials constituted a finely honed system of administration which the inflammatory rhetoric of Guillaume de Nogaret now set into motion against the Templars. For while the Templars were greater in number, the many commanderies and granges of France enjoyed more local autonomy than royal officials. Without advance notice, and in the absence of strong leadership, they were unable to coordinate any opposition or defence.

7

In fact there appears to have been little resistance from the 2,000 or so Templars thought by Pope Clement to have been in France at the time. For the element of surprise was almost total. Moreover, as the result of a series of coincidences, in early October 1307 the most senior officials of the Order were concentrated in Paris. This fact may have prompted King Philip to pounce when he did; certainly, it rendered any organised resistance in the distant provinces even more difficult. The preceptor of the important Templar region of Normandy, Geoffroi de Charney, and the preceptor of Aquitaine and Poitou, Geoffroi de Gonneville, were both captured in the Temple at Paris; as were the Grand Master of the Order, Jacques de Molay, the visitor-general, Hugues de Pairaud, and the equally important preceptor of Cyprus, Raimbaud de Caron. It appears that all were taken without the slightest hint of obstruction, a fact which in turn suggests a total lack of suspicion in the minds of the guards on duty and their immediate superiors. For, as we shall see, the Temple was a formidable fortress that even the royal troops available in Paris would have had difficulty in storming had the garrison chosen to resist. We may imagine verbal protests at the Temple gate, but then rapid aquiescence, since it would not have been unusual for royal officers to appear on legitimate business, especially a powerful figure such as Guillaume de Nogaret who, it seems, made the arrests in person. Indeed the chronicler Belleforest affirms that the king moved into the Temple on the day of the arrests in order 'to supervise the seizure of goods and documents'. This may simply be a reflection of contemporary beliefs about the royal need for money and his financial motivations in challenging the Order. But it might also mean that Philip the Fair himself was present at the moment of the arrests.

Some advance news did of course seep out. Fifteen days before the arrests were made at least one knight fled the Temple in Paris. Later a Templar serving-brother called Jean de Chalon testified during the trial that Gérard de Villiers, the preceptor of France, also managed to flee together with fifty horses and eighteen galleys. Moreover, Hugues de Pairaud appears to have got wind of the imminent arrests: he stated a week earlier that he would fight for his life if rumoured threats against the Temple should materialise. At the same time, however, two centuries of military power and financial prestige, the very physical strength of the Temple complex in Paris, and – above all – the protective umbrella of the Holy See, appear to have induced the Grand Master and other officials to believe that they were invulnerable.

Inevitably too in such a large operation, some brothers managed to avoid arrest on the morning of October 13. A typical example was the knight Pierre de Boucle, who was described during the trial as a *socius* or companion of Hugues de Pairaud. He might therefore have been fore-warned by the visitor-general, and thus succeeded in avoiding arrest. All to no avail, however, since he was recognised shortly afterwards, and captured in spite of having discarded the very visible Templar habit and mantle and shaving off his beard. The problem for such fugitives was quite simply where to run: deprived of their buildings and habit, Templars of long standing were like ducks out of water. Perhaps a score in the whole of France, some of them knights but mostly lower-ranking members of the Order, managed to emulate Gérard de Villiers. Twenty out of 2,000 is a tiny proportion, and even several of *these* were captured soon afterwards – often reduced to dire straits, as the trial transcripts show.

In fact, this proportion serves as eloquent testimony to the efficiency and honesty of the royal administration. At a rough count, at least 400 men throughout France must have known of the arrests weeks before they took place. The system of *baillis*, *sénéschals* and their assistants counted 333 men; and to them must be added royal lawyers who drew up the letter, scribes who made the copies, lesser royal officials, and some inquisitors. Given this high number, the slight leakage is really quite extraordinary. To all intents and purposes, surprise was total.

The most conclusive evidence of unexpectedness comes from the Grand Master himself. Given his recent defence of the Order of the Temple against a much-publicised project for union of the crusading orders, his certain awareness of criticisms of the Order, and his proximity to the royal court now that he was in Paris, Jacques de Molay if anyone should have picked up the signs of impending doom. But he carried on his official duties in sublime ignorance, perhaps betrayed by the apparent respect with which King Philip treated him. For on the very day before the arrests, the Grand Master was amongst high-ranking mourners at the funeral of the royal sister-in-law Catherine, wife to Philip's brother Charles de Valois. As befitted his power and dignity Jacques de Molay was accorded the honour of walking beside the pall and holding one of its cords. Flattered by this prominent role amidst the courtiers and barons of France, proud in his white mantle and red cross with an escort of Templar knights, how could the Grand Master have imagined that within twenty-four hours he would be chained and cast into a dungeon within his own fortress?

9

This episode also illustrates the almost diabolical planning and stealth of King Philip the Fair. With hindsight it is easy to observe that the odds were stacked against the Templars as soon as Philip decided to arrest them. As we shall see, it was generally accepted by contemporary chroniclers that the primary motive behind the royal attack was a desire to acquire the legendary wealth of the Temple. That alone, however, could never have been a sufficient justification, even for such a powerful man as the king of France, to move openly against a religious order. But in the wake of Catharism and other heresies which appeared to threaten the Church in the thirteenth century, the taint of practices associated with heresy and witchcraft *would* be seen by many – especially the recently founded Inquisition – as sufficient reason to bring a deviant Order to trial. Whatever its origins, so-called evidence against the Templars had been surfacing for some time. Perhaps it arose spontaneously; perhaps by design. We shall never know. Certainly, it was damning. And, as references in the *Arrest Order* show, it paved the way towards a formal indictment.

During the trial the preceptor of Payns, a certain Ponsard de Gizy, was to name four 'traitors' who had enabled Philip the Fair to initiate the proceedings. To one of these four in particular historians have assigned the primary role, namely the elusive and ambiguous Esquin de Floyran of Béziers, himself a Templar and prior of Montfaucon in the diocese of Toulouse. His part is beyond doubt since, in a letter to King Jaimé II of Aragon three months after the arrests, he introduces himself in Malcolm Barber's translation of the letter as 'the man who has shown the deeds of the Templars to the Lord King of France'. It appears that he had first attempted to sell his story, as it were, for a large sum of money and rents, to King Jaime during an audience in Lerida as early as 1305. Then, with greater success, although no trace of financial transactions survives, he managed to contact Guillaume de Nogaret and ultimately King Philip the Fair. The Florentine chronicler Giovani Villani – in an account probably tinged as much by Parisian gossip as fact – describes Esquin as a 'criminal and heretic' who sought to save himself from imprisonment and an imminent death sentence by offering his information to the king (Villani also rather melodramatically notes that Esquin soon afterwards died 'by the knife'). Certainly the former prior was ruthless and ambitious: his ruthlessness is suggested by Ponsard de Gizy's assertion in his testimony of November 1309 that Esquin was one of the official torturers of his fellow Templars in Paris. His ambition was also gratified. In spite of

Villani's insinuations, after the suppression of the Order it seems that he came into the possession of former Templar lands. Is this one of the men described by King Philip in the *Arrest Order* as 'worthy of faith'? Whatever the answer to this question, in the autumn of 1307 the accusations made by Esquin de Floyran were of great value to King Philip as he sought a means to lay siege to the Templars. According to the royal lawyer Guillaume de Plaisians, it was as the result of these accusations that twelve spies were sent to infiltrate the Order of the Temple throughout France. Naturally, they soon found the confirmation they sought.

Once formal support for the allegations made by the traitors was obtained, the full weight and efficiency of the royal administration was thrown against the Templars under the guiding hand of the newly promoted Guillaume de Nogaret.

Yet this efficiency only applied to the kingdom of France. Elsewhere in Europe – in Spain, Portugal, England, Germany, and Italy (with the exception of the kingdom of Naples, which was ruled by Charles d'Anjou, an uncle to Philip IV) – the arrests were not made immediately. Members of the Order had time to evacuate their commanderies and preceptories, and to disappear even before the local arrests and trials began. Thousands were never brought to trial.

One of the most plausible estimates of Templar numbers prior to the trial remains that of the American historian Henry Charles Lea who, in his *History of the Inquisition in the Middle Ages* (1908), suggests a total of some 15,000 members of the Order. Given Lea's ratio of one knight to ten brothers (sergeant-brothers, priests, servants, agricultural workers, etc.), this implies around 1,500 knights. In fact, such a ratio tallies closely with information gleaned from the trial transcripts: at the preliminary interrogations carried out by Guillaume de Paris and the Inquisition in Paris shortly after the arrests, there were fifteen knights from a total of 138 prisoners (of the others, seventeen were priests and perhaps as many as forty-one were sergeant-brothers). It also sounds plausible in the light of the few hundred knights known to have been present in the Holy Land at most times, and the total number of deaths in action over 200 years which a witness during the trial placed at 20,000. Furthermore, where details of the manpower of individual Templar houses is available, this ratio also appears to be about right: at Beaucaire (Gard), for example, there were five knights, one priest and fifty-four serving brothers; at Château d'Alais, there were four knights, one priest and twenty-eight serving-brothers. It also tallies with the 9,000 manors the chronicler Matthew Paris ascribed to the Templars in his *English History*, bearing in mind that many of these properties were agricultural and never had more than a handful of men present.

Now, according to the chronology established by Anne Gilmour-Bryson in her *Trial of the Templars in the Papal State and the Abruzzi* (1982), the total count of Templars brought to court in the thirty-two trials or councils held between 1307 and 1311 runs to 1,151 (although some of these may have been counted more than once). Of this number, only sixty-nine are recorded as having been burned at the stake. Others served prison sentences of varying length, often in fact living in relative freedom on Templar (or ex-Templar) estates. This leaves, at a very conservative estimate, 1,086 Templar survivors even amongst those arrested. Few of them seem to have endured long prison sentences, while evidence in the later stages of the trial indicates that most were absolved of their crimes and reconciled to the Church well before 1314. We can immediately see that there is no need to invent elaborate stories of Templars escaping from the dungeons of Paris or eluding the stake in order to account for the perpetuation of the Templar ethos. If a figure anywhere near Lea's estimate of a total number of 15,000 is accepted, it means that at least 14,000 Templars – including 1,000 or so knights – went totally free. For the fact is that outside the kingdom of France the Templars were not treated with the zeal which Philip the Fair instilled in his own officials.

In England, for instance, King Edward II simply refused to accept that there was any truth in the charges when he was first informed of them. Curiously, the news was taken to him by Bernard Pelet, prior of Mas d'Agenais in Lot et Garonne, who was one of the four 'traitors' later named by Ponsard de Gizy. It is interesting to speculate whether this shadowy character's role in the affair was known in advance to King Edward, who was certainly well informed about events in France. In fact, it was only when the information conveyed by Prior Bernard was bolstered by a papal bull in December 1307 that Edward II also made out an order to his officials throughout the kingdom to arrest the Templars. Even then, however, the instructions were carried out with no particular zeal, and with no apparent interest on the part of the king. What appears to have been a desultory process resulted in a relatively small number of arrests in England between 9 and 11 January 1308, and in Ireland on 8 February. By then, of course, many Templars would have been able to evacuate their properties. Moreover, even for those who *were* arrested,

12

vigilance was slack and prison conditions relatively good. Most of the Templars were held in the main castle of the county in which they were captured. They were also provided with a daily allowance of fourpence for each man, to be paid for from revenue of their own lands. High officials were given even better treatment: William de la More, the Templar Master of England, received a daily allowance of 2s 6d and was allowed to leave his prison in Canterbury Castle during the day. He was released from prison altogether in the summer of 1308.

In the Papal State and the Abruzzi the trial did not even begin until the autumn of 1309, exactly two years after the initial arrests had been made in Paris. Inquisitors and notaries travelled throughout these two regions between September 1309 and July 1310. Within the papal states trials were held at Rome, Viterbo, Tivoli, Segni, Castel Fajola, Albano, Assisi and Gubbio; in the Abruzzi at L'Aquila, Penne and Chieti. There were important Templar houses in Italy (at least thirty in Central Italy are mentioned in the trial documents), and ports for the East such as Brindisi. On the Italian peninsula the Templars were administered by a preceptor for Lombardy who controlled central and northern Italy, and a preceptor for Apulia who controlled the Abruzzi, Apulia and Sicily. Total numbers must have run into the hundreds. But with two years of grace between an *Arrest Order* that was barely heeded and the opening of the trial, any man worth his salt had ample time to escape. Results were out of all reasonable proportion to the effort expended: in ten months of travel and painstaking work, twenty-three inquisitors and thirteen notaries managed to try one Templar chaplain-brother and six serving-brothers.

Thus beyond the kingdom of France, few confessed, fewer still were condemned, and none was executed; many were absolved and reconciled to the Church; others joined rival religious orders, continued to live undisturbed on Templar estates, or simply vanished from historical record.

Within France, imprisonment was harsh. As later testimony shows, even the highest ranking Templars were denied decent prison conditions. Following a strict interpretation of the terms of the *Arrest Order*, they were to be kept in isolation under a 'good and secure guard' until they could be questioned by the Inquisitor's commissioners. Confession was paramount, and all means justified in the attempt to obtain it. Prisoners were told in no uncertain terms that the pope and king had been informed of the practices of heresy and sodomy during the initiation ceremony, and that they should confess and return to the faith of the

Church in order to receive a full pardon. 'Otherwise', the instructions continued, 'they will be condemned to death.' We can only imagine the combined effect of such sudden arrest, harsh living conditions in chains on a bread-and-water diet, often total isolation, immediate confrontation by severe inquisitors skilled in the art of interrogation, repeated torture, and frequent threats of death. Some evidence of this emerges during the trial. A written complaint addressed to the doctors and scholars of Paris three months later, for example, refers to the indescribable pains and multiple tortures that the writer had endured in that period.

But this should not shock. For the whole procedure was designed to strike terror into Templar hearts.

2

THE DEFENDANTS

Who were these 2,000 brothers of the Order of the Temple that now found themselves in the dungeons of King Philip IV?

Like many great men and institutions, the Templars nurtured an enhanced view of their own past. They propagated myths of self-aggrandisement, and smoothed over the many episodes of failure in their history. A study of Templar perceptions of the past as they appear in the trial documents shows that living members of the Order in the period from 1307 to 1310 fostered misconceptions and confusion as much as future historians. The common memory was surprisingly short, a fact which prompts the further question: what exactly did the Templars themselves think about the origin, function, history and achievements of their own Order?

One feature of the collective testimony is that recorded memories of the origin of the Order are few and vague. On the afternoon of Friday 3 April 1310, for example, a group of eleven Templar brothers declared to papal notaries in Paris during the course of their defence that 'the religion of the Temple was made and founded in the name of God and the Holy Mary, and was established by monsignor St Bernard and several men of honour, and was confirmed as ours by the pope of that time and reconfirmed by other popes in later years' (it is curious that the expression translated here as 'several men of honour' – *pluseus prudomes* – is the same as that used in the *Arrest Order* for the local men to be charged by the *baillis* and *sénéschals* with the arrests). In the same week another brother, Elias Aymerici, also affirmed that the Order was 'made and founded (*facta et fundata*) by the Blessed Bernard'. Even a more learned witness, Pierre de Bologna, a university-trained lawyer and once the official representative of the Templars at the papal curia in Rome, affirmed just over a month later that the Order was founded for 'the expulsion of the enemies of the cross, that is to say infidels, pagans and saracens wherever they may be, and especially in the holy land of Jerusalem'.

15

In fact, as we shall see, the *Rule*, the monastic code of discipline for duties and conduct, approved by and perhaps written by St Bernard in 1128, itself refers to the foundation of the Order a decade earlier, with the quite different scope of protecting pilgrims in the Holy Land on their way to Jerusalem. The *Rule*, which was re-elaborated almost up to the Order's demise, provides often tantalising clues to their role in the East in later years. Read in isolation, the recurring place names in the text emphasise the importance which the Templars themselves attributed to battle and reverberate like a litany of crusading venture: Saphet, Acre, Beirut, Antioch, Tripoli, Château Blanc, Castle Pilgrim, Caesarea, Tortosa, Jaffa. But of the original purpose of the Order there is little trace.

Most of the precise memories in the *Rule* are of recent events. One of the few references to the situation in the early years appears in #40, which states that knight brothers 'should not presume to go out into the town or city without the permission of the Master' except 'at night to the Sepulchre and the places of prayer which lie within the walls of the city of Jerusalem'. This regulation comes from the original seventy-six paragraphs drawn up with the approval of St Bernard and known as the *Primitive Rule*; but the reference to entering Jerusalem also places it before the loss of that city to Saladin in 1187. Successive sections clearly refer to a quite different everyday reality. Already #77 prescribes that the Master of the Order was to have a 'Saracen scribe' as interpreter, while another later function of the Templars in the Holy Land with their increased wealth and power surfaces in the mention in #119 of a shipyard at Acre. But references to specific events all come from the period of fifty years before the arrests. In #569 we read of a certain 'Brother Roger the German' being compelled to deny his Order and take the oath of the Saracens, and six paragraphs later of contact with the Tartars. This datable reference to the well-known Tartar invasion of 1257 was within living memory for the oldest of the brothers in 1307. But curiously there is little evidence of the life and activities of the Order in the 140 years of its existence before the appearance of the Tartars in Europe.

It is as if the Templars themselves had little knowledge of their past, especially of a kind of 'middle age' between the intervention of St Bernard and the 1250s.

One reason for this may be the fact that, apart from the obvious categories of priests, lawyers, scribes and interpreters, most Templars – including the knights – appear to have been illiterate. The Order of the Temple was founded by a group of nine noble knights and, in the beginning, was imbued with the ideals and convictions of the knightly class of Burgundy – where each of the nine had been born. But in the twelfth and thirteenth centuries, such men were not renowned for their literacy. Moreover, as the Order expanded, the knights became a small minority of the total number of Templars, with a hierarchical structure parallel to that of feudal society in the lay world. Most Templars – serving-brothers, servants and agricultural brothers – were certain to lack any formal education. Indeed illiteracy is often put forward during the trial as an excuse for being unable to provide a defence. One curious testimony before the second hearing of the papal commission, on Monday 9 February 1310, provides a stunning example: the serving-brother Vernondus de Santoni, on being asked by the commissioners if he wished to defend the Order, stated that he did not even understand the meaning of the word 'defend'. In spite of evidence to the contrary, even the last Grand Master describes himself in his second deposition as a 'poor and illiterate knight' (*miles illitteratus et pauper*), who is for this reason unable to provide detailed testimony for the papal commission charged with interrogating the Templars. While in the case of Jacques de Molay this may have been a tactic or an affectation, widespread illiteracy meant that the history, legends and regulations of the Order were transmitted orally, with all the possible consequences of error and a gradual fading of more distant events in the repeated telling. In the formal third-person transcription De Molay seeks to exculpate his Order by vague assertions that '. . . he knew of no other order or no other persons who more readily exposed themselves to death or shed blood in the defence of the Christian faith against its enemies . . .'. Yet no details are forthcoming. In 1307 the real past of the Templars, and the true story of their foundation, were hazy even to him.

This presents us with a curious paradox since, from external evidence, it is clear that the renown of the Templars as a fighting force derived from the rapid expansion and military successes of the twelfth century. Odo of Deuil, the official chronicler to King Louis VII of France on the Second Crusade, which departed in 1146, tells us how during the overland journey to the Holy Land the discipline of the Templars was held up as a model by the king. The consequence of this admiration was that when Louis' army marched south from Constantinople to Antioch it was effectively under Templar command. From then on, Templar contingents were often used in the rearguard of crusading armies. For their sense of discipline rendered them immune to Saracen sniping and harassment techniques, whereas ordinary soldiers tended to flee in the face of these

17

Eastern tactics. In the kingdom of Jerusalem they were assigned the vital southern frontier fortress of Gaza, which was regularly harassed by horsemen from Muslim-held Ascalon, and they held it with striking valour. This was especially true in 1177, when the Templars at Gaza made a vital contribution to the only significant crusading victory over Saladin, at Mont Gisard. The myth of the warrior-monk found resonance in reality: Jacques de Vitry, bishop of Acre, described the Templars as 'lions in war, and gentle as lambs at home' and observed that 'in the field they were harsh soldiers, in church they were like hermits or monks'; an anonymous pilgrim wrote that 'in going into battle they are the first, in returning the last', and relates how they fought in silence and then burst into song at the moment of victory with the *Non Nobis Domine*. Their courage was even acknowledged by Muslim chroniclers: Ibn-Alathir referred to Saladin's 1187 victory over the crusaders at the battle of Safouriyad as 'a signal victory for the Muslims, because the Templars and Hospitallers were, so to speak, the fiery heart of the Franks'. An older crusading order like that of the Hospital of St John changed its original activities to follow the path of success of the Templars. Entirely new orders, those of Santiago and Alcantara, were founded in Spain to imitate the Templars, after their notable role in the *reconquista* of Muslim territories within the kingdom of Castile. The white mantle and red cross was already then, at the end of the twelfth century, a symbol of heroism, courage, and knightly valour. But of all this, which might have been useful in defending the Order, there is virtually no trace in the trial transcripts.

The military victories and glory of the twelfth century brought material wealth through booty, acquisitions, and donations. The German pilgrim Theoderich, who visited the Templar quarters in Jerusalem around 1172, describes a 'wondrous and intricate building resting on piers and containing an endless complication of arches and vaults, which stable, we declare according to our reckoning, could take in ten thousand horses with their grooms', a magnificent palace equipped with gardens, courtyards, antechambers, vestibule, rain-water cisterns, baths, granaries, and a new cloister. 'No man', Theoderich continues with an evocative image, 'could send an arrow from one end of their building to the other, either lengthways or crossways, at one shot with a Balearic bow.' This description represents the Order of the Temple at the height of its wealth and power.

But at the opening of the Paris trial in 1307 the perceptions and memories of the Templar brothers are mainly those of loss, death and defeat. The patina of ancient prestige survived; but beneath it the mental set of the Templars was essentially negative. For it is one of the strangest truths during the defence of the Templars that there appears to be no collective knowledge of successes beyond living memory. The battles that are mentioned, or recalled to illustrate the nobility of the Order, range from the disastrous failure at Mansourah in 1250 to the loss of Acre in 1291. Jacques de Molay himself recalls an incident soon after his recruitment as a knight, when in his own words he was 'young and eager for battle', in the service of the then Grand Master Guillaume de Beaujeu (1273–91), and then refers to Mansourah. When the knight Jean de Montreal – one of the few defendants to bring past victories into his defence – speaks of Templar activities over the seas 'in the past . . . in the days of King Louis, and of the king of England', he too is referring to the Seventh Crusade which disintegrated at Mansourah, and to the unsuccessful crusade upon which Edward embarked in 1272. Perhaps the most common reference is to the defence of Acre, a recent thorn in the Templar conscience, where three hundred knights died together with Guillaume de Beaujeu. Although the Templars fought bravely in these actions, in terms of the crusading venture they must be counted as dramatic failures with huge losses of life.

These curious blanks in the collective memory prompt a further question: was the reason that they did not cite the great victories of the past in order to defend their reputation simply that they had forgotten them?

The written evidence was of course in their own possession, for those who could read. From the first eight paragraphs of the *Rule* itself, from the letters and documents listed in the *Cartulary* of the Order, the official record of documents and letters belonging to the Order, from papal documents and bulls, and from chronicles concerning their own history which it is reasonable to suppose such a great monastic order possessed, together with other documents and letters in their archives, it would have been possible to compile a more appropriate version of events to present in the trial. It might of course be objected that the written material was not available in prison, but in an age in which the art of memory was an important aspect of formal education this should not have been an unsurmountable obstacle. For, as we shall see, several learned Templars did come forward in the course of the seven-year trial.

The *Cartulary* opens with a letter from King Baldwin II of Jerusalem to Abbot Bernard of Clairvaux commending two brother knights, and

19

soliciting the powerful abbot's intercession in their favour with the pope. The king explains that 'the Templar brothers, whom God has raised up for the defence of our province and to whom he has accorded special protection, desire to obtain apostolic approval and also a *Rule* to govern their lives'. But by that time the Templars had already existed as a recognised body of men for several years, their name deriving from the fact that King Baldwin himself had allocated them quarters 'on the north side of the Temple of the Lord'. A document of 1124 already mentions Templar rights beyond the Holy Land, in Marseille, and in 1125 the founder Hugues de Payen is referred to in a grant made by the Patriarch of Jerusalem as *magister Templi*. Then the next year the same Hugues set off from Jerusalem with a twin purpose: to recruit new knights to join the original nine, and to obtain papal approval with the aid of Bernard of Clairvaux. The fact that Hugues de Payens was a relative of Abbot Bernard, and another founder member, André de Montbard, was the abbot's uncle, facilitated his mission.

The abbot lost no time. He convened the Council of Troyes to open early in 1128 with the express purpose of obtaining papal approval for the pre-existing Order. The scribe of the primitive *Rule*, a certain Jean Michel, who names himself in #5, provides a brief account of the event.

> Then we, in all joy and all brotherhood, at the request of Master Hugues de Payens, by whom the aforementioned knighthood was founded by the grace of the Holy Spirit, assembled at Troyes from divers provinces beyond the mountains on the feast of my lord Hilary [i.e. 13 January], in the year of the incarnation of Jesus Christ 1128, in the ninth year after the founding of the aforesaid knighthood.

It was at this council that the regulations concerning Templar dress were formulated, stating that 'all the brothers' habits should always be of one colour, that is white or black or brown' (#17). But far more important for the future direction of Templar activity was the subtle definition of the concept of warrior-monk.

Some precedent existed. The reforming pope Gregory VII (1073–85) had already argued that since the interests of the Church were always to take precedence, so a knight's loyalty to his king or feudal lord was always to be overruled by his loyalty to the Church. For all knights were in the first instance vassals of St Peter. This was not a trivial point of theory. Indeed, without Pope Gregory's idea of offering the remission of sins as just reward for fighting as a *milites Christi*, or soldier of Christ, the First Crusade launched just fourteen years after his death might never have got off the ground. For the move from the simple remission of sins to a fully fledged crusading indulgence, and the promise of martyrdom in the event of death during an overseas campaign in the name of the Cross, was a simple one.

Bernard of Clairvaux's elaboration of the basic concept of *milites Christi* for the Templars was a masterpiece of sophistication. Moreover, it arrived at exactly the right moment, since evidence suggests that the initial enthusiasm which led to the creation of the Order of the Temple was on the wane. In a letter written from France to his brethren in Jerusalem, Hugues de Payen lists the doubts and temptations which the early Templars suffered, and attempts to encourage them in his absence. He works through the problems of the knights in scholastic fashion, setting up the fears and objections and then seeking to demolish them. In the present context, one section of this letter is of particular interest. He first observes that complaints against the Order often concern its military nature, and then replies by asserting that the basic purpose of the Templars is religious: for this reason, the brothers may consider themselves as performing primarily a religious function, and only in the second place a military one. Yet doubts persisted in spite of this persuasive argument, for when Abbot Bernard came to write the short book entitled *In Praise of the New Knighthood* (*Liber ad Milites Templi De Laude Novae Militiae*), in 1135, he addressed Hugues de Payen in the following words: 'Once, twice, three times, if I am not mistaken dearest Hugh, you have asked me to write some words of encouragement to you and your fellow knights, so that, as a result of my status, while I cannot use the lance against the tyranny of our enemies, I can at least take up my pen . . .'.

Seldom can the pen have been imbued with such power. For the thirty or so pages of this little masterpiece of propaganda constitute a carefully reasoned and authoritative justification for the taking of human life in the name of Christ – that is to say, it legitimised for the next century the *raison d'être* of the Knights Templar.

The first problem for Abbot Bernard was to resolve the moral discrepancy between the monastic ideal and the practical requirement for the 'knights of Christ' to kill Muslims in battle. This he does by first asserting that the knight who fights in the name of Christ need have no fear at all:

neither of losing his own life, nor of committing sin in taking the life of an adversary. The next step is to argue that this is more than a merely negative virtue. The killing of infidels actually merits reward and represents a way of attaining Christ, since the soldier of Christ 'is the instrument of God for the punishment of evildoers and for the defence of the just'. From this position it is a simple step to the most notorious assertion of the book: 'In fact, when he kills evildoers *it is not homicide, but malicide*, and he is to be considered as Christ's legal executioner'. Here, surely, is the most magnificent historical version of a licence to kill!

In fact it was so effective that St Bernard's pamphlet was regularly published and translated for the use of soldiers of the papal army, right up to the second half of the nineteenth century. In 1135, with the spiritual backing of perhaps the most influential man in Christendom, it placed Hugues de Payen's nascent crusading order beyond official reproach for the next 172 years. At the time no recorded objections were made to the ambiguous religio-military nature of the Order of the Temple. Perhaps, then, in a sense the later Templars were right to perceive their Order as *facta et fundata* by St Bernard, since he provided the twin impetus – and patronage – which enabled it to expand rapidly in a new form and with a new *raison d'être* after the 1130s: the *Primitive Rule*, and the *De Laude*. With the privileges accorded them in successive decades, and the red cross granted by Pope Eugenius III in 1147, the Knights Templar had in fact become a very new type of warrior-monk.

Yet that was not the original purpose of Hugues de Payen and King Baldwin II. Moreover, from the perspective of 1307, loss of sight of this original scope of the foundation of the Temple could be seen as just one more manifestation of the overbearing pride of the Templars which offended so many contemporaries. What was this purpose?

A few years after the 'foundation' the chronicler known as Michael the Syrian, patriarch of the Syriac Church at Antioch, wrote under the title *Histoire des Phrers Francs* of a Frenchman who came to the Holy Land on pilgrimage, took holy orders, and then decided to stay in Jerusalem for the rest of his life. This man, whom we may identify with Hugues de Payen, was advised by King Baldwin not to take holy orders but to serve in the militia which safeguarded Jerusalem and the sacred places. In his own words, 'to work towards saving his soul, and to protect those places against thieves'. It is likely that Hugues and his original companions were first regarded as a kind of Third Order attached to the Canons Regular

22

of the Holy Sepulchre, the Augustinians, for Archbishop William of Tyre reminds us in the account of the Templar foundation in his *History of Deeds Done Beyond the Sea* that 'nine years after the founding of this order the knights were still in secular garb'. He also substantiates Michael the Syrian's account in stating that the main duty of the original Templars was 'that, as far as their strength permitted, they should keep the roads and highways safe from the menace of robbers and highwaymen, with especial regard to the protection of pilgrims'. Since those early days, to use Jacques de Molay's picturesque turn of phrase, the Templars had 'dreamed of pilgrims as a mother dreams of her children'.

In this context, 'dream' is a fitting term. When, in 1187, less than a century after the Christian conquest, the holy city of Jerusalem was lost to the great Muslim leader Saladin, the very idea of reconquering the holy city was as much a dream as a realistic prospect. Moreover, the apparently innocuous and self-explanatory concept of 'pilgrim' was soon overlaid with ambiguous meanings. For pilgrimage was considered not only in the modern sense of an 'act of religious devotion' (*COED*), but also in terms of penance undergone to obtain absolution from sin. Hence the later systematic use of minor and major, or local and more distant, pilgrimages on a sliding scale in proportion to sins confessed (for example, the inquisitor Bernard Gui in Toulouse considered minor pilgrimages those to churches in Carcassonne, Albi and Palmiers, and major pilgrimages those to Rome, Compostella and Canterbury). But the indulgences granted to crusaders rendered these armed knights a special category of pilgrim, and henceforth crusade could be defined as an *armed pilgrimage*. In fact, in the twelfth century the 'crusades' were referred to as 'pilgrimages'. The French chronicler Villehardouin, for instance, in his celebrated account of the Fourth Crusade, *The Conquest of Constantinople*, uses the term 'pilgrim' where a later writer would have used 'crusader'. Only in the following century did the Latin term crusader come into use.

The Order of the Temple followed this usage, and thrived under the umbrella of ambiguity which 'dreaming of pilgrims' offered. The produce of the 9,000 manors in Europe of which the later chronicler Matthew Paris writes, the financial operations, the farming and husbandry, the land reclamation, the fleet and shipyards, the commanderies and houses along the major routes from north-west Europe to the Holy Land, and the hierarchical organisation, were all conceived originally for the primary purpose of protecting pilgrims. Banking operations such as transmittal of money, payments of pensions at a distance, loans and advances, and deposits were initially developed to serve pilgrims (although they were soon honed to provide financial services for the English and French thrones, and tax collection for the Holy See). All became vital instruments of the rise to military power.

Papal privileges to sustain the Order, once again under the impulse of St Bernard, came thick and fast. Already in 1139 Pope Innocent II could write in his bull *Omne datum optimum* (from the opening words 'Every best gift and every perfect gift is from above . . .') that 'your Order and venerable institution is famous throughout the whole world'. The Templar ethos that was maintained intact until the fall of Acre emerges from the well-chosen phrases of this momentous papal bull: 'you have most conscientiously sworn on your breasts the sign of the living cross, because you are especially reckoned to be members of the knighthood of God'; the Templars are 'warriors most versed in holy battle', 'on fire with the flame of true charity', and 'defenders of the Church and assailants of the enemies of Christ', and are charged with the duty 'to rid that part of the Church which is under the tyranny of the pagans from their filth'. That this bull, ostensibly to create a new category of chaplain-brothers for the Templars, was extremely personal and friendly in its terms is shown by the introduction in which the pope presents himself as 'Bishop Innocent, to our dear son Robert, Master of the knights of the Temple'.

The consequences of *Omne datum optimum* were of crucial importance in terms of the later Temple trial, and were the legal source of the Pope Clement V's jurisdiction over the Temple, since this bull freed the Templars of all ecclesiastical authority save that of the pope himself. It states quite explicitly that the House of the Templars would thenceforth be under the tutelage and protection of the Holy See, and that the newly created chaplain-brothers would be free from all diocesan control and responsible only to the Grand Master of the Temple. Furthermore, the bull gave the Templars the right to construct their own churches without the need to obtain episcopal approval. These freedoms and rights developed into a major bone of contention with local bishops, for, together with the secrecy of the Order, it effectively allowed for the existence of a parallel religious organisation beyond diocesan control. In fact, in the full list of accusations against the Templars drawn up in August 1308 the right for the Master to absolve fellow brothers of their sins was a prominent feature. From a logical point of view, it left the way open for the Templars to commit any form of heretical act within the ample cloak of

24

the Order, and then to be absolved by their own Master. This in turn meant that the purity of the entire Order was dependent on the probity of the Grand Master: a leader of heretical inclination would have had the power to absolve his followers and thus to nurture deviant ideas within the Order. Here, in other words, the privileges granted to the Temple with the best of intentions generated contempt for local ecclesiastical authority and an aura of secrecy which would create much resentment in future years. The bull *Omne datum optimum* has with justice been described by a modern historian as the Magna Carta of the Knights Templar.

In fact it was repeated many times in the following century, and initiated a spate of equally favourable edicts. Pope Innocent's successor Celestine II issued the bull *Milites Templi* in 1144, awarding indulgences to benefactors of the Temple and allowing the Templars themselves to hold an annual collection in their favour in their own churches. But the most significant support after *Omne datum optimum* came with the election of Pope Eugenius III in 1145. For, as Bernardo Pignatelli, the pope had been a monk in the abbey of Clairvaux, and was both a personal friend and a loyal disciple of Abbot Bernard. He did not wait long to make a show of his allegiance: on 7 April, only seven weeks after his election, Pope Eugenius promulgated the bull *Militia Dei* in favour of the Templars. This reinforced the Templars' right to build their own churches, and added the right to bury dead brothers in their own private cemeteries. Two years later, when he was invited to a general chapter of the Order of the Temple in Paris, it was the same pope who granted the Templars the right to wear the red cross on the breast of their mantles. Hence the guiding influence of St Bernard held firm two decades after the Council of Troyes.

It was the red cross more than any other element of their history and legend which came to symbolise the Knights Templar, from the pontificate of Eugenius down to Edmund Spenser's Red Cross Knight and the Templar Master in *Ivanhoe*. No prisoner made reference to its origin during the trials, but its relevance and symbolic value continued to impress members of the Order. During the 1310 interrogations of the Templars of the preceptory of Mas Deu, in Roussillon, for example, Berengar de Collo spoke eloquently of the extreme reverence in which the Order held the cross while defending himself against the charge that they spat, trampled or urinated on it in their chapters. Such was this reverence, Berengar maintained, that the Templars wore a cross of red cloth stitched on their mantles and shed their own blood against the Saracens, Christ's enemies, just as 'Jesus Christ shed his own blood on the cross for us'.

Acting in tandem, Pope Eugenius and Bernard of Clairvaux were also the prime movers of the Second Crusade, in which for the first time the Temple participated as a fully fledged military order. Following the loss of the County of Edessa in 1144 to the new Muslim leader Imad ed-din Zengi, Eugenius addressed a papal bull to King Louis VII of France urging him to go to the rescue of the crusading kingdoms. After an initial stalemate, when the king failed to interest his vassals in a new crusade, king and pope together appealed to Abbot Bernard. Thus it was Bernard himself who preached the Second Crusade in Vézélay on 31 March 1146, which was Easter Sunday. He managed to instill in the huge crowd – which gathered before a platform set up in a neighbouring field because even that vast cathedral was too small for the occasion – such enthusiasm that the men present began to shout for crosses to stitch on to their garments immediately in sign that they were to leave. The Grand Master of the Temple, Everard de Barres, and a contingent of Templar recruits sailed with the royal fleet, and it was de Barres who negotiated the passage through Constantinople at King Louis' request. Odo of Deuil wrote of the Grand Master that he 'should be revered for his piety', and that he 'furnished the army an honourable example' of courage and loyalty in battle.

But, as so often, the rise to sudden wealth and power generated envy and hostile criticism.

Already within a few years of St Bernard's elaboration of their *raison d'être*, another Cistercian Abbot, Isaac of Etoile, referred to the Templars as 'this dreadful new military order'. In a remark of astonishing perspicacity concerning the concept of warrior-monk, Abbot Isaac also observed: 'We do not maintain that all they do is wrong, but we do insist that what they are doing can be an occasion of many future evils'.

According to William of Tyre, however, problems emerged even as Pope Eugenius was increasing their power. Writing from the biased point of view of an archbishop in the Holy Land, he reports that soon after their foundation the Templars 'withdrew from the patriarch of Jerusalem, from whom they had received the establishment of their order and their first privileges, and refused him the obedience which their predecessors had shown him'. At the same time, they became 'very troublesome' in their attitude towards ecclesiastical authority. If anything this observation is an understatement, since, in 1154, the Templars shot

26

arrows at the door of the patriarch of Jerusalem when he complained about their abuse of the privileges accorded them. Neither was it merely a matter of conflict between different branches of the Church, for there is evidence that the existence and abuse of these privileges irked the lay inhabitants of the kingdom of Jerusalem just as much. In 1160, Pope Alexander III was forced to issue a bull to prevent people pulling Templars from their horses as they passed by in the street. After executing twelve Templar knights for the crime of treachery, and suffering the indignity of seeing Ismaili ambassadors to his court murdered by them, King Amalric I of Jerusalem (1162–74) seriously considered expelling the Order of the Temple from the Holy Land.

Although many books give the idea that the Templars led impeccable lives until Philip the Fair launched his attack against them, severe papal criticism of the Order came early. After discussion of the alleged abuse of their privileges at the Third Lateran Council of 1179, a formal motion of censure was passed. Then, in 1207, came Pope Innocent III's explicitly named bull *De insolentia Templariorum* (*On Templar Pride*). In this far-ranging analysis of the Order, Innocent III argued that it was the inordinate pride of the Templars which had induced them to abuse privileges granted to them by his predecessors. The Templars were accused of lacking in respect for papal legates in the Holy Land, of committing apostasy, of burying excommunicates, usurers and adulterers in their cemeteries, and of accepting recruits into the Order on payment. This virulent formal reproach was repeated by Pope Honorius III in 1222, and further reprimands came from Pope Clement IV (1265–8), Pope Gregory X (1271–6) and Pope Boniface VIII (1294–1303).

In view of the protestations of piety and holy intentions which emerge during the trial, Clement IV's comments are of particular interest. He not only suggested that the Templars display greater humility and mildness, and accused them of mendacity and accepting new brothers on payment, but even went so far as to excommunicate the then Grand Master of the Order, Etienne de Sissi. Ominously, he also reminded the Templars that without papal support they would have no defence at all against the hostility of bishops and secular princes.

It would have been wise to take heed. For throughout the thirteenth century, the current of protest increased – as the chronicles show. Matthew Paris, for example, in his *English History from the years 1235 to 1273* refers with contempt to the Order as 'these proud Templars' and relates a specific series of Templar actions in and around 1243.

During this time the Templars persecuted fiercely the Hospitallers in the Holy Land, so that they were not allowed to carry their dead out of their house (which was in Acre) to be buried. Moreover, the same Templars, in derision of the emperor, drove out and banished from their territories, the brothers of the Teutonics, of the Church of St Mary, thus bringing on their heads the anger of God, and promoting the views of the enemies of the cross.

Then, under the year 1279, the *Chronicle of Bury St Edmunds* makes another specific accusation against the Templars.

On the vigil and on the day of Palm Sunday the Christians and the infidels met in battle between Acre and Safed. First eight emirs and eighteen columns of infidels were killed, then eventually the infidels were victorious, but not without very great loss of men. The Christian army was nearly wiped out because of the sedition of the Templars.

Later in the same chronicle it is alleged that 'Hugh of Lusignan, king of Cyprus, his son and others of his household were killed by poison by the knights of the Temple'. While the modern editor correctly observes that there is no evidence at all of such an event, this entry and those of Matthew Paris clearly represent deep feelings against the Order of the Temple such as must have existed in the monasteries of other orders throughout Christendom.

Both the great victories and the criticisms seem to have been forgotten in 1307. Templars of every rank appear to have a distorted view of the history of the Order. The events recalled during the trial are mostly military losses and instances of failure, for the Templars did not, strangely, cite their successes as a defence. The tone is often one of bickering, with conflicting accusations made against brother knights or lay rivals, or even of abject apology.

Three examples of military loss or defeat, Tortosa, Mansourah and Acre, as they emerge in evidence during the trial, will suffice to illustrate the extent of the bickering and the confusion in the minds of the participants.

During the interrogation of Ponsard de Gizy, the Templar preceptor of Payns, on Thursday 27 November 1309, a letter was produced which de Gizy agreed had been written by him. Indeed he had addressed it to his gaoler, Philippe de Voet, the provost of Poitiers, in the hope of obtaining permission to appear before the Pope and his commissioners. In this letter de Gizy alleged that in the last Templar chapter held by the Visitor of France, a brother called Renaud de la Folie and another unnamed brother had accused the preceptor for France, Gérard de Villiers, of wilfully losing the island of Tortosa in 1291, and thereby causing the death or imprisonment of many Templars. But the facts do not bear out such allegations. For Tortosa was evacuated on 3 August 1291 *after* the fall of Acre, when the garrison would have been unable to resist the advance of the Mameluke sultan, Al-Ashraf. The sultan had made his decisive move in March of that year, capturing Acre, Tyre, Sidon (where the Templars held off his army for a month) and Beirut. The castle of Tortosa had been destroyed on 14 July, so an evacuation of the island would appear to have been a sensible move rather than an act of treachery. The Templars had held many properties and castles in the Holy Land but, by August 1291, only two remained: Athlit, or Castle Pilgrim, which was evacuated on 14 July; and Ruad, an island fortress off Tortosa, which was held for another twelve years as the last Templar possession in the East. It is difficult to see how Gérard de Villiers could have done much more. But Ponsard's evidence indicates the degree of confusion concerning a relatively recent event, and the existence of controversy within the Temple.

The next day Jacques de Molay, in his second deposition before the papal commission, recalled another great failure of the crusading armies: the battle of Mansourah in February 1250. It was as the result of the fighting qualities of the Order of the Temple, he argued, that the comte d'Artois (i.e. Robert I of Artois, one of the three brothers of Louis IX) 'wished that the Templars should be in the avanguard of his army' when they moved up the Nile delta from their base at Damietta towards Cairo. But then the comte, de Molay continues, disobeyed the royal orders and obliged the Templars to follow him into a disastrous attack on the Muslim fortress of Mansourah, about one third of the distance upriver. The Muslim chronicler Maqrizi records that the Templars fought valiantly and even killed the emir of the Muslims, Fakhr ad-din. But the victory was temporary and the attack a failure. Had the comte d'Artois listened to the advice of the Grand Master of the Temple, de Molay tried to argue in defence of his Order, neither he nor the Master himself would have died.

But again all is not as it seems. In the account of the chronicler Joinville, for example, the defeat at Mansourah comes across more plausibly

29

as the consequence of rivalry based on the pride of the two parties involved. For in this version the Templars accused Robert d'Artois of gravely insulting them 'in assuming the lead when he should have followed after . . .'. Joinville even suggests that the real cause of the defeat was a deaf knight, a certain Foucaud de Merle, who simply did not hear the Templar remonstrances and therefore failed to report them to the comte. Whether or not this is so, the result of this classic case of rivalry over leadership was a headlong gallop into the city. Mameluke troops attacked the crusading knights in narrow streets, where they were unable to manoeuvre their horses. The Muslim chronicler Ibn Wasil suggests that the defeat was inevitable, since it was the result of tactical inferiority. Unknown to the Christian forces, while they achieved what seemed to them an easy conquest by entering the city, a message had been sent by carrier pigeon to Cairo. Then, at the moment of apparent victory, when in Ibn Wasil's words 'Islam seemed mortally wounded', the Mameluke army arrived in force from their capital: 'Everywhere the Franj were taken by surprise and massacred with sword or mace'. Thus the great defeat at Mansourah may be interpreted as the consequence of a blind rush into ambush provoked by knightly rivalry. Guillaume de Sonnac and the Templars were every bit as guilty as Robert d'Artois.

Moreover the Templars themselves were not unblemished earlier on the same campaign. Joinville tells us that the previous December 7, the Marshal of the Temple blatantly disobeyed royal orders and attacked Muslim fugitives. His words provide a vivid and contemporary comment on Templar behaviour and impetuosity:

> One of the Turks bore a Knight Templar to the ground, right in front of the hoofs of the horse on which Brother Renaud de Vichiers, at that time Marshal of the Temple, was mounted. On seeing this, the Marshal cried to his brother Templars: 'For God's sake, let's get at them! I can't stand it any longer'.

This sounds magnificent, and compatible with the myth of courage and knightly valour which the Templars nurtured. But the fact is that the knights who pursued the fugitives then had difficulty in rejoining the army.

Since it is hard to see how the Christian forces might have won at Mansourah a few weeks later, the Grand Master's argument before the papal commission reads like the special pleading of a man desperate to find something positive in the recent history of his Order. By any reckoning, Mansourah was a failure: of 290 Templar knights in the field only five are said to have survived.

Acre was worse still, although once again the Templar knights fought valiantly. The Muslim offensive opened on 6 April 1291 with mangonels and petraries launching rocks against the city walls, archers firing over them, and engineers undermining the defences with tunnels. The siege lasted until 12 May, when in the words of the pilgrim Ludolph von Sachen 'the most noble and glorious city of Acre, the flower, chief and pride of all the cities of the East, was taken'. In the midst of the siege of Acre three episodes concerning the Templars stand out: one entirely risible, one heroic, and one demonstrating unexpected gullibility.

The risible episode presents an intriguing contrast to the conventional image of the red-crossed knight galloping at full tilt into battle. On the moonlit night of 15 April a group of Templars made a sortie into the enemy camp, at first taking the sleeping Muslims completely unawares. But once the element of surprise was lost, the Muslims counterattacked. In a scene which smacks of early Hollywood comedy, experienced knights found a successful sortie degenerating into a rout: for, in the darkness, they seem to have forgotten that tents are supported by guy-ropes. Tripping and falling to the ground, they were easy prey for Muslim troops. According to the youthful soldier and chronicler Abu'l-Fida, who was present in the camp and later described this episode, one Templar suffered a particularly ignominious end by tripping straight into a latrine ditch and dying there. Once again, it was a shameful failure. 'The next morning,' the Muslim eyewitness relates, 'my cousin al-Malik al-Muzaffar, lord of Hama, had the heads of some dead Franj attached to the necks of the horses we had captured and presented them to the sultan.'

On the same day the sultan's forces launched a ferocious attack against the wall between St Anthony's Gate, one of the main landward gates to the northeast of Acre, and the Patriarch's Tower at the southern extremity of the walls. The Grand Master of the Temple, Guillaume de Beaujeu, was wounded in the right shoulder by an arrow and had to be dragged to the Temple – which was on the opposite side of the city at the point of the promontory on which Acre stands (some 1200 yards from St Anthony's Gate as the crow flies). There, shortly afterwards, he died. But even in this case it is worth noting that the Grand Master died in vain, since it was during a hopeless counterattack on the so-called Accursed Tower, near St Anthony's Gate, that he was mortally wounded.

The third episode concerns the taking of the Temple itself, a fortress which was protected on two sides by the sea and which had once been the palace of the Muslim governor of the city. A week after the main battle, Sultan al-Ashraf offered Peter de Sevrey, marshal of the Temple and then acting Master, safe conduct to Cyprus in exchange for a complete surrender. Seeing the impossibility either of resisting any longer or of escaping, the marshal accepted these terms and allowed the sultan's banner to be raised over the Temple. But Muslim troops who then entered the fortress to guarantee the safe-conduct began to pillage the contents and rape the women and girls inside it. This naturally provoked a violent Templar reaction, and many of the Muslims already within the Temple were killed as the gate was barred against al-Ashraf once again. There was a fresh stalemate, but the conditions for the Templars remained unchanged: there was no hope of escape, and little chance of receiving reinforcements. So once again a safe conduct was negotiated. But this time marshal de Sevrey seems to have been too gullible. He and his escort were captured as they left the Temple, and immediately beheaded. Then 2,000 Mameluke troops stormed the fortress and massacred all but a handful of the Templars present.

Yet again, this incident demonstrates a striking lack of understanding of the Muslims and their strategy, at the human cost of 300 lives. It must be said, however, that this weakness may have been the result of the death of the Grand Master. For, on the authority of Jacques de Molay, we know that many years earlier Guillaume de Beaujeu had maintained good relations with the sultan in order to protect Templar interests. Presumably, he also knew the enemy better than Peter de Sevrey.

These episodes led to the virtual dissipation of frontline Templar fighting forces. According to Sir Steven Runciman in his *History of the Crusades*, 'subsequent travellers to the East spoke of seeing renegade Templars living squalidly in Cairo and of other Templars working as wood-cutters by the Dead Sea'. In a sense the Order of the Temple died its real death at Acre in 1291: the guy-rope episode illustrates the lack of experience and ingenuousness of much of the Templar force; Guillaume de Beaujeu's death was afterwards recalled as heroic, but it may be seen as a futile waste of an experienced commander in a situation in which defeat was inevitable; Peter de Sevrey's actions were part of the panic and confusion into which the Temple – and other crusading forces – were thrown by this massive attack.

With hindsight, it is possible to read the defeat at Acre as a wilful waste of human life in search of superficial glory. For the fall of Acre was very much a foregone conclusion. This had in fact been clear to the Grand Master of the Temple and the Master of the rival order of Hospitallers for some time. Two years earlier they had dispatched two envoys, a Templar named Hertrand and a Hospitaller named Pierre d'Hèzquam, on a mission to the recently elected Pope Nicholas IV in Rome with the hope of obtaining papal support and extra finances for the defence of this last bastion of the crusader kingdom. But, as far as gathering fresh funds and manpower was concerned, the mission had failed. In 1291, the knights of the two religious Orders besieged in Acre faced impossible odds. The Muslim chronicler Abu L-Mahasin describes the numbers of men under the command of the sultan as 'unnumbered', for it was a vast popular army in which volunteers outnumbered regular troops. Modern authorities have put the numbers of the besieging army as high as 66,000 horse and 160,000 foot soldiers, pitched against 14,000 Christian foot soldiers and possibly 800 knights then present in Acre.

It was very much a matter of sending lambs to the slaughter; the Templars themselves never engaged in a major battle again.

The destiny of the Order was already to some degree marked even before Acre – although the Templars during the trial once again appear to have overlooked this crucial fact – as an indirect result of the mission of Hertrand and Pierre d'Hèzquam to Rome. For, while the embassy produced no cash, their pleas fell on the ready ears of a new pope with vast experience of the East. In that way, they served to rekindle a project which had been formulated nearly twenty years before and then forgotten: a union of the crusading orders which would sound the death toll for the Templars as an independent fighting force.

On 15 February 1288, Girolamo Masci, Cardinal Bishop of Palestrina, was elected to the Holy See and took the name Nicholas IV. In the early 1270s, during the pontificate of Pope Gregory X, this Franciscan friar had been appointed apostolic legate to the Holy Land and had resided there for some years. From that moment the problems of the Holy Land and of crusade were never far from his mind and, when he became pope, they were one of the main concerns of his policy. Yet his four-year pontificate was plagued by the loss of prestige of the papacy after wars in Sicily and by the lack of a potent secular ally. He planned to establish the Inquisition in Acre and, in a remarkable move which illustrates his knowledge of the East, sent a fellow Franciscan, Giovanni di Montecorvino, on a mission to the Mongol court in Peking in order to enlist

Qubilai Khan's support against Islam. Above all, however, he revived the project of creating a permanent standing army in the Holy Land.

The project had been discussed at the 1274 Council of Lyon, presided over by Pope Gregory X, which had the specific purpose of reviving the old crusading spirit and organising the departure of a new large-scale crusade. Three years earlier, as Archbishop Teobaldo Visconti of Liège, Pope Gregory himself had visited the Holy Land and, like Girolamo Masci, had been inspired by first-hand knowledge to operate in its favour. But already in 1274 it was hard to generate enthusiasm for crusade in kings with severe local difficulties. Neither King Philip III of France nor King Edward I of England went to Lyon, where the only royal participant was King Jaimé I of Aragon – who had ruled since 1213 and was only two years away from his death. Worse still, reports requested by Pope Gregory on the difficulty of persuading men to take the cross were extremely negative: one, by Bishop Bruno of Olmutz, suggested that the crusades were pointless and outmoded; another, by the Dominican Humbert of Romans, said that few men now believed in the spiritual benefits which had been promised to crusaders; others thought that the conquest of the Muslims would be better attempted through peaceful missions. In practical terms, the Council of Lyon failed in its declared task of inspiring a new crusade. Yet the idea of a permanent standing army took root, with its necessary corollary of a union of the crusading orders. St Louis had dreamed of it even before the Council of Lyons, as did Charles II of Anjou, Jaimé of Aragon and, of course, Pope Gregory himself. As was to be expected, the newly appointed Grand Master of the Temple, Guillaume de Beaujeu, who was present at the Council in person, opposed the idea vigorously. This he did on the logistical grounds that first it would be hard to recruit enough men, and then it would be equally difficult to guarantee supplies of arms and food. In the midst of general disagreement, and, given the absence of the most powerful Christian monarchs, the idea was shelved.

But the presence of three exceptional delegates among the 500 bishops gathered in Lyon had been of special significance for future developments. One was Raimon Lull (c.1232–1315), a Mallorcan knight who, at the age of thirty, had undergone a conversion which led him to become a celebrated mystic and missionary, and who, in 1274, had just completed nine years' study both of the Arabic language and of Islam; another was Fidenzio of Padua, a widely travelled diplomat who was at that time the Franciscan Provincial Vicar in the Holy Land; and the third was

Girolamo Masci, at that time still the apostolic delegate to the Holy Land but within the year to become vicar-general of the Franciscans. Each of these men was to have a significant role in the future of the idea of union, and more or less indirectly therefore in the destiny of the Templars. The seed that was sown at Lyon in 1274 may have initially appeared wasted, but was to bear unexpected fruit nearly twenty years later.

One of Pope Nicholas' initiatives in favour of the Holy Land was to commission from his colleague Fidenzio of Padua the book known as *Liber Recuperatione Terrae Sanctae* (*On the Recovery of the Holy Land*), which was published in 1291. In this work, Fidenzio begins with a history of the Holy Land and the earlier crusades. Then he goes on to discuss the practical problems of crusade, such as the type of army required, the numbers of men, strategy and tactics to be adopted, and the best routes from Europe to the East. It is the work of a learned man who knows the Holy Land well and has devoted much thought to the problems. At the Council of Salzburg in the same year the idea of union of the military orders was again discussed, and even formally approved, but there were no practical consequences. More important, Fidenzio's book seems to have stimulated a series of similarly titled works which appeared in the next two decades. In a sense, each new book could be seen as a nail in the coffin being prepared for the Templars.

In 1294, Raimon Lull entered the fray with his *Petitio pro recuperatione Terrae Sanctae* (*A Petition for Recovering the Holy Land*). The next year a French doctor at the royal court, Galvano de Levanti, published a work dedicated to Philip the Fair, the similarly titled *Liber sancti Passagii Christicolarum contra Saracenos pro recuperatione Terrae Sanctae* in which he implicitly proposed the French king as the single leader of a great crusade. But King Philip was then engaged in disputes with Normandy and England, and had little interest. Crusade as a vital idea was moribund. In fact the very concept had been debased by Pope Boniface VIII (1294–1303) with his innovation of a 'crusade' against a personal Christian enemy within the walls of Rome, the great Colonna family. Here the crusade had degenerated to no more than a cynical instrument of papal power, following in the tradition of crusades against the heretics in Albi, or that announced against Emperor Frederick II. In real terms the Holy Land was lost, and forgotten. By then, Jerusalem had become the symbolic goal of a pilgrimage to eternity rather than a physical entity to be reconquered by feats of arms.

Yet the propagandists did not relent. Around 1305 Raimon Lull began a period of lecturing at the University of Paris which continued almost throughout the Templar trials. It was in the French capital that he wrote a new work entitled *Liber de Fine*. In this he again advocated a new crusade, with the Temple and Hospital united as the core of the army. The major innovation in his new concept of crusade was the simultaneous importance of preaching: the idea was for a crusading army to support and protect a specialised missionary force of friars who knew Arabic and who could attempt to *convert* the Muslims instead of fighting them. In setting out the way in which the crusade he advocated should be carried out, in the second part of the pamphlet entitled *De modo bellandi*, Lull argues that the leader of this great crusade should necessarily be a man of royal blood. There was nothing particularly novel about this, since many crusades had been led by kings and Galvano de Levanti had already proposed King Philip the Fair for this role. But Raimon Lull went further: in his project all the crusading orders were to be united under a *dominus bellator rex*, or 'warlike king', who would then command both secular and papal knights. Since this tract was composed in Paris, it may be read as a piece of blatant royal flattery.

The decisive move was made by Pierre Dubois, a lawyer in the service of Philip the Fair. A Norman by birth, Dubois had studied first at the University of Paris and then at the law school in Orléans. Most of his working life was spent as the royal advocate in the *bailliage* of Coutances, with no apparent desire to transfer from his native Normandy to Paris. Then, probably early in 1306, he composed his seminal pamphlet *Concerning the Recovery of the Holy Land*, the most striking aspect of which is not the expected bias in favour of King Philip but the vehemently anti-Templar stance which Dubois assumes.

The royal lawyer opens his argument with the sensible premise that the first requirement for a successful crusade in the East was peace in the West: it should be Philip the Fair's responsibility to resolve the conflict between Edward I of England and the Scots, and that between Jaimé II of Aragon (1291–1327) and Charles II of Anjou King of Sicily and Naples (1285–1309). Once peace was achieved, the next step would be to acquire sufficient financial support for a crusade. This is where ominous signs for the future of the Order of the Temple begin to appear. For in #14 of his pamphlet Dubois advances the suggestion that if the properties of the Temple and the Hospital, which he states were then 'divided and confused', were to be united, then it would be possible to find the necessary funds. Even worse from the Templar point of view is #107, where Dubois advocates setting up a common treasury for the Holy Land, to be held in the cathedral of each diocese. Since for over a century the treasuries of the Templars had been the primary repositories for crusading finance (especially in London and Paris), this apparently reasonable suggestion amounted to a direct attack on the Temple and its prerogatives. But the final blow comes in the *Appendix* to Dubois' pamphlet, which is thought to have been written in the summer of 1307 – just before the Templar arrests. Here his intentions are made explicit, since in #5 he writes that 'It was decided with the approval of the Council that the Order of the Templars was to be abolished, and that according to justice it would be totally annulled, and it was decided to order as mentioned above that their wealth be used towards a general crusade'. Dubois does not specify which Council, but it may be that as an expert propagandist he was being deliberately vague, referring implicitly to the 1291 Council of Salzburg. Be that as it may, his argument was extremely persuasive.

It was with Dubois' pamphlet and the earlier 'recovery' and 'union' arguments in mind that in June 1306 Pope Clement V (1305–14) initiated an inquiry into the feasibility of union of the crusading orders. He invited the Grand Masters of the Temple and the Hospital to commit their opinions on the matter to paper.

Jacques de Molay wrote a careful and well-reasoned reply. Certainly the arguments were not new to him. At that time he had been Grand Master of the Order of the Temple for thirteen years, having achieved that honour after Tibald Gaudin's brief Mastership (1291–3). Shortly afterwards, in 1294 and 1295, he had travelled through Europe on a recruitment and finance-seeking trip to make up for losses at Acre. During this visit it is likely that de Molay heard about, and even discussed, the union of the two major crusading orders. When he and the Master of the Hospital were ordered by Pope Clement in June 1306 to visit him in Poitiers to give advice on how to send aid to the kings of Cyprus and Armenia, Jacques de Molay travelled to Europe again from his base in Cyprus with Raimbaud de Caron, the preceptor of Cyprus. They probably arrived in France in late 1306 or early 1307, during which period the Grand Master produced two memoirs: in the first he attempted to persuade Pope Clement to preach a general crusade; the second is that preserved under the title *Jacques de Molay's Report to Pope Clement on the Union of the Orders of the Temple and the Hospital*. Both memoirs

37

survive in the Bibliothèque Nationale, the latter was published by Lizerand in the *Dossier*.

That the latter memoir is a direct reply to Pope Clement's request is made clear in the opening words: 'Most Holy Father, to the question you ask me concerning the union of the orders of the Temple and the Hospital, I, Master of the Temple, reply as follows'. De Molay goes on to provide a brief review of the history of the idea of union. Whether or not the self-styled *illitteratus* composed this memoir in person, the detailed arguments offered illustrate beyond doubt that Jacques de Molay and the other leaders of the Temple were fully cognisant of the background to the delicate situation in which they found themselves. He refers to the discussions at the 1274 Council of Lyon, and to the role of Pope Nicholas IV.

Then he provides the arguments for and against union, with a clear bias towards the latter: fifteen reasons *not* to unify the crusading orders are followed by a mere two arguments in favour of union. His reasoning offers a rare insight into the mental processes of Jacques de Molay and the other Templar dignitaries who may have helped him in writing the memoir.

The Grand Master begins by asserting that it would not be honourable to unite ancient orders which have performed many good services to Christendom in the past. The second disadvantage sounds shaky to a modern ear: the knights themselves would place their souls in jeopardy in being forced to change the habit, everyday lifestyle and morals of an Order which they had chosen of their own free will for that of another which they did not wish to join. But de Molay is on surer ground – given a long history of disputes in the Holy Land – when he says that the present rivalry between the Orders would continue to exist, and that members would be instigated by the devil to quarrel. This, he adds, would be dangerous because the quarrelling knights possess arms. Echoes of modern arguments against company mergers appear when he suggests that further discord would result when they came to decide which of the existing preceptories would be suppressed, and which holders of duplicated offices (i.e. Marshal, Commanders, Draper) would lose their rank. In view of the allegation during the trial that charitable offerings and hospitality were not provided as they should have been (#94), it is interesting to read de Molay's argument that a united order would have less surplus to offer for the provision of alms and food for the poor than the two separate orders did at present; pilgrims, too, would be worse off for the same reason. In fact, he argues with a certain coherence, the rivalry which has always existed between the orders is a positive fact which has been to the advantage of the Christian cause, rather like the rivalry between Franciscans and Dominicans. Finally, he comes to what he believes is the clinching military argument. When kings, dukes and counts go to the Holy Land to fight the Saracens, he asserts, it has always been the custom for one of the orders to march as the avanguard (*avangarda*) and the other to form a rearguard (*reregarda*). Thus, in his picturesque turn of phrase, 'covering and enclosing the foreigners as a mother does her infant'. This was an excellent arrangement because of their expert knowledge of Saracen customs, and also because the Saracens recognised and respected the Temple and the Hospital. So, if the orders were united, he continues with a striking absence of logic, it would be necessary to find others to perform these tasks.

The advantages are dismissed in nineteen lines of the printed text, as if the author suddenly remembered at the last moment that he should offer some counterargument. The Grand Master argues with obvious reluctance that in a modern world where people lack respect for the religious, a combined order would be able to defend itself better against attack and criticism. But his principal argument in favour is that union of the Orders would bring about a reduction of costs, owing to the reduced number of preceptories both in Western Europe and in the Holy Land. Finally, in a general defence of the concept of crusading order and explicit rejection of the idea of a permanent standing army, he presents the case that the religious orders are better adapted to the reconquest of the Holy Land than other men. 'That', he states with confidence, 'is certainly true, because they are less expensive, and more obedient in their houses, in the fields and in combat.'

In short, Jacques de Molay rejects the idea of union in this memoir as assuredly as his mentor Guillaume de Beaujeu had done at the 1274 Council of Lyon. But could a Templar of such long standing have done otherwise? The Grand Master, probably born at Molay, in Franche-Comté, around 1243/4, had been received into the Temple at Beaune in 1265, thus having seen forty years of service in the Order. From his own confessions during the trial we know that he served in the Holy Land as a young man under Guillaume de Beaujeu, who was Grand Master from 1273 to 1291, and that he himself was a survivor of the battle of Acre. His mind was steeped in the traditions and power of the Templars, to the extent that another way of life seems to have been inconceivable to him. For this reason it is hardly surprising that he rejected union so forcefully.

In his memoir to Pope Clement he is very much on the defensive. He and the other Templar leaders must have been aware that the Order of the Temple was under pressure from propagandists like Pierre Dubois, and that much of its *raison d'être* had been swept away with the loss of Acre. They must also have suspected from the sophistry of Dubois' pamphlet that Philip the Fair aspired to their wealth and power. Yet at the same time they had no grounds to fear anything as dramatic as the arrests which were now just weeks away. Jacques de Molay wrote with serenity and confidence. For, since the time of St Bernard of Clairvaux, the Order of the Temple had been a religious order under the jurisdiction of the Holy See. And they had, after all, even if many of them seemed to have forgotten, survived Saladin, Baybars and Al-Ashraf.

But this time the forces ranged against the Temple were both more insidious and more powerful than the infidel in the East.

3

THE ACCUSERS

One accuser stands head and shoulder above the others: King Philip IV of France, named 'the Fair' or 'the Handsome' because of his blond hair and handsome features. The other principal figures in the trial may be divided into secular and religious camps: the royal lawyers Guillaume de Nogaret and Guillaume de Plaisians, and the royal counsellor Enguerrand de Marigny, fall into the former; Pope Clement V, Inquisitor-General Guillaume de Paris, and Archbishop Gilles Aicelin of Narbonne belong to the latter. But, as we shall see, the demarcation was never that keen. In a sense, all the main participants became instruments of a grand strategy against the Order of the Temple. For ecclesiastical acquiescence in royal schemes was one of the main issues at stake, and led to greater emphasis being placed on the trial of the Templars than accusations and evidence perhaps warranted. The trial may in fact be seen as part of the broader spectacle of an emergent nation-state entering into head-on conflict with a traditional supra-national power – the Church.

In 1307, Philip IV had been on the throne of France for twenty-two years. The grandson and a fervid admirer of the crusading king Louis IX (St Louis, 1226–70), he was the eleventh in direct male descent of the Capetian dynasty which had ruled France since 987. Born at Fontainebleau in 1268 and crowned at Reims in 1286, in 1307 he was at the height of his powers. Two years earlier his wife Jeanne de Navarre had died at the age of thirty-two, leaving four surviving children (three others died in childhood): the eldest son Louis, who would succeed his father as Louis X, was eighteen in 1307; his daughter Isabelle was fifteen and already engaged to the future Edward II of England, whose queen she was to become; his second son, fourteen-year-old Philippe, who would succeed his brother Louis as Philip V; and his youngest son, thirteen-year-old Charles, later Charles IV of France. The kingdom was at that time divided into two parts: the *domaine du Roi*, or kingdom proper, which consisted of the lands traditionally owned by the Capetians, and *la mouvence*, which consisted of fiefs dependent on the king and ecclesiastical fiefs and *appanages* held by Philip's sons. It has been estimated that a few years later, in 1328, the *domaine* consisted of just over 300,000 square kilometres, with a population of around twelve million people; at the same time, the *mouvence* was just over 100,000 square kilometres with a population of five million. In brief, the France of Philip the Fair comprised about four-fifths of the area of the present Republic, with about one third of the present population.

King Philip ruled with an iron hand. His absolute faith in the God-given legitimacy and power of the dynasty, and in his divine right to rule, manifest itself in a conscious attempt to imitate the saintly qualities of his grandfather. The result was a cultivated coldness and aloofness. But he lacked the spiritual warmth of St Louis, and the aloofness was tarnished by a hard streak of pride. The handsome features too were tempered by this chill aspect, so that a contemporary could observe that 'the king stares at men fixedly, without uttering a word . . . He is not a man, not a beast, he is a graven image.' He was tall and robust with a fair, rosy complexion, blond hair and a strong nose. His passion for hunting suggests physical strength. The portrait on the royal seal shows a figure with longish hair and slightly upturned lips, while the deathbed scene represented in a miniature in the *Grandes Chroniques de France* depicts him with a short beard. Contempt for the wordly achievements of man and a deliberate stoicism marked Philip's character, perhaps influenced by continual reading of his favourite author Boethius, whose *Consolations of Philosophy* was specially translated into French for him. But the message of Boethius was not perfectly received, since this apparent stoic calm was punctuated by bouts of fierce rage which terrified onlookers.

Austerity was usually the mark of his public comportment, as may be seen in the 1294 edict which sought to curb extravagance by specifying the amount of money his subjects could spend on clothing. He even tried to establish how many dishes they should eat at each meal, and the ingredients. Expenditure was to be strictly regulated according to rank: a bishop could spend twenty-five *Tournois sous* on his clothing, a cathedral canon fifteen *sous*, and a squire six *sous*. Although this, and another similar attempt in 1306, eventually failed, the expense of the royal court were always severely controlled, down to the number of maids allowed to Queen Jeanne. In fact, if anything, this royal austerity and contempt for luxury increased after the queen's death. The only element of extravagance to be conceded was the vast sum spent on the rebuilding and expansion of the royal palace on the Ile de la Cité, on the site of the present Palais de Justice. But that was a matter of dynastic prestige rather than personal comfort. Cost was irrelevant. King Philip wished to create a palace equal to his status, building it around the site of the Sainte Chapelle which St Louis had built.

The same utter certainty about the divine origins of his rule enabled the king to ignore criticism, and pushed him to defy and challenge popes. While he was respected by his subjects, and followed the Capetian custom of walking openly round Paris, the general impression of historians is that his reserved and taciturn nature meant that he was never loved by the common people as his grandfather had been. Bernard de Saisset, Bishop of Pamiers, who knew the king's wrath, described Philip as 'more handsome than any man in the world'; but he then went on to dismiss him as a man 'who knew nothing at all except to stare at me'. Yet de Saisset was a declared enemy of the king, and a brief description by a Scots monk known as Guillaume l'Ecossais, at the Abbey of St Denis, suggests a different side to his character. Guillaume writes that King Philip 'was noted for his sweetness and modesty, fleeing with horror from bad conversations, precise at holy offices, a faithful observer of fasts prescribed by the Church, subduing his flesh with a hair-shirt'. This description has been regarded as false just because it contradicts the image constructed from other sources. Yet it could well be the case that the same silent stare which froze some men in terror provoked admiration in those with less to fear.

He was certainly able to create and maintain good personal relations with a small group of loyal men to whom he delegated much more than most contemporary medieval rulers. Thus Philip was able to spend much of the year outside Paris, at a series of lodges where he could indulge in his great love of hunting. Ministers and lawyers in Paris formulated his policies, and paid officials such as the *baillis* and *sénéschals* executed them in the towns and villages of the provinces – as we have seen in the case of the Templar *Arrest Order*. In just the same way, he had delegated many financial operations to the Templars so that, during his reign, the Temple in Paris had become the centre of financial administration for the entire kingdom. Complete banking services provided by the Order to King Philip included payment of rents, pensions, gratuities and pledges, reimbursement of war debts incurred in Navarre and

Normandy, advances made to members of the royal army, and collection of taxes and other sums due throughout the kingdom. All this was regularly rendered with detailed accounts: the *Compte de la Chandeleur* (or Candlemas Statement) for 1287, for instance, published in the nineteenth century, lists as many as 290 separate sub-headings for financial operations. Given this excellent financial administration and the quality of legal services provided by his ministers, King Philip was able to concentrate on overall strategies.

The trial of the Templars provides a good example of this delegation of authority, for while the impetus was provided by Philip the Fair the everyday running was carried out by royal ministers and lawyers – with the exception of a handful of key moments when the royal patience was pushed to the limit and he intervened personally.

Another prominent figure with a legal background, Gilles Aicelin, Archbishop of Narbonne, and the financial counsellor Enguerrand de Marigny, must also be considered among the leading royal players in the Paris trial. With Guillaume de Nogaret and Guillaume de Plaisians, they rose to prominence in the later part of Philip the Fair's reign, after another celebrated lawyer, Pierre Flote, who was succeeded as keeper of the seals by Guillaume de Nogaret, had dominated the royal court throughout the 1290s. There were close links between some of them, and each worked in apparent harmony with the others under the guidance of King Philip.

In the context of the Templar trial Guillaume de Nogaret is the most prominent of these men. He was born in Toulouse in the 1260s, although his family came from the village of Saint Félix de Caramon. He first appears in history in 1287, when he was professor of jurisprudence at the school of law in Montpellier and a legal counsellor of the king of Mallorca. It is almost as if the creation of a series of law schools and universities was carried out by the great twelfth-century series of lawyer-popes in view of the later trial: in 1229, Pope Gregory IX founded the University of Toulouse; Montpellier itself became a university under Pope Nicholas IV in 1289 (with the three faculties of arts, law and medicine), for the purpose of providing suitably trained lawyers for the Church and the Inquisition; in 1303 the University of Avignon was founded by Pope Boniface VIII, together with Charles of Anjou; the school of law at Orléans was changed into a university by an authorisation of Pope Clement V in 1305 (and properly founded in 1312 by King Philip). Something of the skill of Guillaume de Nogaret as professor of law may be imagined from the rapidity with which he was drawn into the royal circle: in 1294 he became the senior judge in the *sénéchaussée* of Beaucaire, in the following year he appeared as a member of the *parlement* in Paris, and in 1296 he became a member of the *curia regis*. During the next decade he performed delicate and important tasks for King Philip as one of the most trusted royal counsellors. He was honoured by being raised to the nobility in 1299 and, after the death of Pierre Flote in 1302, de Nogaret became the dominant minister in the royal court. Legal success entailed financial success, and he came to own a large estate near Nîmes which has been estimated at some 400 square miles in size, including jurisdiction over forty or fifty villages. His career reached its apex with the office of keeper of the seal in 1307 and the early stages of the Templar trial. But his power seems to have faded during the last years, perhaps as the result of sickness or old age. He died in 1313, before the trial came to its real conclusion with the execution of Jacques de Molay. There exists no genuine portrait of Guillaume de Nogaret, but the iconography presents him as a forceful man with prominent nose and chin and thick lower lip, and wide-open strong eyes; if this were anything close to the truth, then he would clearly have been a man to avoid in litigation.

It seems de Nogaret could be a loyal friend once gained. For it is likely that Guillaume de Plaisians was his close friend and protégé for nearly two decades. De Plaisians himself was born at the village of Plaisians in the Dauphiné, near Vaison la Romaine and just a few miles north of Mount Ventoux. He was sent to study law at the University of Montpellier, where he was probably one of Guillaume de Nogaret's students. Certainly he followed his master in his own career: in 1301 he succeeded de Nogaret as *juge-mage* in Beaucaire, and two years later he too appeared in Paris. From that moment he was often to act in de Nogaret's stead, which indicates a special relationship of trust. He has in fact been described as his master's *alter ego*. In surviving speeches made during the Templar trial, de Plaisians shows himself to have been an elegant and persuasive speaker at ease with the techniques of legal argument and sophisticated in his use of scriptural texts. He too was ennobled by Philip the Fair, and his services to the king were further rewarded by large estates near those of Guillaume de Nogaret.

The career of Gilles Aicelin is even more fascinating. He was the scion of a powerful southern noble family whose estates in Auvergne were on the southern borders of the kingdom of France and thus of vital strategic

importance. Born around 1250, he too was a student of law and perhaps
for some time a professor of canon law. But his early advancement was
owing to the fact that he was a nephew of Pierre Flote, the all-powerful
keeper of the seals, who seems to have adopted Gilles as his special
protégé while also elevating the entire family to positions of importance:
one of Gilles' brothers, Hugues, filled the key post of cardinal bishop of
Ostia; another, Jean, became the secular abbot of Bourges and Clermont.
Gilles himself first achieved prominence as provost of Clermont, a position he reached at the age of thirty-five. In 1288 he was sent to the papal
court in Rome by Philip the Fair to review the perennial dispute over
taxes with the newly elected Pope Nicholas IV, who appears so often in
the background of these royal lawyers. The pope appears to have ap-
preciated his diplomatic and legal skills as much as King Philip had done
and, from that moment, Aicelin enjoyed papal patronage as well. First
he was made a papal chaplain, and then in 1290 Pope Nicholas appointed him archbishop of Narbonne.

From this ecclesiastical powerbase he carved out for himself a role as
one of the foremost royal lawyers and counsellors, accomplishing crucial
missions as royal ambassador and negotiating treaties on behalf of King
Philip. In 1292 he established himself permanently in Paris, having appointed vicars-general to manage the day-to-day business of the vast
metropolitan diocese of Narbonne (which comprised the bishoprics of
Agde, Lodève, Nîmes, Elne, Bézier, Maguelonne, Carcassonne, Uzès and
Toulouse). Some idea of his status at the royal court may be gleaned
from the fact that in 1293 he was chosen as godfather to the royal baby
Charles, later to rule as Charles IV (1322–8). By then a man noted by the
chroniclers for his learning, his legal skill, and his opulent clothes, in the
following years he worked closely with Pierre Flote, travelled on several
missions to Rome, negotiated with ambassadors from King Edward I,
and participated in the *parlement* in Paris. In 1301 he played a vital role
in the affair of Bishop Bernard de Saisset, and in 1303 was in Montpellier
working together with Guillaume de Plaisians. Two years later he was
instrumental in the election of Bertrand de Got as Pope Clement V, with
whom he always maintained good relations.

When Philip the Fair needed to put forward an acceptable name for
the presidency of the papal commission set up by Clement V in 1309 to
inquire into the Order of the Temple, it was natural that he should suggest the archbishop of Narbonne. With the formidable prosecution team
of Guillaume de Nogaret and Guillaume de Plaisians executing the strat-

46

egy of King Philip, odds were already stacked against the Templars. Then the archbishop of Narbonne, a friend and colleague of the prosecutors, became in effect their judge.

To make matters worse, this team was further strengthened by two other important royal men. The first of these men was the inquisitor-general of the diocese of Sens, Friar Guillaume de Paris. Born in Paris around 1250, when Guillaume was a young man he entered the Order of the Dominicans in the Parisian monastery of St Jacques, now demolished but which then stood on the Left Bank near the Panthéon (on the area enclosed between the present streets of rue Soufflot, rue Cujas, and rue Saint Jacques). Nothing else is known of his early life, but he achieved renown as a scholar and author of specialised theological tracts and was appointed inquisitor-general around 1303. Like Gilles Aicelin, he managed to achieve the delicate balancing act between high ecclesiastical office and membership of the royal court. Two years later, in December 1305, he became the personal confessor to Philip the Fair. In a letter written to the inquisitors and Dominicans of Toulouse and Carcassonne in September 1307 ordering them to interrogate the Knights Templar within their jurisdictions, Guillaume de Paris described himself with memorable comprehensiveness as 'papal chaplain, royal confessor, and inquisitor-general'. His loyalty throughout the Templar trial was rewarded on 17 May 1311, when Philip the Fair made Guillaume one of the executors of his will. This was the man who formally began proceedings against the Knights Templar *in the name of the Church*.

The second man was the royal chamberlain Enguerrand de Marigny who, by the end of the trial, had replaced Guillaume de Nogaret as the most influential of royal counsellors. De Marigny was a Norman of noble origins, a knight and landowner, who differed from the other royal participants in the trial in being a financial administrator rather than a lawyer or cleric. From manuscript descriptions of a now-lost statue which stood near the entrance to the royal palace in Paris, his modern biographer, Franklin J. Pegues, attempted to construct an identikit of Enguerrand: he was short and stocky, with a strong head and good posture; his face was cheerful and pleasant, and his hair probably blond or reddish since he was sometimes referred to as 'the Red'. The hair on the statue was long, curled in a semicircle on his neck. He was born around 1275, the son of a royal official in the district of the provost of Andelys. That he entered royal favour early is suggested by the fact that his marriage to Jeanne de Saint Martin about 1295 was arranged by no less a person than Jeanne de Navarre, queen of France, the bride's godmother. From this marriage two children were born: Louis, who was made a knight in 1313 and became chamberlain first to Louis of Navarre and then to King Louis X; and Marie, who became a nun at the convent of Maubuisson. On the death of his first wife, Enguerrand married Alips de Mons, a cousin of Jean de Grès, the marshal of France – another indication of status and favour. From this marriage two further children were born: Raoul, who became a cleric; and Thomas, who became a knight in royal service. He probably moved to Paris on marrying Jeanne de Saint Martin and, around 1295, took up residence in the Louvre as squire. From that moment his career moved rapidly, and he was soon in in a position to acquire houses nearby. In 1308 he was appointed the royal minister of finance, and as such became the controller of the Treasury. This key position, of vital importance given Philip's perennial financial shortage, placed Enguerrand at the heart of the court and of the royal administration. Perhaps he was more cynical and less sincere in his faith and duties than the legal advisors. Certainly he enjoyed the same success as the result of royal favour, ending his career with large estates which included land and twelve castles between Dieppe and Gisons.

Thus Enguerrand de Marigny was a constant and powerful presence behind the scenes. In a sense, however, his real contribution to the story of the Templar trial was the pressure he exercised for the advancement of his brother Philippe de Marigny. At a crucial moment of stall during the trial Philippe became archbishop of Sens on the suggestion of King Philip, and was immediately responsible for one of the most dramatic actions carried out against the Templars. Moreover, Enguerrand de Marigny's career differed from the other royal participants in the trial in one other major respect: while the others weathered the storms of rage of King Philip, and in the case of Gilles Aicelin even managed to maintain a certain independence, Enguerrand was to fall into disgrace, ironically, following another trial in which charges of heretical and magical practices were made. He was hanged in 1315 after being condemned for using image magic against Philip's son King Louis X (1314–16) and his brother Comte Charles of Valois.

These men – Guillaume de Nogaret, Guillaume de Plaisians, Gilles Aicelin, Guillaume de Paris, Enguerrand de Marigny – were the prime movers immediately behind King Philip the Fair. They provided the intellectual and organisational momentum which directed hundreds of royal officials throughout the kingdom during the lengthy trial of the Templars.

But such a complex administration required huge funds, in addition to those needed for the king's constant warmongering. Chronic cash shortages had already led to the spoilation of the Lombard bankers in the kingdom of France in 1291, and that of the Jewish population in 1306. This led contemporary observers to believe that King Philip's real motive in attacking the Order of the Temple was to lay his hands on their treasury. Giovanni Villani, who was in Paris at the time, uses the terms avarice (*avarizia*) and cupidity (*cupidigia*) in his succinct account of the trial. A more celebrated Italian, Dante, refers to Philip in the *Purgatory* as the 'new Pilate', as Pilate is supposed to have informed the Judeans that he could find no basis of guilt on which to condemn Jesus. But in Dante's imagination this already interesting parallel achieves greater poetic force with the astonishing epithet which he employs to describe King Philip: as attacking the Temple in piratical style with 'avaricious sails'.

> Veggio il nuovo Pilato si crudele
> Che ciò nol sazia, ma senza decreto
> Porta nel Tempio le cupide vele
> (*Purgatario* XX, 90–3)

More specific still are the words of the Genoese merchant Christian Spinola in a letter addressed to King Jaimé II of Aragon less than three weeks after the arrests in France: 'I understand, however, that the pope and the king are doing this for the money . . .'

The story is not that simple. For while King Philip was certainly both ambitious and ruthless, other sources show that his actions were inspired by a strong belief in law and the concept of divine order. Above all, he was a medieval king. This sounds like a truism, but it is necessary to consider his actions in context. For an English reader, it is pertinent to recall the consequences of disruption of *order* or *degree* in Shakespeare's history plays and tragedies, which were often set in the reigns of kings who lived later in the fourteenth century – for example that of Richard II (1377–99). The fear which haunts many of those kings is expressed succinctly by Ulysses in *Troilus and Cressida*:

> Take but degree away, untune that string,
> And hark, what discord follows.

'Discord' is symbolised by the descent of human reason into madness, or in the feigned bestiality of a character such as Edgar in *King Lear* when he disguises himself as Poor Tom and 'eats cow-dung for sallets'. In the same way, the emphasis on bestiality and inhumanity in the Templar *Arrest Order* is meant to show that their supposed heresy is an abuse of God's gift of reason. The preamble contains the following sentence: 'Certainly the spirit of reason suffers when it passes the limits of nature, and in suffering is tormented by that which, forgetting its origins, ignorant of its dignity, wasting itself and given to reprobate feeling, has not understood why it has been held in honour'. This is a notion which could easily be inserted into *King Lear*. In forgetting the origins of their Order by indulging in heresy, so the argument runs, the Templars have forsaken their position in the Chain of Being and descended to the point at which, in Guillaume de Nogaret's words, they may be 'compared to beasts completely deprived of reason'. Just like Edgar, and Lear himself.

The Chain of Being represented the order of God's creation, and was underpinned by the Catholic faith. It was because King Philip feared – at least on a formal level – stepping out of line that he took care to present himself in terms of a defender of the faith. Guillaume de Plaisians stressed this fact in a speech made to Pope Clement at Poitiers on 29 May 1308. The king of France, the royal lawyer asserted, is coming into the presence of His Holiness 'with no intention of personally assuming . . . the judicial role of accuser, denunciator, examining magistrate or promoter against (the Templars), but as a zealot of the Catholic faith, defender of the Church, defender of the walls of Jerusalem, and as the extirpator of heretical depravity'.

A modern French historian, Robert Fawtier, has concluded after years of studying the period that 'the mainspring of Philip the Fair's actions in both the secular and the religious fields was probably his faith: faith in the Capetian dynasty, faith in his kingly office, and religious faith too, deeply rooted'. Yet while in Philip's mind religious faith was always secondary to faith in himself and his dynasty – the exact opposite of the view of Pope Gregory VII cited above – in exploiting the efficiency of the Inquisition against the Temple, he was careful to observe the trappings of legitimacy in bringing one institution of the Church to bear against another. He recognised as well as any man the truth of the statement of his ancestor Louis VI (1108–37), as reported in the *Life* written by Abbot Suger of Saint Denis: 'For the king to break the law is wicked and foolish, for the law and the king draw their authority from the same source'.

The paradox is that King Philip *needed* the Church to legitimise his actions, while at the same time his actions were aimed at *subverting* the Church. In this sense, the trial of the Templars represents the violent resolution of a conflict which had been simmering since the beginning of his reign. When he succeeded in obtaining the consent of Pope Clement and the use of the Inquisition, his struggle for domination of the Church was complete. Pope Clement and Inquisition became the last two great accusers of the Temple.

Before presenting them in the context of the trial it is necessary to review the struggle between Church and State in the years before the trial of the Templars. Ideas appearing towards the end of the thirteenth century threatened to upset the established scheme of things. Scholars at the University of Paris had recently argued on scriptural grounds that royal power was in fact obtained directly from God, so that the king of France was in no sense dependent on the pope for his authority. In a twist which could only endear him to Philip the Fair, the royal lawyer Pierre Dubois went so far as to suggest that Church should be governed by the State. As a consequence of the spread of these new ideas, King Philip had already come into conflict with Pope Boniface VIII (1295–1303) in three incidents which help us to understand the forces at play during the trial, and in which two of the protagonists of the trial first came into prominence.

The first incident concerned ecclesiastical taxes. In February 1296 Pope Boniface issued the bull *Clericis laicos*, which placed all secular rulers who taxed the clergy without explicit papal permission under interdict – that is to say, they would be debarred from ecclesiastical privilege if they demanded the payment of taxes. King Philip responded with two shrewd moves: first, he forbade the export of money or precious objects from France without royal permission; and second, royal permission was also made mandatory for the the residence of papal legates and other ecclesiastical officials within the kingdom. These conditions made it impossible for clergy in France to send taxes to Rome, The diplomatic stalemate was so effective that the following year Pope Boniface was obliged to issue a further bull which allowed the king to decide when the clergy in his kingdom should be taxed. He also canonised Louis IX in April 1297, a move designed to mollify the saint's grandson.

The truce was shortlived. For, in 1301, a second, more serious, incident occurred. Without consulting the king, Boniface had created a new diocese of the ecclesiastical district of Pamiers (previously in the diocese of

Toulouse). This might sound innocent enough, and well within papal powers, yet it was also a deliberate provocation. Since Carolingian times France had been divided into seventeen ecclesiastical provinces or Metropolitan areas, corresponding to the Roman administrative provinces of Gaul. This structure had been remarkably stable, and the last time new bishoprics were created had been in the ninth century. Thus the slightest change would be perceived by King Philip as creating discord. But Pope Boniface went one step further on a course of inevitable conflict. He appointed as bishop the notoriously anti-French abbot of the abbey of Saint Antonin in Pamiers, Bernard de Saisset, the son of a Languedoc knight. Since Languedoc had only been annexed and united with the *domaine* in 1271, anti-French sentiment remained amongst local lords. By upbringing, de Saisset was hostile towards France; by nature, he was a proud and contentious man. Earlier he had been involved in a bitter dispute with the count of Foix, the secular lord of the territory in which his abbey stood. Pope Nicholas IV assigned Cardinal Benedetto Gaetani to carry out an enquiry into the matter, and we may imagine that the Roman cardinal sympathised with an abbot who stood up for the rights of the Church against a secular lord. King Philip issued an injunction requiring Bernard de Saisset to appear before him in Paris. The abbot refused. Then Cardinal Gaetani became pope as Boniface VIII, and Bernard de Saisset travelled to Rome to seek exile and protection. Pope Boniface's solution was to provide immunity by making de Saisset bishop of Pamiers.

In other words, the appointment was a calculated affront to the dignity of Philip the Fair.

Bernard de Saisset was not prepared to leave the matter to rest. He began to put word about that, many years before, while he had been the abbot of Saint Antonin, King Louis IX – now St Louis – had told him that the kingdom of France would be destroyed in the tenth generation of the Capetian line, in other words under Philip the Fair. Nothing could have been better calculated to arouse the king's ire. The last straw, however, came when de Saisset sought to conspire with his old enemy, the count of Foix, to separate the Languedoc from France, and thereby re-establish the ancient independence of Toulouse. The loyal count sent word to Paris via the archbishop of Toulouse, after which a royal commission was set up to investigate the issue. Witnesses who appeared before the commission confirmed everything, for it seems that, under the influence of drink, Bishop de Saisset allowed his imagination to gallop, and much more besides. A long list of insults he had made included the charge that Philip the Fair was actually a bastard through his mother, and not descended from Charlemagne as he claimed.

Though this matter was well beyond normal challenges as in the case of the Templars, the king moved with caution. For the whole affair fell under the jurisdiction of his own trusted counsellor, Gilles Aicelin. As the archbishop of Narbonne, Aicelin was de Saisset's Metropolitan. While he now spent most of his time on royal business, he maintained an independence of mind and was rigorous in the application of law. When news reached him that royal officers had ransacked the bishop's palace at Pamiers, arresting the servants who were there and taking them to Toulouse for torture, he was forced to act because such an attack constituted a violation of canon law. At the same time, he too was no friend of Pope Boniface nor of Bernard de Saisset. In an embarrassing situation which served as good preparation for the circumstances of the Templar trial, he managed to walk the diplomatic tightrope with consummate skill. After stalling the royal ire with a series of legal objections which enhanced his role as a man of the Church, he then wrote a letter of formal reprimand at the royal behest. Shortly afterwards the bishop of Pamiers was transferred to Senlis, near Paris. This too was an advance echo of future proceedings, illustrating the skill of royal lawyers in choosing their battlegrounds. The point here is that the diocese of Senlis was part of the Metropolitan area of Reims, where Archbishop Robert de Courtenay – as becomes clear later in the trial – was very much a royal man and subject to court influence, unlike the stubborn and independent archbishop of Sens, Etienne Bécard, who might have blocked the matter if it took place under his jurisdiction in Paris. At Senlis, on 24 October 1301, the prisoner appeared before a court composed of Philip the Fair, the papal legate, other barons and prelates, and of course the archbishop of Narbonne. De Saisset, in what may be seen as a dry run for the trial a few years later, was formally charged with heresy, treason, simony and blasphemy.

Ambassadors were sent to Rome with a letter written by Gilles Aicelin which may have suggested the future tactic against the Templars. For it asserted in a phrase used in the *Arrest Order* that 'Certain important *persons worthy of faith* have informed us that this bishop was a manifest simoniac ...'.

A long-distance battle of wits and power ensued, a preview of the contest between Church and State during the trial of the Templars. Pope

Boniface immediately published a bull which asserted that only the pope had the right to intervene in ecclesiastical matters. Then he demanded not only that the king of France release Bernard de Saisset, but also summoned him to respond for his actions at a Council which would be held in Rome. In a direct attack on Philip's lawyers, Pope Boniface argued that 'Those who assure you that you have no superior, and that you are not subject to the supreme hierarchy of the Church, are deceiving you.'

King Philip's answer was to summon the first ever Estates-General within the friendly atmosphere of Reims, where prelates, barons, and burgesses from the chartered towns met in a *parlement*.* The purpose of this gathering was to bolster the king's own position by obtaining the explicit support of his subjects, including the clergy – who, like the archbishop of Narbonne a few months earlier, found themselves sitting on a very sharp fence.

Events precipitated. In November 1302, during the Council which had been announced to deal with the dispute, but obviously in the absence of Philip the Fair, Pope Boniface issued one of the most famous of all medieval papal bulls, *Unam Sanctam*. In it, he argued that the Church was necessarily a single and unique organisation. In his metaphor it possessed 'one body and one head – not two heads, which would make it a monster', but at the same time had two swords, the spiritual and the temporal: 'the one to be wielded for the Church, and the other to be wielded by it'. The former sword, *for* the Church, should be used by kings and other secular rulers, while the latter, *by* the Church, was the exclusive prerogative of ordained priests. The key affirmation of the bull was that the former must *always* remain subservient to the latter – a position which was in evident contradiction to the thoughts of the scholars at the university of Paris. In a transparent reference to the case of Bernard de Saisset, the bull continues: 'If a temporal authority should err, it is to be judged by the spiritual authority, but if an inferior spiritual authority should err it is to be judged by its own superior authority'. Moreover, in a message for King Philip's ear, willing submission to the pope was said to be a necessary step towards salvation. Pope Boniface was prepared to go further still to enforce his authority. During the summer of 1303, news came to Paris that he was preparing the text of

*It was convoked by lawyer Pierre Flote with the idea of legitimising Philip's position by showing it as representing all the social classes and groups in France: clergy, nobility and even the Third Estate or 'commons'.

54

another bull for the purpose of excommunicating Philip the Fair, to be promulgated in early September. This news provoked the third incident in the series.

In late summer the royal lawyer Guillaume de Nogaret rode to Italy with an assault force of French knights. Near Siena he joined up with Sciarra Colonna, of the great Roman family which Boniface had exiled from Rome and excommunicated, and together they marched on Anagni. This was the walled hilltop town in the Gaetani territory, south of Rome, where Boniface had been born and where he was then in residence. On 7 September 1303 – exactly one day before the excommunication of King Philip was due to be published – the combined forces of Nogaret and Colonna, estimated at around 600 cavalry and over 1,000 infantry, launched an attack against Anagni. Some sources say that during the assault the troops shouted 'Death to Boniface! Long live the King of France!' Despite strong defences, Anagni fell quickly. The defenders, together with the majority of cardinals there, fled almost at once. French and Colonna troops then sacked and pillaged the town, burning down the doors of the cathedral, while de Nogaret and Sciarra Colonna searched for Pope Boniface. According to legend, when they found the pope at prayer in the presence of the two cardinals who had stayed with him, Sciarra struck the pope on the face. Guillaume de Nogaret acted with greater calm, and managed to restrain his new ally. He demanded that the pope summon yet another Council to judge his own sins. Naturally, Pope Boniface refused.

Then, three days later, a popular uprising routed de Nogaret and the French troops. Pope Boniface VIII was liberated from his imprisonment and returned to Rome. Free, but a broken man, he died there a month later.

Thus King Philip the Fair emerged from this series of incidents the victor. Now at the apogee of his reign, he was able, through the presence of Gilles Aicelin at the conclave held in Perugia in 1305, to influence the election of Boniface's successor, Bertrand de Got, the archbishop of Bordeaux, who took the name Clement V. It was under this first of a series of French popes that the papacy was transferred to Avignon, and Clement himself soon found himself one of the major participants in the trial of the Templars.

Bertrand de Got came from a Gascon family whose prominence was derived entirely from the Church. His own ecclesiastical career probably originated with his maternal uncle Bertrand, bishop of Agen. At an early age Bertrand entered the monastery of Deffends, and progessed to studies at the universities of Bologna and Orléans. By the age of eighteen, he was already a canon of Saint Caprais in Agen, from which position he began his rise to the archbishopric of Bordeaux. By the time he became Pope Clement he was a sick man, weak, and characterised by an almost hopeless generosity which may have been the root-cause of his flagrant nepotism. The entire family advanced with him in a blatant manner that was unusual even then. The son of his eldest brother Arnaud, Raimond de Got, was elevated to cardinal. Four of the sons of his sister Marquise (who married Bérenger Guilhelm de Fargues) achieved high office: Raimond de Fargues became a cardinal; Bernard was the bishop of Agen (briefly, in 1306), and then archbishop of Rouen and Narbonne respectively; Béraud became the bishop of Albi (1311); and Amanieu was also the bishop of Agen later (in 1314). In addition, his youngest sister Vitale's son, Gaillard de Preyssac, became the bishop of Toulouse. At least four and possibly five other relatives were made cardinals.

Portraits show a roundish gentle face, with a single tuft of hair above his forehead, doleful, almost pleading eyes, and a small soft mouth. The coronation in Lyon, in the presence of Philip the Fair, his brother Charles de Valois, his half-brother the count of Evreux and the duke of Brittany, could hardly have been more inauspicious: during the procession which followed the ceremony a wall collapsed on the participants. The new pope was thrown from his white hackney, and a precious stone dropped out of the papal tiara. Charles de Valois was wounded, while the duke of Brittany died in the accident.

Pope Clement came further under the manipulating influence of Philip the Fair, often acting as though he were responsible for the spiritual extension of Philip the Fair's temporal strategy. In the next few years he annulled Boniface VIII's bull *Clericis laicos*, tempered the full force of *Unam Sanctam*, absolved King Philip and Guillaume de Nogaret of all accusations made against them after Anagni, and transferred the papacy to Avignon.

Yet he was not totally malleable, and stubbornly refused continuous pressure exerted on him to obtain a formal condemnation of Boniface VIII, and maintained a certain distance from the royal court. When he decided to establish his residence in Avignon it was in part because of that town's proximity to the forthcoming Council of Vienne, but also partly because it stood just beyond King Philip's realm. For the bridge celebrated in song was not only the southernmost bridge on the Rhône.

While Avignon, inside a great curve on the left bank of the river, was within the lands of the Angevin counts of Provence, at the other end of the bridge was a tower built to mark the limits of the kingdom of France.

A certain degree of papal acquiescence was essential to King Philip's strategy concerning the Templars. Memories of the scandal which his attack on Bernard de Saisset had created throughout Europe meant that whatever course of action he and his councillors decided upon should remain within the realms of formal legality. There was only one international and capillary organisation capable of mounting a challenge to a supra-national Order such as the Temple, and it too fell under the jurisdiction of Pope Clement: the Holy Inquisition. That was the reason why King Philip insisted in the wording of the *Arrest Order* that in acting against the Templars he was merely 'following the just request' of the inquisitor-general for France, Guillaume de Paris. Thus the Inquisition may be considered the last major participant in the trial of the Templars.

The Inquisition derived its name from one of the three main forms of legal action used in medieval episcopal courts, the *accusatio*, *denunciatio* and *inquisitio*. This last became the standard procedure against heretics after the Council of Verona in 1184, but it was a half-century later under Pope Gregory IX that the Inquisition came into being. He first set up special courts to search out and try heretics, and then in 1231 issued the constitution *Excommunicamus*, which was the first papal document to provide detailed legislation for the punishment of heretics. This included the surrender of heretics to secular authorities for punishment, the excommunication of all Cathars, Waldensians and their defenders, followers and friends, a formula by which suspected heretics automatically became heretics and subject to punishment after a year if they did not formally swear their innocence. The sentence was life imprisonment for impenitent heretics. Moreover, suspected heretics were neither allowed to appeal, nor to be defended by a lawyer (which to medieval eyes would be tantamount to the lawyer himself being heretical). But Pope Gregory did specify that the friars would be the ideal inquisitors since, unlike most clerics, they were trained both in theology and in pastoral work.

This legislation was reinforced by Pope Innocent IV (1243–54), who, in the ominous-sounding bull *Ad Extirpanda*, 'to extirpate', pronounced the elimination of heresy to be the chief duty of secular rulers. It was also Innocent IV who introduced torture as a legitimate means of extracting confessions, and proposed death at the stake as the punishment

57

for persistent or relapsed heretics. Coercive practices were justified by scriptural authority, for it was St Luke who told the followers of Christ to 'go out to the highways and hedges, and compel people to come in ...' (Luke: 17,23). The seeds of a capillary organisation were also sown by Innocent IV: Italy and Europe were divided into inquisitorial provinces overseen by the Franciscans and the Dominicans. Eastern France south of the Loire went to the Franciscans, while western France south of the Loire and Northern France were assigned to the Dominicans. The inquisitorial province of Paris, which included the dioceses of Rouen, Reims and Sens was the largest in France and, since its area corresponded to the royal *domaine*, the senior inquisitors were usually referred to as *inquisiteurs in regno Franciae* or *inquisiteurs généraux de France*. In the opening remarks of the first interrogation of the Templars in Paris, Guillaume de Paris is described with precision as 'inquisitor into heretical depravity within the kingdom of France'.

Some observations on the men who worked as inquisitors, and on the working methods and procedures of that tribunal, will enable us better to follow the trial of the Templars.

The inquisitors themselves were often men of exceptional theological and legal talent and, from about 1300, were usually university-trained doctors of law. Pope Innocent IV had specified that they should be 'forceful in their preaching, and full of zeal for the faith'. To this the Dominican friar Bernard Gui, one of the most celebrated of French inquisitors and author of a manual for practical use, added that 'the inquisitor should be constant, and should persist amidst dangers and adversities even to the point of death; he should be prepared to suffer in the course of justice, neither inviting danger nor avoiding his duty out of fear'. He was also to be diligent, zealous, honest and to maintain self-control at all times, taking care to arrive at the best possible judgment. To ensure that this was the case, the inquisitor's job was from the beginning performed in pairs. Towards the end of the thirteenth century, each pair was also provided with a companion known as the *socius*, with substitutes known as *comissari*, with armed *servientes* (servants), and finally with the scribes who kept detailed records of interrogations and trial proceedings. Although the inquisitor was in effect both prosecutor and judge, this complex structure served as a brake for the unscrupulous.

The procedures were also carefully regulated, and were codified during the thirteenth century in a series of practical manuals such as that of Bernard Gui mentioned above. One such manual, widely used at the time and known as the *Processus inquisitionis*, was compiled by Bernard de Caux and John of St Pierre in 1244 on the orders of Pope Innocent IV and the archbishop of Narbonne for use in that ecclesiastical province. Still in use at the time of Gilles Aicelin's archbishopric (the bishop of Mende, Guillaume Durant, who also sat on the papal commission, came from this Metropolitan district as well), it provides a fascinating insight into the mental climate in which the minds of such men were formed.

The *Processus* first explains how inquisitors should preach a general sermon in the locality in which they are to carry out their inquisition, and then issue a summons to heretics in the area to appear before them. There then follow eight sections on the main areas of procedure. The first, on the 'Method of Citation' (*Modus citandi*), provides a formulaic announcement of the inquisition, leaving gaps to be filled in with names of priests and localities. All heretics – men over the age of fourteen, and women over twelve – are summoned to appear, but given a period of grace before doing so. The second section, on the 'Method and Form of Abjuration' (*Modus abjurandi et forma jurandi*), provides a format to be used by the heretics: first he or she should acknowledge the true Catholic faith and deny all heresies, then swear obedience to the Pope and the Church; last of all, he or she should indicate belief in the holy sacraments, and promise to have no further truck with heretics. Next comes the 'Formula for the Interrogation' (*Formula interrogatorii*), which contains the questions to be asked by inquisitors. It specifies that a notary or scribe must authenticate confessions in the presence of at least one of the two inquisitors involved and in the presence of 'at least two other persons qualified for careful discharge of this task associated with us'. The questions sent out to provincial inquisitors in 1307 by Guillaume de Paris, and the 'Instructions for the Trial against the Templars' issued in 1309 by the bishop of Paris, both adopted this formulaic model.

To these provisions the modern reader should be especially grateful, since one of their consequences was the careful transcription of the Templar trials. The records of the trial in the Papal States describe the journeys, the public readings of citations, the posting of the edict on churches and other buildings, details of the thirty or so churches and monasteries used, and even – reminiscent of the reference made by William Morris in *News from Nowhere* to Horrebow's snakes in Iceland – details of inquisitorial sessions at which no suspects or witnesses at all appeared. In the same way, the transcripts of the papal commission in Paris allow us to reconstruct itineraries and identify places employed as prisons during the trial. Sometimes details we would not expect to find are given without the slightest trace of the embarrassment a modern mind would feel: in the trial at Florence and Lucca between 1310 and 1311, for example, the notary takes care to distinguish between testimony obtained with torture and that obtained without torture. In Paris, complaints about the use of torture were also faithfully recorded.

The fourth section, 'Method of Summoning Individuals' (*Modus singulos citandi*) provides yet another specific formula, interesting for the stress it places on the right of defendants to a legitimate defence. It also states that officers of the Inquisition should follow standard legal procedures, as we shall see in the detailed account of the trial when Templar defendants come forward to present a well-reasoned defence of the Order. There was, however, one major difference between inquisitional proceedings and standard legal practice for, in the words of the *Processus* 'we do not make public the names of witnesses', that is to say the delators.

The final sections concern the punishment of convicted heretics. They deal with such matters as the procedure for heretics who had been reconciled to the faith after abjuration of their crimes, an explanation of the classes of penance (where, how, how often, and for how many years they should be performed), and the sentence to be used for releasing convicted heretics to the secular arm for execution. For from a formal and technical point of view, the Inquisition did not punish heretics at all: in the sophistic reasoning of the *Processus*, the condemned heretic 'is to take himself to the prison prepared for him and make it his permanent home'. Punishment was therefore voluntary! The last section provides the 'Formula for the Sentence against those who died as Heretics' (*Forma sententie contra eos qui heretici decesserint*), in which the pernickety thoroughness of the Inquisition is shown to follow heresy quite literally into the grave. Even death could not provide a haven; once a target of the Inquisition, there was little chance of evasion whether alive or dead. For in dying the heretic had contrived to evade the strictures of the Church. So dead heretics too were to be condemned, and their bones to be exhumed and burned in punishment – a macabre procedure of which there is an interesting example during the Templar trial.

These meticulous procedures clearly left little space for manoeuvre for the Knights of the Temple once they found themselves under the gaze of the Inquisition. It was a ruthless tribunal, and to be accused was virtually to be condemned. Moreover, on the side of the accuser there was ample space for ambiguity and political manipulation, as the shrewd royal law-yers fully understood. The authors of the *Processus* candidly admit that 'we do various other things, indeed, in procedure and in other matters which cannot easily be reduced to writing . . .'.

Such provisions offered a man of Guillaume de Nogaret's ability and character a virtual licence to destroy the Order of the Temple, for *his* ruthlessness was totally at the service of King Philip the Fair. As was the skill of Guillaume de Paris, private confessor to King Philip and inquisi-tor-general of Paris, who carried out in person the first interrogations of the arrested Templars. Throughout the trial, procedures were meticulous-ly followed, so that even the Templar lawyers who eventually came forward found little on which to peg their objection and defence argu-ments. For the techniques developed and honed by inquisitors for nearly a century were perfectly suited to Philip the Fair's purpose.

4

FIRST INTERROGATIONS: OCTOBER 1307–NOVEMBER 1309

Guillaume de Nogaret lost no time once the Templars had been locked up in prison. On Saturday 14 October, just one day after the arrest, he summoned the leading theologians and lawyers of the University of Paris to the chapter-room of Notre Dame. Given the surprise and lack of information alluded to by Bernard Gui, we may imagine the buzz of excitement and curiosity as the scholars crossed the Petit Pont on their way from their abbeys and hostels on the Left Bank. In the medieval equivalent of a press conference, shock, horror and disbelief competed for space in the minds of those present as the royal lawyer outlined to them the reasons for the arrests and the nature of the accusations made against the Temple.

This gathering, which would today be described as an exercise in public relations, affords an insight into the mind of Philip the Fair and his concern for maintaining 'order' and the trappings of legality; it is not a procedure readily associated with the notion of a medieval king. Neither was the speech by Guillaume de Nogaret the sole event in the exercise. For, according to Jean de Saint-Victor, on Sunday the outlines of the affair were announced to a wider audience. This time, the clerics and the ordinary people of Paris were invited from every parish of the city to hear a sermon preached by Dominicans whose names the chronicler did not record, in the garden of the royal palace. Now the accusations were public knowledge.

The stage was set. On the following Thursday, 19 October 1307, preliminary hearings began inside the fortress of the Temple.

The initiative passed to Guillaume de Paris who, as inquisitor-general, presided in person over this first phase of the trial. The odds were stacked against the Templars. For the proud, expert interrogator in his black Dominican habit, rested and well fed, would have been a match for any lawyer on the niceties of theological controversy and heresy. But the

62

Templars who appeared before him were neither theologians nor lawyers: they were stunned, frightened and often broken men. The shock of arrest, a week of harsh imprisonment on a bread-and-water diet, the deprival of sleep, repeated threats of torture, use of the strappado and the ordeals of fire and water, had quickly broken the resistance of men who were mostly middle-aged or elderly. Gautier de Payen, for example, who had been initiated into the Order at Payen thirty-six years before, is said in the transcript to have been 'around eighty'. Jacques de Molay himself was in his mid-sixties, Hugues de Pairaud was about sixty, and Geoffroi de Charney about fifty-six. Each must have been exhausted by decades of harsh military discipline, debilitating travel, long-term residence in the East, and the sores of battle. For them, resistance to the skilled interrogation of Guillaume de Paris would have required almost inhuman feats of endurance.

The first witness to appear, the Templar priest Jean de Folliaco, set the pace on this opening day by affirming that during his reception ceremony he had been threatened with harsh imprisonment if he refused to deny Christ. In fact – as he tells us in his testimony – he was a recent recruit, having been received into the Order in the Paris Temple three years earlier by the treasurer. He is also thought to have been one of the spies infiltrated in the Order by Philip the Fair. Certainly the dates fit. But, whether or not he was a spy, his testimony set the ball rolling. He was followed by the serving-brother Rainier de Larchant, a Templar of longer standing who had been received into the Order twenty-six years before at the house of Beauvoir in the diocese of Gastines, Sens et Marne, by the then treasurer of the Temple at Paris, Jean de Tour. To those present, Rainier's brief confession must have seemed a terrifying confirmation of the accusations made by Guillaume de Nogaret: after having sworn to obey the statutes of the *Rule* he had been required to kiss Jean de Tour three times, 'first at the base of the spine, second on the navel, and third on the mouth'; next he had been ordered to deny a cross which was brought before him and to spit on it three times; then he was informed of the virtues of carnal relationships with other brothers. Last of all, he confessed to having worshipped a bearded idol which he had seen in twelve separate chapters of the Order, especially in the Paris Temple. The next day, Friday 20, a fifty-year-old serving-brother called Pierre de Tortaville, who had also been received into the Order in the diocese of Sens by Jean de Tour twenty-six years before, confirmed these 'errors' with only minor variations. He claimed that his recollections of the reception were not clear, but stated under oath that after an initial promise to obey the rules and statutes of the Order he had been allowed to put on the Templar mantle. When this was done, he had been taken to another, more secret place where a cross with an image of Christ had been shown to him. He had been instructed to deny Christ, and to spit on this cross. He too was then kissed by the receptor on the navel, on the base of the spine and on the mouth, and informed that it would be permissible for him to engage in carnal relations with other brothers – and for others to do so with him, if they so wished.

Here, exactly one week after the arrests, the essential elements of accusation against the Templars had already emerged: the denial of Christ, the practice of an 'obscene kiss', and sodomy.

Nor were Rainier and Pierre alone. On Saturday a far more important man, Geoffroi de Charney, the preceptor of Normandy and the putative uncle of the Geoffroi de Charny in whose possession the Turin Shroud later came to light, appeared before Guillaume de Paris. The reception ceremony he related had been carried out at Etampes by Amaury de la Roche, Master of the Temple in France, and in the presence of the then preceptor of Paris, Jean Le Franceys, some thirty-seven or thirty-eight years before. He too had been presented with an image of Christ and told not to believe in the Saviour because he was 'a false prophet, and not God'. He confessed to having denied Christ three times, although he claimed that it was only done with his mouth and not in his heart (an attempted escape clause which often appears in the confessions). Although he refused to be led by the inquisitor into more damning confessions, de Charney did confess to kissing the Master of the Temple in France on the navel.

Then, on Tuesday 24, came the turn of the Grand Master. In his testimony, Jacques de Molay declared under oath that he had been received into the Templars forty-two years earlier at Beaune by the then Master of the Temple in London, Humbert de Pairaud, who was Hugues de Pairaud's uncle. The key and condemning part of his testimony was the confession that he too had denied Christ in this ceremony. In the words of the inquisitorial notary: 'And he who received him had brought into his presence a bronze cross on which was a figure of Christ, and told him and ordered him to deny the Christ whose image was before him. And he, in spite of himself, did so. Then he was ordered to spit at it, but he spat on the floor.' In spite of this last contrivance, such a confession was more than sufficient to condemn him in the eyes of the Inquisition.

Worse still, while the Grand Master denied the more serious charges of 'carnal union with his brothers' he did – given his rank and responsibility – inculpate the entire Order of the Temple by implying that ceremonies for other initiates to the Templars were the same as his own.

The strategy of Guillaume de Nogaret and Guillaume de Paris was already evident, for the 'errors' these Templars were being coerced to confess were intended to establish in the willing minds of listening inquisitors and scholars a link between the Order of the Temple and the most pernicious heresies of the previous century.

For we must recall that the Inquisition had come into being because of the heresy of the Cathars. The first step towards becoming a Cathar was a formal renunciation of Christ, and they also practised the *osculum infame* or 'obscene kiss' – which was usually offered to the Devil. On meeting a *perfectus*, or initiated priest, the Cathar performed the *salutatio* which consisted of an embrace and a kiss. This ritual greeting constituted one of the five ceremonies of their doctrine. The leap from the *osculum infame* to the kiss on the buttocks and navel, and then another leap on to sodomy and other heretical practices, would have resembled a series of smooth transitions in the imagination of men trained to perceive these links. Study of Cathar doctrines was an integral part of the training for an inquisitor, and the ceremonies were referred to as examples in their instruction manuals.

Even worse was the implicit connection with nascent witchcraft. Just seventy years before these proceedings, Conrad of Marburg, the first man to bear the title 'inquisitor into heretical depravity', had been sent to Germany by Pope Gregory IX to suppress supposed outbreaks of heresy. Marburg, who had won his spurs in the confusingly named Albigensian Crusade against the Cathars, launched into his task with such zeal that chroniclers claimed even king and bishops in the Rhineland feared for their lives while he was at work. The archbishop of Mainz complained to the pope that this fanatical inquisitor forced innocent people to confess by the simple expedient of threatening them with the stake. Pope Gregory's reply was a bull issued in 1233 which informed the archbishop of the heretical practices within his diocese. These practices bear such a striking similarity to those the Templars were charged with that they could have been used by Guillaume de Nogaret as a blueprint for drawing up the accusations in 1307. First the initiate into these sects was led into a meeting where the Devil appeared (usually in the form of a black cat), he was then required to kiss this figure either on the mouth or on the buttocks, in this way formally renouncing the holy sacraments; next, he was required to kiss the master of the sect. Finally, after a short liturgy, lights were extinguished so that an orgy could take place.

In other words, what might seem to a modern observer to be implausible or exaggerated confessions of denying and spitting on the cross would have sparked hideous comparisons in the mind of a zealous inquisitor around 1300.

Later, of course, Jacques de Molay and the other prisoners sought to retract these early confessions. For, in spite of the formula added by the notary at the end of his interrogation, in which the Grand Master affirmed that his confession had not been made 'as the result of violence, the fear of torture or prison or some other cause', and swore that 'he had stated the pure truth for the salvation of his soul', these immediate confessions were clearly extracted under torture. The preceptor Ponsard du Gizy later claimed that he had made his confession after three months of brutal torture, and there is evidence that some Templars died during this period of torture and deprivation. Most Parisians seem to have accepted that Templar confessions had been extracted under torture. In the words of the verse chronicler Geoffroi de Paris:

> Et puis ont dist communement
> Que, par la force du torment,
> Et dist et confessé avoient
> Celz de l'ordre.

(And then it was commonly said/that by the use of torture/they had made their confessions/those of the order.) Yet while the confessions were falsely obtained, the subtle hand guiding the process had excogitated a plan the Templars could not forestall. The seeds of heresy were sown in the minds of clerics and populace alike, in spite of the fact that they knew torture had been employed. When, later in the trial, circumstances made rectraction feasible, and a defence of the Order was organised, it was too late. The die had been cast in these early days.

The pressure applied by Guillaume de Paris allowed no respite. On Wednesday 25 October, the very day after his first appearance before the Inquisition, Jacques de Molay and other prominent Templars were paraded before an audience comprised of the theologians and lawyers of the University of Paris who had been addressed by Guillaume de Nogaret eleven days before. But this time, the summons was to the Temple rather than to Notre Dame: inside the prison.

With the previous week's rhetoric and dramatic accusations still fresh in their minds, the scholars now gathered to hear the Grand Master make a *public* confession of guilt. We may imagine a broken Jacques de Molay, exhausted and confused, something like the maltreated pilots wheeled before television cameras by Saddam Hussein during the 1991 Gulf War to atone publicly for their 'sins'. A pitiful and plaintive old man, referring sycophantically to his accuser Philip the Fair as 'the bringer of light' as though he believed it would help his case, de Molay again confessed to denial of Christ and spitting on the cross. He pleaded with the scholars to intercede on his behalf with Pope Clement, so that the Templars could be absolved of their crimes and receive suitable penances. From the point of view of the royal court this was yet another superb example of public relations, since the 'astonishing bestiality' and 'supremely abominable crimes' of the arrest order had now been rendered credible to an audience with immense influence by means of an authoritative confession.

An astonishing transformation had taken place in just twelve days: on Thursday 12 October, Jacques de Molay walked beside the coffin of Catherine of Valois with the highest dignitaries of Church and State; on Friday he was thrown into the dungeons of the Temple; on Tuesday 24, after being racked by torture, he had confessed before Guillaume de Paris; now, on Wednesday, he confessed in public to crimes and heretical practices no one would have believed of him just a fortnight ago. This carefully orchestrated series of events betrays the subtle hand of Guillaume de Nogaret, a publicist and propagandist whose skills would have been invaluable in any epoch of history.

The scandal was international, and potential defendants of the Templars would have needed vast reserves of courage to speak up now. Here, in a certain sense, in the brief period from 13 to 25 October is the essence of the downfall of the Order. Other Templars, whether high-ranking like Hugues de Pairaud or simple serving-brothers, had little reason to resist their interrogators or suffer torture. For their own Master had already betrayed them. In fact, only four Templars of the 138 questioned under Guillaume de Paris denied all the charges, possibly because all four were of a younger generation with little or no experience of life in the East or of the glorious past: Jean de Chateauvillars was thirty, Lambert de Toysi and Henri de Hercigny were both around forty, and Jean de Paris was only twenty-four. In any case, their denials made little impact because damning evidence rapidly mounted against the Order and the arrests were formally justified. In a series of well-planned, decisive, brilliantly executed moves Guillaume de Nogaret had out-manoeuvred the most powerful of crusading orders. The coup was made; now the trappings of legality would – it must have seemed to him – complete the operation in short order. It is likely that towards the end of October 1307 the royal lawyer believed that the whole affair would soon be concluded.

If so, then he was too optimistic. First, as we have seen, the arrests in France were not followed by equal enthusiasm throughout Christendom. Templars of all ranks still, on 25 October, enjoyed total freedom and revenues from the Order's property in Scotland, Ireland, England, Germany, Portugal, Spain, Italy and Cyprus. Now Pope Clement too made an unexpected show of independence.

For although the author of the *Arrest Order* claims that preliminary investigations into the Order of the Temple had been carried out 'after having spoken with our most holy Father in the Lord, Clement', the pope seems to have had no advance notice of the arrests. Bernard Gui is quite explicit on this point:

> Lastly, the Roman See, to which the fact at first seemed incredible and which tolerated the above-mentioned capture with ill-will, was given further information at Poitiers, where the curia was at that time . . .

The Dominican friar's observation is confirmed by the fact that on 27 October Pope Clement wrote a formal letter of complaint to Philip the Fair from Poitiers.

Clement seems to have understood that the attack against a religious order under the exclusive jurisdiction of the Holy See was tantamount to a full-frontal attack on the papacy itself – every bit as violent as earlier confrontations with Boniface VIII. So when the written complaint brought no change in the situation, the pope used his own considerable powers. On 22 November he issued the bull *Pastoralis preeminentiae*, which ordered the recalcitrant rulers of Europe to arrest the Templars within their kingdoms and cited the spontaneous confession of Jacques de Molay as an argument to convince them. Now while this might sound like capitulation to the French king, phrases citing the possibility of doubt and the need to investigate the truth of allegations against the Templars more fully also suggest that the pope was following up his earlier letter of protest. It was a shrewder move than might appear at first sight. For with this bull Pope Clement brought the trial, at least to a certain extent, under his own control. Another consequence of the bull was that henceforth the trial of the Templars would be an entirely public affair, prolonged and under full international scrutiny. It would also remain catalogued for posterity, a matter of no small importance for long-lived institutions like the Roman Catholic Church and the Capetian monarchy.

The immediate effect was cataclysmic. Pope Clement sent Cardinal Bérengar Frédol and Cardinal Etienne de Suisy to Paris to represent his interests. But as so often later in the trial, the men chosen to perform this delicate duty had one foot in each camp. The former, a learned scholar from Laverune near Montepellier, who was to play an important role throughout the trial of the Templars, had been made cardinal by Clement two years previously; but, like Gilles Aicelin, he was as well regarded in the royal court as in the curia. The latter had actually been a member of the royal chancellery before his elevation in 1305. Now they entered Paris as representatives of the pope and it was only after some initial skirmishing – peacock-like displays of independence – between king and pope that the cardinals were allowed to enter the Temple and interview the Grand Master and other members of the Order. Faced with what must have seemed to him friendly questioners, Jacques de Molay retracted his confession. He claimed that it had been made out of fear of torture.

In effect, then, Pope Clement's bull stemmed the floodtide set into motion by Guillaume de Nogaret and Guillaume de Paris. A groundswell of resistance gathered force. There were rumours of wax tablets circulating inside the Temple with messages in the Grand Master's name encouraging other prisoners to retract their confessions before the cardinals. Letters written at the time consider the possibility of the Templars' innocence; memoirs defending the Order were also circulated. Geoffroi de Paris expressed his doubts in these terms:

> Je ne sai a tort ou a droit
> Furent li Templiers, sanz doutance,
> Touz pris par la royaume de France;

(I do not know whether rightly or wrongly/the Templars were, without doubt/all imprisoned by the king of France.) In the minds of the imprisoned Templars, hope deriving from the rumours must have been increased by hints that they were to be judged by a papal commission. Perhaps the visiting cardinals had even made such a suggestion. In that case, it must have seemed to them – perhaps naïvely – a judgment in their favour was bound to follow. When Pope Clement formally suspended the activity of the inquisitors working under Guillaume de Paris, their confidence must have soared.

For, after the relentless drama of the autumn of 1307, the year 1308 found the opposing forces in stalemate. No real progress was made in the trial as Philip the Fair and Pope Clement indulged in a debilitating tug-of-war over the right to try the Templars.

In February 1308, King Philip sought to gain support in this tug-of-war by putting a series of loaded legal questions to the scholars of the University of Paris. Once again we see evidence of his respect for 'order'. The first question may be seen as a explicit criticism of Pope Clement's procrastination. It concerns the formal problem of whether in a case of heresy a secular prince has the right to act, even though it is technically a matter for the Church, in cases where it is clear that the lack of justice may create a scandal. The second question struck even closer to the heart of the problem: in the case of the affair of the Templars, a 'unique sect formed by several damned, horrible and abominable persons', should the secular prince not proceed in spite of the fact that they are members of a religious order, since their heresy is 'so huge and pestilent'? To this end, King Philip – or Guillaume de Nogaret – presents a subtle argument designed to isolate the separate categories of 'warrior' and 'monk' which St Bernard had brought together in his *De Laude*. Now that confessions had demonstrated the truth of the accusations beyond all doubt, he argued, the dignities and privileges of the Templars should be cancelled. Then they would be mere knights rather than clerics, and therefore fall within the jurisdiction of the king. Surely the confessions of the Grand Master and more than fifty other Templars were sufficient evidence to condemn the Order without any further ado, and even enough to deny the prisoners their status as true Roman Catholics? Some of course had denied the charges made against them, which brought up the question whether their denials were sufficient to save the Order as a whole from condemnation; or, on the contrary, whether the confessions were enough to condemn it. The final questions concerned the matter of Templar property, which the chroniclers and observers believed to be the real object of the king's strategy. There were two real problems here: first, whether properties confiscated from the Order should go to the secular prince within whose jurisdiction they are found, or to the Church to be used for the Holy Land; and second, who should administer these properties in the event of their being destined to the Holy Land? The Church

70

itself, or the secular prince – especially in the case of the kingdom of France?

The replies to these sticky technical demands came just over a month later, on 25 March. The independence of the scholars may be judged from the fact that these replies were by no means wholly in King Philip's favour.

The fourteen masters in theology who signed the document first apologised for the time they had taken to reach their conclusions. The task had been a difficult one, requiring 'diligent, mature and repeated deliberation' on the seven main issues. This may be taken to indicate the enormous difficulty of reconciling the provisions of canon law with the threat implicit in Philip the Fair's presence across the Seine. But they had now prepared the replies, which were brief in order to 'avoid prolixity and spare the time of the royal majesty'. The questions and answers may be represented schematically as follows:

	Question	Answer
1.	May the king judge the Templars alone?	No
2.	Are the Templars knights rather than clerks?	No
3.	Are the confessions sufficient to condemn the Order?	Yes, or at least to require a thorough inquiry
4.	Does apostasy render the Templars no longer Catholic?	Yes, but with reservations
5.	Should Templars not confessed retain status?	As for questions 3 and 4
6/7.	Should confiscated property go to King or Church?	Ambiguous: property wasn't given to Templars; should be used for same purpose & administered in best way

These indecisive replies indicate the ambiguities, hesitation and hedging which must have characterised the discussions of the scholars. The real problem was that the conflict over jurisdiction which marked the struggle between King Philip and Pope Clement was reflected in the persons of the masters of theology. In their reply, they describe themselves to the king as 'your humble clients', and as 'humble and devoted chaplains' of the king of France who are offering their 'complete submission to render whole and devoted service to the royal majesty'. But at the same time, the masters of law are clerics. Five of them sign the replies as members of religious orders, implying direct obedience to the Holy See (one Franciscan, two Dominicans, and two Augustinians). They are courteous and humble in tone, and assure King Philip that they desire 'with all our heart . . . to obey the royal orders'; but they also assert in no uncertain terms that they will 'obey the truth'. This is perhaps the crux of the reply. For while the masters appear to accept the possibility that confessions obtained from the Templars *might* justify condemnation of the Order, there is no explicit encouragement in their letter. Certainly there is no mandate to the king to take the whole matter in his own hands – as he must have hoped.

Failure on this front meant that more fuel was needed for the propaganda machine. Fresh arguments and justifications had to be sought for King Philip to assume absolute control of the Templar trial and, as a consequence, the fate of the Order. Who could have provided them better than Pierre Dubois and Guillaume de Plaisians?

Dubois pitched in with two finely reasoned pieces of propaganda in favour of Philip the Fair. The first was an undated and anonymous pamphlet with the title *Remonstrance of the People of France*, written in French some time early in 1308 and replete with learned references both to canon law and to the Bible. The main thrust of this piece is an *ad hominem* attack on Pope Clement on the grounds of his notorious nepotism. It asserts that the subjects of King Philip are dissatisfied with the delay in condemning the *bougrerie* and the denials of Christ of the Knights Templar. Both these charges, he argues, are wholly beyond doubt. He goes on to insinuate that the inadequacy of the pope in this affair, and the fact that Clement has done nothing beyond offering verbal condemnations, are thanks to his own corruption. He even allows himself to make the irreverent suggestion that Pope Clement may have been bribed by the Order of the Temple. The fact that the important dioceses of Rouen, Toulouse and Poitiers had been assigned to papal relatives is offered as proof of papal corruption.

Although this diatribe may have been written just before the masters of theology of Paris made their judgment, it provides a fascinating example of the measures King Philip – and the lawyers working on his behalf – were prepared to take in order to bring the Templar trial to a rapid conclusion. It would require only a short step from this position to make formal accusations against Pope Clement.

The next Dubois piece, *Populi Franciae ad requem supplicato*, or *Public Entreaty on behalf of the People of France*, was written after the judgment of the masters of theology. Published in April or early May of 1308, its main task was to encourage the king in person to strike the Templars. This shorter, more tightly argued piece has for its basic premise the idea that the particular heresy of the Templars differs from that of normal deviants from the Catholic faith. While most heretics accept much of Christian doctrine and only differ from orthodoxy in detail, in this way remaining fundamentally Christian, the Templar heresy is of a different order. According to 'the people of the kingdom of France' – aka Pierre Dubois – these miserable individuals 'are entirely beyond the power of the Church' even on the terms of their own confessions. Judgment of their sins should now be transferred from Church to State. This assertion is given scriptural authority from St Paul's first letter to the Corinthians (5,12): 'For what have I to do with judging outsiders?'

The author then moves on to a more spectacular example taken from Exodus. 'For Moses punished the worshippers of a golden calf by having 3,000 men killed without seeking permission from the high priest, who was his own brother Aaron.' (In Dubois' *Entreaty* the actual figure is 22,000, but the Revised Standard Version from which quotations are taken gives 3,000.) The point here is that Moses was not a priest, just as the king of France is not a priest, and the homicidal and apostate Templars were every bit as bad as the calf-worshippers of ancient Palestine. Starting from this Old Testament authority, Dubois moves on to quote a passage from The Letter of Paul to the Romans in explicit support for immediate action by Philip the Fair: 'For whatever was written in former days was written for our instruction, that by steadfastness and by the encouragement of the scriptures we might have hope' (15,4). The logic of the 'people of France' is there for all to see: if Moses killed 3,000, what matter if King Philip condemn 138? It is his duty as a good Christian king to do so.

But what of the 138 Templars? While these discussions and debates reached fever pitch, and must have been the stuff of everyday gossip among the learned men of the Left Bank, the imprisoned brothers languished in prison. Months of harsh diet and torture had reduced many to inhuman conditions; some, perhaps as many as thirty-six, had died in the Temple at Paris alone (though they were perhaps better off than the group of around 100 Templars said in one of the defence memoirs to be held in Saracen prisons – *in carceribus Babilonis*). A dramatic letter written to King Jaimé II of Aragon at this time claimed that Jacques de Molay stripped off before Pope Clement's visiting cardinals, in order to show them the lacerations and marks of torture on his racked body. In this one-sided battle, no possibility of reply was granted to the Templars, save the circulation of wax tablets and necessarily anonymous letters.

The pope himself stayed with his court for sixteen months in Poitiers, which remained the principal papal residence until the move to Avignon the following spring, where he created a semi-permanent papal palace and court.

There were good reasons for his residence beyond the reach of Paris. Poitiers stood just outside the royal *domaine*. Furthermore, it was the northernmost diocese of the metropolitan area of Bordeaux, which also included Agen, so, in a certain sense, Pope Clement was on home territory. The bishop of Poitiers, Arnaud d'Auch, was another of his relatives and had been appointed to this position soon after Pope Clement's accession to the Holy See. Bishop Arnaud was also a Gascon, born in the village of La Romieu south of Agen. He appears to have known Bertrand de Got in their youth, and perhaps studied with him as a student at the abbey of Deffends. Certainly they enjoyed a relationship of intimate trust. It was for this reason that Pope Clement had sent the bishop on diplomatic missions to France and England in 1306 and 1307, and again to England in 1312. In 1312, Arnaud d'Auch became papal chamberlain, which was a position of enormous influence within the curia. For, apart from the formal functions of controlling papal finance and official acts, the chamberlain also acted as close personal advisor. In this capacity he was to play an important role behind the scenes during the Templar trial. We shall see later that Bishop d'Auch was a member of the commission of cardinals which eventually passed judgment on Jacques de Molay and the other leaders of the Order.

This, then, was the man with whom Clement sought refuge in the early phase of his papacy. Poitiers was a well defended city, having been fortified by the counts of Poitou, and was situated on a hilltop between the rivers Clain and Boivre on a site reminiscent of Durham. Pope Clement resided in the monastery of the Franciscans, which had been founded in 1240 opposite the royal palace. Towards the end of the century it had been enlarged by the acquisition of the nearby convent of the friars known as the Sachets, and by the appropriation of the new cemetery of Notre Dame la Petite. But distance from Paris was a double-edged sword: Pope Clement was physically safe but, at the same time, unable to exert pressure on behalf of the imprisoned Templars. Papal business continued as normal, with daily hearings of pleas and meetings with ambassadors from the courts of Europe. But the shadow of the trial of the Templars must have hung over him. Powerless, almost as if he were waiting for the furore of Pierre Dubois' polemics to pass over, the pope engaged in a waiting game of cat and mouse with Philip the Fair.

Events were precipitated by a distant and unexpected death. On 1 May 1308, the Holy Roman Emperor Albert I of Habsburg died. He had reigned since 1298. A new emperor was needed, and the desire of Philip the Fair was to elect his own brother Charles of Valois. Thus he could exert a stranglehold over both Church and Empire. If he could influence the election in his favour and at the same time obtain the treasure and lands of the Templars, King Philip would become beyond question the strongest ruler in Christendom. For this reason, astute and unpredictable as ever, he suddenly departed from Paris for Poitiers in mid-May with what seems to have amounted to a sizeable army. He arrived on 26 May with Charles of Valois, several French barons and prelates, and other representatives who had gathered at Tours earlier in the month. These men and their accompanying knights and soldiers represented a serious threat to the undefended pope. It has in fact been suggested that Pope Clement became so acutely aware of his vulnerability, so near to Paris with no fixed residence, that the idea of settling the papal court permanently in Avignon came to him during the weeks of pressure from this army in the summer of 1308 at Poitiers. King Philip established himself squarely in Poitiers, and papal business was suspended as if in anticipation of a lengthy and claustrophobic royal presence. The distant battle of nerves was transferred to one small provincial town, with the protagonists each feigning their pleasure at the presence of the other while seeking the destructive blow. King Philip and his court were housed in the royal palace, which had been built by the counts of Poitou at the highest point of the city, and which was now the residence of the royal *sénéschal*; Pope Clement was quite literally across the road from him in the Franciscan monastery, on the south side of the palace. The third party, the Order of the Temple, was represented by brothers who were held in the important Temple of Poitiers – from which the Templar province of Poitou and Aquitaine had been controlled. This was a stone's throw away from both pope and king, opposite the door of the church of Saint Etienne on the Grande Rue (on the site between the present rue de la Cathédrale, rue Montgautier, and Grande Rue).

The issue all of them were there to settle was brought out into the open on 29 May 1308, when Pope Clement held a public consistory in the presence of both the papal and the royal courts inside the palace of Poitiers. Now, after Pierre Dubois' opening salvos, came the big guns of the expert theologian and lawyer Guillaume de Plaisians with a speech possibly written by – and certainly composed in collaboration with – Guillaume de Nogaret. Here, from the point of view of the Templar trial, was the real purpose of Philip the Fair's presence in Poitiers: first to intimidate the pope by force of arms; second, to embellish the physical intimidation with legal and theological argument.

Guillaume de Plaisians' harangue before Pope Clement that morning contained an exuberant display of rhetoric, comparable to the opening paragraph of the previous year's *Arrest Order*. After an initial invocation to Christ, the royal lawyer insinuated into the minds of the listeners the parallel between Christ as a saviour-king and Philip the Fair as his minister on earth. In so doing, he was seeking not only to justify the royal action in taking the initiative against the Templars but also to praise it. At the same time, there was implicit in his argument a condonation of any future move:

> After the universal victory gained on the wood of the cross, against the ancient enemy in defence of his Church and for the redemption of man, by Jesus Christ himself, who reigns and rules and who merits more than any other to be known by antonomasia and through his excellence to be called king . . . even Jesus had not won against the enemies of his Church and the orthodox faith a single victory as admirable, great, quick, useful and necessary, as he has recently, in our own time, by means of his ministers and delegates, in uncovering the affair of the perfidious Templars and their heretical depravity . . .

It is for this reason, de Plaisians continued, 'to make this victory manifest to you, most Holy Father', that King Philip has come with his prelates, clerics, barons, knights and people of his kingdom into the presence of the pope. Not, as we have seen in an earlier chapter, to assume the role of accuser and denunciator in the royal person, but to act as zealots of the Catholic Church and as 'extirpators of heretical depravity'.

Poor King Philip, the argument might be summarised, had not really wanted to arrest the Templars at all. The first accusation came from men of little importance – a probable reference to Esquin de Florayn – and was made against a rich and powerful religious order which had long-standing links with the French crown, and had also enjoyed the king's own patronage. Moreover, the hideous nature of the crimes for which they were accused made the matter most unpleasant, and it had been painful to be forced into a decision to act. So, the argument runs, King Philip's actions had been dictated almost against his own will out of a profound sense of duty and his deep faith, and had been carried out in the name of Christ. With magnificent sophistry Guillaume de Plaisians turns the chief accusation *against* King Philip on its head, so that it appears in *his favour*. While contemporaries suspected his cupidity, and modern observers might see his action against the Templars as an example of arrogance against the Church comparable to his attacks against Pope Boniface, here the king is praised for his *courage* in taking action: 'In fact, no other living person would have dared to do something so grandiose; and he was obliged to do it for many reasons, above all because he swore to do so at his coronation'.

Now, the lawyer continued, the arrests had been made and confessions had been recorded throughout the kingdom of France. The Grand Master himself had confessed both to the Inquisition and before the masters of theology, so there could not possibly be any lingering doubt concerning the heresy of the Templars. Suspicion about the Order had been gathering for some time, especially concerning their secret reception ceremony and the holding of chapters at night, 'which is the custom of heretics'. This, too, constituted convincing proof. Guillaume de Plaisians even charges the Templars with responsibility for the loss of the Holy Land – as a result of their shortcomings and their conniving with the Saracens. The facts, he concludes, are 'clearer than the light at midday' and, for this reason, it is the special duty of the pope to sustain the cause of the faith. Pope Clement must not concern himself about *how* these crimes became known, but rather with the fact that their existence is now known. Moreover, their gravity is such that he would be justified in taking steps which in normal circumstances would be considered outside the law.

Decoded, this last affirmation meant: Pope Clement, the situation is so unusual that you should simply charge King Philip with the task of condemning the Order of the Temple.

Pope Clement, to his credit and in spite of the strong military presence of the king, resisted the pressure as far as the Templars were concerned. He also stalled on the business of electing a new emperor: that was something King Philip could not force him to do. According to Giovanni Villani, Clement manoeuvred against the king while orally assuring him that Charles of Valois would be the new emperor. The papal stalling was rewarded in November, when Count Henry of Luxembourg was elected emperor at Frankfurt by the elector-princes, German princes and archbishops. After Henry was crowned as the Holy Roman Emperor Henry VII, at Aachen on 6 January 1309, the risk of total suffocation of papal powers by Philip the Fair diminished. Pope Clement gained valuable breathing space.

For the moment, however, he was still under ferocious pressure. Guillaume de Plaisians returned to the charge on 14 June. Then, in words which were replete with scriptural quotation, the screws were turned one notch further in what amounted to a blatant threat. Pope Clement was forcibly reprimanded for his disdain, and for his refusal to accept that he too might be guilty of sinning through inaction. Just as St Peter had been reproached twice by God and once by St Paul, de Plaisians argued, so should his successors be prepared to accept accusations of sinful conduct. Even in their 'eminent dignity', popes should sometimes be willing to accept advice from lesser persons if that meant 'avoiding sin and the consequent scandal'. In a subtle turn of phrase, he manages to suggest that King Philip had acted as the result of direct revelation from God: 'For it is better to intervene before an affair is compromised than seek a remedy later; and the Lord may, through the divine word, reveal to lesser persons things which may be profitable to the great'.

This second harangue developed into an explicit attack on Pope Clement's refusal to take action. Such a refusal could have dangerous consequences, de Plaisians argued. First, it gave the impression that the pope wished to protect the Templars, which was itself tantamount to heresy; second, it allowed the Templars time and hope which might serve to restore their strength and enable them to achieve ultimate victory, which amounted to abetting heresy. Worse still, while the heresy of the Templars was previously hidden, it had now been made manifest 'like a kindling fire which has smouldered for a long time and which flares up so much the more as one delays extinguishing it, and which burns down the neighbour's home'. This image seemed to kindle de Plaisians' own rhetoric, for he goes on in these dramatic terms:

Hence, holy Father, you see the flames of the blazing fire-place, burning the homes of the best; the entire Church of France, where

78

this fire, hidden up to now, in the same way as in other kingdoms, reveals itself in flames, the Church of France, I say, cries out in the breath of its piety: 'Fire! Fire! Help! Help!'

The audience in the great hall of the castle of Poitiers must have been held spellbound by this fiery language. We can imagine him winding up his voice to a shouted climax which stunned them into silence.

'The fire must be stopped before it devours the Church, and destroys Pope Clement himself.' While the effect of his words reverberated through the hall and the minds of those present, de Plaisians moved in for the kill with three specific demands in the name of the 'zealot' king. Each of the three actions, he affirmed, was 'necessary for the extirpation of the above-mentioned perfidy'. First of all, Pope Clement should instruct the prelates of Europe to take action against individual Templars in their dioceses; second, he should arrange that the papal suspension of the inquisition into the Templars be revoked; and third, the Order of the Temple, 'which must be considered as a condemned sect', should be removed totally from the Church by apostolic provision 'as a vase which is truly useless and full of scandal'.

Then, just in case the theological argument and rhetoric failed to move Pope Clement, the royal lawyer concluded with an explicit threat:

If you do not do these things promptly, consider the great confusion which will result for Your Holiness; assuredly great, since the princes and the peoples, seeing that you do not do them, will do them themselves, in default of you.

The gauntlet was down.

Still Pope Clement refused to budge from his position that a religious order could not be judged by a lay authority. Time, he insisted, was necessary in order to ensure a judicious decision. Once again, King Philip was thwarted. For all the power he wielded and the threats which were made in his name, his profound sense of faith and order made papal consent essential. He was frustrated, but not defeated. Once again, he moved with decision.

Two weeks after Guillaume de Plaisians' second harangue, a group of seventy-two Templars was brought from Paris to Poitiers on King Philip's orders to be tried in the presence of the pontiff. The brief trial-within-the-trial which ensued was clearly a showpiece made to measure for papal consumption, with prisoners carefully picked from the hundreds of Templars available in Paris. The depositions of over half the men who appeared in Poitiers survive, and all but one of them confessed to the crimes with which they were charged. But none was later to appear in the list of over 500 Templars who, two years later, constituted the defence movement, and none was of high rank in the Order.

From 29 June to 2 July, the pontiff and the cardinals who were with him at Poitiers listened to the confessions. The now-familiar ingredients emerged: secret rooms, denials of Christ, obscene kisses, sodomy, and the mysterious head which the Templars worshipped. It was, in modern terms, a blatant framing. Yet for Pope Clement it must have been quite a different matter to hear from the horse's mouth what had previously been confined to abstract words in the dry language of inquisitors, or to the letters of the king. Now he was able to address the prisoners in person, and he seems to have been genuinely shocked by their replies. Bernard Gui reported that

> ... some Templars were led into the presence of the pope and here again in the presence of several cardinals, confessed and recognised that the confessions which they had made earlier were true, including their own confessions. The result of this was that it was ordered that the Templars should be arrested everywhere and that the truth should be brought to the light.

For three papal bulls issued immediately after these hearings illustrate how effective King Philip's pressure had been.

The first of these bulls, *Subit assidue*, was promulgated just three days after the hearings concluded, in the heat of the moment. In it, Pope Clement reveals how much he had been touched by the arguments of Guillaume de Plaisians. He claims, plausibly, that he had suspended the powers of the inquisitors because Guillaume de Paris had never informed him of the plans for the arrest of the Templars. Now, however, having heard for himself the confessions of heresy, he is willing to forgive the king for his hasty action. He is also prepared to revoke the suspension of the inquisitors, and would allow bishops and inquisitors to begin fresh inquiries. A further, strained compromise was worked out concerning the imprisonment of the Templars: in theory they would be handed over to the Church; in practice they remained in royal hands. In this way both Pope Clement and King Philip had saved face after the showdown, and the way was open to proceed with the trial of the Templars. A few days later, Pope Clement announced the conditions for episcopal inquiries into the Templar heresy: each commission was to consist of the bishop in whose diocese the inquiry took place, two canons of the cathedral church, two Dominicans and two Franciscans. These provisions, in effect, paved the way for the great trial in Paris from 1309 to 1310 which forms the centrepiece of this book. Philip the Fair was evidently satisfied, for towards the end of July he returned to Paris.

Then, on 12 August 1308, after further negotiations with Guillaume de Plaisians, Pope Clement issued the two bulls *Faciens misericordiam* and *Regnans in coelis*. The former repeats the papal version of the story so far, and explains how Clement had gradually come to believe the accusations against the Templars. Then, after repeating the institution of episcopal commissions or inquiries into the heresy of individual Templars, it adds the new element of the creation of an inquiry *against the Order as a whole*. For while he was willing to concede ground on the question of individual guilt, any global judgment on a religious order had to remain the prerequisite of the Holy See. To resolve the issue, in the second bull Pope Clement announced a General Council of the Church to be held at Vienne in order to judge both the guilt of individual Templars and that of the Order of the Temple as a whole, and also to consider the possibility of a new crusade to the Holy Land. This Council was to open on 1 October 1310, still far off and in the event to be postponed still further. While acceding to the royal demand for action, the pope had contrived to refuse pressure for immediate intervention and even to impose his own timetable.

Philip the Fair had also obtained nearly everything he desired. Two of the three requests made by Guillaume de Plaisians at Poitiers (that the prelates act against Templars in their dioceses, and that the suspension of the Inquisition be revoked) had been granted. In addition, there was the prospect of a General Council to decide the fate of the Templars. All things considered, the bulls of 12 August were substantially in his favour. It appeared that King Philip had brought Pope Clement firmly into his camp. The next day, however, Clement departed from Poitiers.

Once again the trial of the Templars went into abeyance as the pope eluded direct royal control. He had expressed a desire to travel to Rome, perhaps even to place himself permanently beyond physical intimidation. For the moment he announced that from 1 December 1308 he would set up the papal court in Avignon, which was part of lands bought for the Church by Pope Gregory X thirty years before. There he would be on his own land, inside the territory of the Angevin kings of Naples and separated from the kingdom of France by the famous bridge. In March 1309 Pope Clement took up residence in a wing of the Dominican monastery in Avignon, while the Templars languished in their prisons throughout the kingdom of France.

Then, in late 1309, momentum picked up again. During the summer Pope Clement had asked the bishop of Paris, Guillaume de Baufet, to prepare a set of instructions on the method to be used in interrogating the Templar prisoners. They were intended for the use of the provincial commissions, whose members might be expected to have less experience in these matters. Once again, however, we see how difficult it was to choose a high-ranking cleric in France who did not have at least a degree of allegiance to Philip the Fair. For Guillaume de Baufet, also known as Guillaume d'Aurillac after his birthplace, had begun his career as a doctor and had ministered in this role to King Philip himself. At the same time, perhaps as a direct consequence of his success in curing the king, he had become a canon in the diocese of Paris. It was from this powerbase, the almost unique double role of canon–doctor, that de Baufet was appointed Bishop of Paris in 1304 and consecrated by Archbishop Etienne Bécard of Sens on 17 January 1305. Thus he too was a member of Philip the Fair's intimate court, and it is more than likely that he was a friend of the inquisitor-general, Guillaume de Paris. Certainly he too was named an executor of the king's last testament, in 1311. When he died, on 30 December 1319, Guillaume de Baufet was accorded the honour of burial in the chapel of the infirmary of the royal abbey of St Victor. This was the abbey of the canons regular, known in Paris as 'victorins', which had been founded in the eleventh century and which until its demolition from 1811 to 1813 stood on a huge site on the Left Bank, today occupied by the universities of Paris VI and Paris VII (between rue des Fossés Saint Bernard, rue Jussieu, rue Cuvier and the Seine).

The instructions de Baufet now compiled drew their inspiration from the manuals of the Inquisition, and we may reasonably assume that he received advice from Guillaume de Paris. The principal difference from normal inquisitorial procedures lay in this document's emphasis on elements relevant to the specific charges made against the Templars. For example, extra care was to be taken with Templars who had denied the charges against them: they were to be questioned more than once, and discrepancies were to be sought between the various versions of their confessions. Questions were to be asked about the time and place of their reception into the Order, the person who carried out the reception and the way in which it had been done. Then the prisoners were to be asked whether after the 'public' part of the reception they were taken to some secret room; if so, then inquiries were to be made into who had been present with them, what they did there, and how it had been done. If any Templar did confess to participating in such a secret ceremony he was to be guarded in solitary confinement while information was sought about those he had mentioned as being present at the reception.

Confession was all, as in regular inquisitions. Absolution and penance would then follow. This is stressed in the next section of the bishop's instructions. For if any Templar should be stubborn enough to persist in denying all charges, he was to be put on a bread-and-water diet; if this was not enough, then a brother Templar who had already confessed should be used to persuade him of the wisest course of action; failing that, he was to be threatened with torture and shown the instruments which would be used to support the threat; last of all, in Guillaume de Baufet's chilling words, 'torture should be applied by an experienced cleric, in the normal manner and without excess'. If a prisoner persisted in his heretical ways and refused to confess, then he was to be denied the privilege of ecclesiastical burial – an affirmation which presumably takes for granted that he will die under torture. There could be no escape. But on the other hand, those Templars who did confess were to be well treated and fed, and would of course receive absolution (although they were not to be released from prison). With these instructions in hand, the papal commission at last opened its inquiry into the Order of the Temple in August of 1309.

Or at least tried to open it. For the procrastination was not over. In Paris, a commission was named by King Philip during the summer. The president was to be Gilles Aicelin, the archbishop of Narbonne. Other members of the commission were to be: Guillaume Durant, the bishop of Mende; Guillaume Bonnet, the bishop of Bayeux; Renaud de la Porte, the bishop of Limoges; the apostolic notary Matthew of Naples; Jean de Montlaur, the Archdeacon of Maguelonne; and Jean de Mantua, the archdeacon of Trent. Another member, the provost Jean Agarni, was nominated to the commission but never in fact appeared during the trial. There was clearly a strong bias in favour of the French king in the commission, especially in its president and the French bishops. Guillaume Bonnet in particular was as much a royal man as Gilles Aicelin, and was later often absent from the commission on business for Philip the Fair.

Yet Pope Clement accepted the proposed names without demur, knowing that within the kingdom of France such a degree of influence was inevitable. The first session was formally opened on 8 August at the royal abbey of Sainte Geneviève in Paris, now demolished but on a site behind the present Panthéon. That morning, summonses were sent to Templar prisoners and witnesses to appear before the commission at the episcopal palace beside Notre Dame (also now demolished) on Wednesday 12 November. But on that day two commissioners were missing, and no Templars turned up. On Thursday it was the same; and Friday; and Saturday; and the first two days of the following week. No one seemed to have been informed that they were to appear, and it was only after the intercession of the bishop of Paris – and a personal visit to Jacques de Molay and Hugues de Pairaud inside the Temple – that a new date was established.

5

THE OPENING OF THE PAPAL COMMISSION, NOVEMBER 1309

After the series of almost farcical adjournments and excuse letters the first series of hearings of the papal commission actually began in Paris on Saturday 22 November 1309. But after such a build-up, it sounds like a dismal affair. At last the great trial was to begin, a trial – in the eloquent words of the transcript – for 'monstrous apostasy, detestable idolatry, the execrable vice of sodomy, and various heresies' which had been committed by the brothers of the glorious military Order of the Temple of Jerusalem.

We may imagine the scene: in the great Gothic vaulted hall of the episcopal palace of Paris, Bishop Guillaume de Baufet himself appeared that morning with the commissioners. Given the time of year, the bishops present would have been dressed in opulent full-length cloaks held at the front by a heavy clasp or brooch, and a tall arch-shaped mitre not dissimilar to those worn today. The bishop of Paris himself would be seated on his throne, and there would be another for the archbishop of Narbonne. The other members of the commission seem to have been seated on wooden benches. Then, around these great men of the church, there were scribes, junior priests, assistants and servants.

Now, at last, all was ready.

The appearance of the first witnesses bordered on the ridiculous. A man named Jean de Melot claimed to have been a Templar for some ten years but now to be no longer part of the Order. The commissioners, without much beating about the bush, judged him in forthright fashion to be *non bene compos mentis*; that is to say, not in complete control of his mind. Far from a random observation by prejudiced clerics, this was a judgment based on the evidence of de Melot's general appearance, his way of acting, his gestures and his speech. In fact reading between the severe lines of the trial transcript brings out a vivid image of a scruffy, filthy, ragged and demented-looking man. Such an image is light years from the concept of the elegant, white-mantled knight in immaculate white robes and shining armour and mounted on a fine destrier (war-horse) ready for battle with the infidel. And de Melot's self-definition is no better: he describes himself as a pauper. From his confession it sounds as though he bothered to turn up to the hearings neither to defend the honour of his Order nor to defend his own personal conduct; nor did he have any intention of betraying the Order, or of making delations against brother Templars. More simply, he had come in the hope of a cash payment in exchange for his appearance in court.

On the same day, a certain Pierre de Sornay of Amiens appeared before the commission. Now Pierre, although fresh to the Order after only three months service, appears to have been one of the few Templar brothers who had taken heed of the rumours in Paris in the weeks leading up to their arrest. He had fled from the Temple at the end of September 1307, probably to Amiens. On being asked the reason for his return to Paris from what we must assume to be the safety and freedom he had enjoyed, he replied that 'he had come to Paris to earn money in order to live and sought employment as a servant, because he was a pauper, without any means, and humble'. In other words, he had returned because he had heard there was financial advantage to be gained by appearing in the trial.

Other Templars came forward merely to exculpate themselves in person from any responsibility for the charges made against the whole Order. Their defence was often that they were simple men (*simplices*), and therefore both unwilling and unable to defend either themselves of the Order. Even the visitor in France, Hugues de Pairaud, from whom the commissioners must have expected more, limited himself to a formal statement to the effect that he was only prepared to speak in the presence of Pope Clement.

The Grand Master was hardly better. The following Wednesday he appeared before the commission at what was perhaps a more private audience in a smaller room behind the episcopal hall. As so often during the course of the trial, he was segregated from his fellow Templars. After two years of harsh prison conditions where, in Bernard Gui's words, the normal diet was 'the bread of suffering and the water of tribulation', and now in his mid-sixties, he must have presented a gaunt, haggard and broken sight. The lacerations resulting from torture which he had shown to visiting cardinals a year earlier could not have healed well on such a diet. Furthermore, it is likely that torture continued. Jacques de Molay was brought into the room by two officials, Philippe de Voet, the provost of Poiters, and Jean de Janville, a royal gaoler, who claimed that, on hearing the summons of the bishop of Paris, the Grand Master had said 'that he wished to come into the presence of the said commissioners'. Yet this verb is reminiscent of the manifestly false 'free and spontaneous' confessions made under torture, and the instruction in the inquisitorial manuals that the penitent heretic 'is to take himself to the prison prepared for him, and make it his perpetual home'. Reading between the lines, it is legitimate to picture the Grand Master being dragged or half-carried before the commission, especially in view of the contradictions, confusion, and incoherence which he then displayed during the hearing.

The Grand Master was on the defensive, weak and rather pathetic. In an ingenuous show of faith in the pope, he first stated his disbelief that the same Holy See which had granted the Templars so many privileges should now wish to destroy them. But he asserted that he would be 'vile and miserable' if he did not attempt to defend his Order, and that it was his intention that the full truth about the charges against the Templars be known. But after this promising protestation, his actual defence consisted of a series of trivial complaints that can only have increased the pathos of the situation. It would be difficult for him, he argued, to present an orderly defence because he was a prisoner of both the pope and the king and had no money to finance his purposes, 'not even four *denarii*'. Moreover, there was no one but a simple serving-brother to advise him. He therefore requested help and counsel. But this was to ignore the nature of the hearings against the Order, as the reply of the commissioners made clear. For they said that they 'wished him to understand that in a case at law concerning heresy and the faith they were to proceed in a straightforward and unceremonious manner, without the clamour and formality of lawyers and judges'. They could hardly have been more explicit.

The real problem was that the Grand Master had voiced these timid complaints two full years after his arrest, and in the lair of his main accuser – whose newly built palace was only a few hundred metres away at the other end of the Ile de la Cité.

The commissioners' reply indicates what little hope there was for Jacques de Molay, or indeed any other Templar brother, to put forward a convincing defence. Once in the clutches of the inquisitor-general, the Templars had already in a certain sense been condemned. The procedures were no personal whim of Guillaume de Paris, or even of Guillaume de

Nogaret, but an integral part of the *raison d'être* of the Inquisition. A modern reader must cast off notions such as the right to a defence, and always bear in mind that at the best of times the purpose of an ecclesiastical trial was not to establish the objective 'truth', which to the medieval mind was an alien concept, but to obtain a confession and conduct the suspected heretic back into the fold of the faith. Here matters were worse still. For the declared purpose of this trial was to condemn the Templars, a fact underlined by the presence that morning of no less a person than the third of the legal trio which sustained Philip the Fair's attack. Guillaume de Plaisians, while not a member of the commission (and the transcript is careful to point out that the royal minister was not present on the orders of the commissioners), defied the secrecy of the hearings by his obtrusive presence at the episcopal palace that morning.

Neither did Jacques de Molay's evidently frail mental condition help him, for Jean de Melot was far from being the only prisoner *non compos mentis* that week. While a clerk was reading the passage of documents concerning the case which referred to the Grand Master's repetition of his confession to the cardinals, he feigned astonishment and protested 'by twice making the sign of the cross before his face and *by other signs*', and by asserting that he would have much more to say. Behind the dry language of the transcript a dramatic scene must lie concealed for, after this outburst, the commissioners retorted that they had not come into the court to accept a challenge to battle. What 'other signs' would have been necessary to provoke such a response? Jacques de Molay must have been shouting and gesticulating wildly. In something of a rage, he declared that the customs of the Saracens and Tartars to cut off the heads of sinners and split them down the middle should also be used in this case. In this matter, he was treading on very dangerous ground, since any recommendation to follow Muslim customs could be read as a confession of having adopted heretical and infidel ways. In any case, sudden angry outbursts and bluster would do him no good before such severe judges, as their reply again emphasises. For with language in the purest style of the Inquisition, Gilles Aicelin – or one of the other commissioners, since it is not made clear – pointed out that it was up to the Church to judge heretics, whereas 'persistent heretics were given up to the secular arm'. (Or, in plain words: calm yourself, or we'll cart you off at once to be burned.)

It was an ominous start to the trial. But folly immediately led Jacques de Molay to further heights. For, in casting his eye around the room in search of help, he chose no less a person than Guillaume de Plaisians, and informed the court that 'he would very much like to be able to converse with Guillaume'. It is worth recalling that when the Grand Master was in Paris, at great occasions such as the state funeral of Catherine of Valois or a *parlement*, he would have been treated with great respect by the very lawyers and clerics who were now prosecuting him. All the major participants of both sides had been acquaintances, if not friends, for many years; not only the team of royal lawyers and councillors. In fact the request was granted, and the royal minister spoke to him in private for a few minutes. No report of this exchange exists, and it would be fascinating to know what they whispered off the record in some corner of the room. When they had finished, de Plaisians – as if to mollify the prisoner and encourage him in his naïvety – announced publicly that he had loved and still loved the Master since they were joined by the common bond of knighthood. Then, with consummate hypocrisy, for this was the man who had spoken in such virulent terms at Poitiers, he added that de Molay 'should take care neither to blame himself nor to waste himself without good reason'.

This curious and rarely noticed exchange casts doubt on the fitness of Jacques de Molay to represent the Order of the Temple in such formidable circumstances. The mouse may as well have sought safety in the cat's basket.

Could it be that the Grand Master had never heard about the harangues at Poitiers, or of Guillaume de Plaisians' role in the negotiations with Pope Clement? Did he really believe that because he had once spoken with the royal lawyer as a friend at the court, he could approach as a confidant now? Perhaps it is a further indication of the fundamental naïvety of Jacques de Molay: just as he genuinely believed that Pope Clement would eventually save him and the Order of the Temple, so he believed that friendly words and courtesy shown to him by Guillaume de Plaisians in better times now guaranteed the lawyer's backing. This of course begs another question: how on earth did such a man manage to become Grand Master of a great religious order? It is likely that the answer to this query is that he achieved the office as a result of seniority or long experience of the East rather than for his intellectual qualities. At the same time, however, it is clear that two years of prison and repeated torture would have broken a younger and stronger man. Moreover, de Molay was aware of the predicament in which he found himself. In a graphic moment of self-illumination, he observed under

89

interrogation that 'he would have to reflect carefully to avoid hanging himself in his own halter'.

After a brief postponement, Jacques de Molay appeared before the commission again at Prime on Friday 28, that is to say, at the first canonical hour, around 6 a.m. On that occasion the role of royal intimidator was assumed by Guillaume de Nogaret himself. Perhaps it was for this reason that the Grand Master presented himself in the humble role of an 'illiterate and poor knight' rather than exhibit himself in a show of pride. He asserted that he did not wish to make a formal defence, but begged instead to be brought before Pope Clement. This was no mere pathetic repetition, and he appears to have been on his mettle since there was evidence in his testimony that morning that two days of reflection had allowed him to put some order into his thoughts. In the first sign of a response to the charges, he made three observations to the commissioners: first, that he knew of no other order in whose chapels and churches divine offices were performed better and with a finer array of ornaments and relics, with the sole exception of cathedrals; second, that he knew of no other order which gave so many alms, three times every week in every Templar house as the *Rule* commanded; and third, as we have seen earlier, that he knew of no other order which had so readily shed its blood for the Christian faith. These observations did not of course amount to a coherent defence, but at least they showed him to be *compos mentis*.

Furthermore, reflection over those two days seemed to have helped him to repress further emotional outbursts. For he displayed a new contrition in his behaviour in court. Rather than shout and gesticulate, he humbly prayed the commissioners and the royal chancellor that he be allowed to use his private chapel in the Temple to hear mass and other divine offices, and also that he be permitted the services of his personal chaplains. Now this may have been part of a strategy to present himself in a more favourable light, but it might also be a sign of genuine piety – and even penitence. Certainly it shows us the Grand Master in fresh light. Even Guillaume de Nogaret seems to have been impressed, for the transcript specifically states that the commissioners and chancellor 'praised the devotion which he demonstrated'. In a sense, that might be said to clinch the issue of the personal guilt of Jacques de Molay: if a man who dared to assault a pope believed the Grand Master's sincerity, who are we to doubt it?

In substance, however, save a new insight into the personality of Jacques de Molay, little had changed.

90

Yet *something* appeared to be changing, as if a concerted effort to construct a rational defence were being made via messages sent from cell to cell in the Temple. The first glimmer of a sustained defence of the Order had in fact surfaced in court the day before, when the preceptor, Ponsard de Gizy, had said that he would be prepared to defend the Templars if he were allowed the counsel of two fellow brothers. These men, Renaud de Provins and Pierre de Bologna, had already advised Ponsard before he appeared in the hearings. It seems reasonable to suppose, especially in view of their later testimony, that it was these highly trained Templar lawyers who had counselled – directly or indirectly – Jacques de Molay in the two-day interval.

The commission formally closed this first session on 28 November 1309, with a striking lack of tangible achievement. Neither the pressure of Philip the Fair at Poitiers, nor the intimidating presence of Guillaume de Plaisians and Guillaume de Nogaret at the hearings in Paris, had been sufficient to force the issue. In this sense, in spite of his relative weakness the stalling techniques of Pope Clement had been more successful. To the commissioners leaving Paris in early December, it must have seemed that the trial would now drag on to the Council of Vienne two years hence with no dramatic novelty.

The second and most important series of hearings of the papal commission was due to begin in February 1310.

PART II
THE HEART OF THE TRIAL: PARIS 3 MARCH–30 MAY 1310

MAP OF PARIS c. 1310
showing sites mentioned in the text

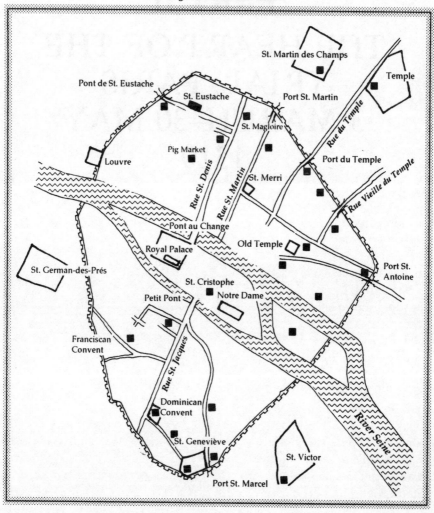

St. Martin des Champs

Temple

Pont de St. Eustache

St. Eustache

Port St. Martin

Rue du Temple

St. Magloire

Pig Market

Louvre

Rue St. Denis

Rue St. Martin

St. Merri

Port du Temple

Rue Vieille du Temple

Pont au Change

Royal Palace

Old Temple

St. German-des-Prés

Port St. Antoine

St. Cristophe

Notre Dame

Petit Pont

Franciscan Convent

Rue St. Jacques

Dominican Convent

St. Geneviève

St. Victor

River Seine

Port St. Marcel

⌐_¬ Walls built by King Philip Augustus c. 1200

■ Identifiable sites where Templar prisoners were held

6

PARIS IN 1310:
SITES OF THE TRIAL

Between 1307 and 1314 there were trials of the Templars in sixteen other towns or regions of France, and also in Portugal, Spain, Italy, Cyprus, England, Scotland and Ireland. Most of them were brief in duration and involved small numbers of Templars, often in single figures. Fewer still were condemned. In fact these trials were peripheral to the main event, which took place in a limited geographical area and a very limited period of time. For the heart of the trial was in Paris, during the second series of hearings of the papal commission from 3 February to 30 May 1310.

The extreme precision of the trial transcripts, together with references in contemporary chronicles, enables us to identify the buildings and squares in which the main events took place. It also allows us to elaborate a map of the trial which, with references to the modern city, should make the sequence of events easier to follow.

Around 1300, Paris had the highest population of any urban area in Europe. The walled city occupied a shallow valley between the rise known as the Mont de Paris on which the royal Abbey of Sainte Geneviève stood (just behind the present Panthéon), at sixty metres above sea level on the left bank, and La Butte Montmartre, at 130 metres on the right bank. The walls were still those of Philip the Fair's ancestor King Philip Augustus (1180–1223). In 1190 that king had ordered the citizens of Paris to finance a wall nine to ten metres high and three metres thick at its base to encompass the city on the Right Bank. At the same time the Louvre was built as part of the defence system, just *outside* the wall. Then, in 1212, Philip Augustus began at his own expense another wall to enclose the area on the Left Bank as far out from the river as Sainte Geneviève. The ends of these two walls faced each other over the Seine, near the Louvre and across the islands later formed into the single mass known today as Ile St Louis. Within these walls the skyline was marked by the royal palace, pitched-roof wooden hostels and merchants' houses, and tall church towers; beyond them was open countryside, often marshland, with scattered abbeys almost forming a loose circle around the city within walking distance of the gates. The main streets, in the words of a chronicler, were paved in 'hard, strong stone'. At that time, the Left Bank was still sparsely inhabited, so Philip Augustus encouraged abbeys and other landowners to fill up the empty spaces with new building projects. In this way the physical fabric of the University came into being, with the Dominicans (whose teachers later included Albertus Magnus and Thomas Aquinas) established in 1217 and the Sorbonne founded in 1257. Around thirty further colleges were founded during the thirteenth century, including the prestigious college of Navarre.

Thus in Philip the Fair's day, although the terms were not used in this sense until later, Paris had already assumed the distinctive tripartite form dictated by the twin branches of the Seine: the Cité, with the newly enlarged royal palace, episcopal quarters, and the parliament building, on what is today called the Ile de la Cité; the Ville, which included the quarters of the merchants and artisans, and the principal markets, of the Right Bank; and the Université, with the student quarters, on the Left Bank. The River Seine was some forty metres wider than it is today and, since the first *quais* were only built in 1312, during the time of the trial the course of the river was marked by stakes. It was only crossed by two bridges, each cluttered with shops and workshops like the Ponte Vecchio in Florence: the Petit Pont and the Grand Pont (today the Pont au Change).

While the royal palace, city churches and abbeys were built of stone, most private homes were sharp-roofed buildings constructed with timber from surrounding forests, and *paillefart* like wattle and daub – with its characteristic visible beam-ends whitened with chalk to prevent fire. In 1310 the population was around 200,000, perhaps as high as 250,000, with a student population on the Left Bank of some 12,000. The contemporary chronicler Jean de Jandun asserted that to count the houses, palaces, churches and chapels of Paris would be like 'counting the hairs on one's head'. In fact, the walls built by Philip Augustus were to provide the form and sufficient space for the expansion of Paris for two centuries. Beyond them were outlying churches and abbeys sited between the city and the marshland, which was formed by an ancient northern branch of the Seine. These ecclesiastical complexes can be recognised today by the suffix 'des champs', and several of them figured in the story of the Templar trial: St Paul, St Martin, St Nicholas, St Antoine. Today this marshland survives only etymologically in the area known as the Marais, comprising most of the third and fourth arrondissements.

Little of the Paris of 1310 has survived physically intact. The Palais de Justice occupies the site of the royal palace and incorporates parts of the original structure, such as the four towers on the north side. Only a handful of the large number of medieval abbeys and churches within the old city still exist in some form today, and fewer still – like Notre Dame and the Sainte Chapelle – can be seen in something close to their medieval form. Fragments of the original buildings remain in Saint Merri and Saint Julien le Pauvre. Churches which were then outside the walls have fared little better: Saint-German-des-Prés is probably the best preserved; St-Pierre de Montmartre and St Denis de la Chapelle survive in heavily restored form, while the attractive cluniac church of St Martin des Champs is now a museum of historic cars and aeroplanes. Other medieval survivals include short sections of Philip Augustus' walls, the palaces of the abbots of Cluny and archbishop of Sens, the Clisson Tower, and the Tower of John Without Fear. In a city which had been dramatically rebuilt, especially after the Revolution but also in the nineteenth century by Baron Haussmann, many of the buildings and churches mentioned in the Templar trials – for instance, the episcopal palace, Sainte Geneviève (although the original tower may be seen inside the Lycée Henri V, just behind the Panthéon), St Christophe and St Magloire, have disappeared altogether.

The study of medieval toponymy is more fruitful. On the Right Bank the principal thoroughfares named for Saints Denis, Martin, Honoré and Antoine still serve vital functions, while smaller medieval streets exist in rue de la Verrerie, rue de la Tacherie, rue aux Ours (in the old sense of geese rather than bears), rue du Roi de Sicile (where the Anjou palace stood), and quai de la Mégisserie. Also on the Right Bank are several streets which recall the presence of the Temple: rue Vieille du Temple, rue du Temple, square du Temple, and carreau du Temple (although the two last named would have been outside Philip Augustus' walls). Among the most important survivals on the Left Bank are rue Saint Jacques, rue de la Bucherie, and rue de la Parcheminerie, while rue des Fossés St Jacques and rue des Fossés Saint Bernard reveal in their names the fact that they mark the line of the broad moat outside the walls in that section of the city.

With a little imagination, however, these apparently meagre clues are sufficient to visualise the extent of Paris in 1310. In crude terms, and

97

using present-day street names, we may first isolate the cross formed by the roughly east–west line from Place de la Bastille along rue de Rivoli to the Louvre; then the north–south axis formed by rue St Jacques and rue St Martin, from Porte St Martin to the Panthéon (similar to the *grande croisée* on which Haussmann based his plan of Paris in the mid-nineteenth century). A circle touching the four points of the cross would indicate the approximate area of Paris at the time of Philip the Fair.

More precisely, downstream – or to the west – the walls of Philip Augustus passed just beyond the point of the present Ile de la Cité, so that both the present area of the Louvre and the abbey of St Germain des Prés were *outside* the city. Upstream, the walls actually passed across the present Ile St Louis, so that its easternmost end was virtually outside the city while the walls on the Right Bank extended as far as the present boulevard Bourdon. (This boulevard and its continuation in boulevard Beaumarchais actually trace the area of no-man's-land which was beyond the walls.) To the south of the Seine, the walls extended far enough to encompass the Sorbonne and the abbey of Sainte Geneviève. For the greatest expansion of the walled city was north of the river, on the Right Bank, where Philip Augustus' walls reached Porte St Denis and Porte St Martin, which were situated at the end of the modern boulevard de Sébastopol.

Now, with a clear idea of the plan of Paris in 1310 in our minds, we can focus on the principal sites of the Templar interrogations in the spring of that year. These were the Temple itself, the episcopal palace, and the Chapel of Saint Eloi.

The original Templar house in Paris was built in 1146 much closer to the Seine than the area now referred to as the 'Temple', near the ancient church of Saint Jean en Grève. The fluvial port along what is today called the Port de l'Hôtel de Ville, between Pont d'Arcole and Pont Louis-Philippe, where once boats could be hauled up from the river on to a sandy shore, was one of the earliest inhabited areas in Paris. The now disappeared Saint Jean en Grève and still existing (but completely rebuilt) Saint Gervais and Saint Protais were amongst the first churches to be built in the city. The whole area, from the Seine back to rue de Rivoli, was known in medieval times as the Grève. It was the logical place for the Templars to found their first house in Paris, comparable in situation to the London Temple between Fleet Street and the Thames as it was near the river on a dry, raised prime site with a port. The actual site was probably on or very near that of the present Hôtel de Ville. Other early properties of the Order included a small port and some warehouses, opposite the Ile St Louis between Pont Louis-Philippe and Pont Marie, a mill on the Grand Pont, and lands beyond the city walls known as the 'Enclos du Temple'.

It was on the land of the Enclos that the Templars soon afterwards built the complex known until the French Revolution as 'Le Temple', which functioned as the headquarters for the Order in France until its abolition. By 1310 it was a huge fortified complex standing outside the city walls almost like an extension to the north-east, an irregular square protected by massive walls and towers which were visible from almost any point within the city. It was reached along the still existing rue du Temple, which begins opposite the Hôtel de Ville and may once have linked the two Templar properties. Then one of the longest streets in Paris, rue du Temple was recognised as having two distinct parts: one section was referred to as 'within the walls', and the other as 'outside the walls'. The wall at the time passed near the junction of rue du Temple with rue Réaumur and rue de Bretagne, which separated these two sections. In the thirteenth century, a new gate was built into the walls of Philip Augustus at this point to provide direct access to the Temple: it was usually known as Porte du Temple, but also as Porte Sainte Avoie after a convent which was built nearby around 1288 (and demolished around 1535). Just beyond this junction on the left today is a smaller street called rue des Fontaines du Temple. Exactly opposite this street was the main gate of the Temple, a massive structure some three metres wide and six to seven metres high between strong flanking towers, with a drawbridge.

The approximate extent of the irregular square which formed the Enclos can be superimposed on a map of modern Paris. The eastern wall of the Temple continued along rue du Temple from the original gate as far as the present place de la République. From that point it turned southwest, roughly along the line of the present rue Béranger; the much later Boulevard du Temple was built through what was once the marais or no-man's-land beyond the Temple walls. The western side of the Enclos followed the modern rue Charlot down to a now-disappeared lane called rue de la Corderie which followed the southern perimeter – roughly on the line of rue de Bretagne.

In many ways it was less than an ideal site; at first it had limited access to the city. But in 1287 Philip the Fair himself granted the Templars permission to build yet another gate in Philip Augustus' walls. The new gate, known as Porte de Chaume, was opened between the Porte de Temple and Porte Barbette, a less fortified postern gate. Long after their demise, when the area of the city was extended under Charles V (1364–80), the Enclos became a kind of fortified buttress to the north-eastern corner of the new city walls. The fortified walls and towers which had once protected the Templars *outside* the city then became, in effect, the defences of the city itself.

The total area within the Enclos was calculated by the nineteenth-century historian Henri de Curzon on the basis of documentary evidence to have been about 60,000 square metres, that is to say around fifteen acres. The buildings within the Enclos were said to be large enough to house 300 knights together with their horses and full retinue of squires and servants. The fortifications were reputed to be so strong that King Philip III, 'the Bold' (1270–85), usually took up residence in the Temple when his wife was away from Paris, and even his son Philip the Fair seems to have resided there until the extensions to the royal palace were completed towards 1310. For the first twenty-two years of his reign the Temple served as the royal treasury, and just a year before the arrests King Philip and his court took refuge within the Enclos during a popular uprising against his financial policies.

The crenellated walls of the Enclos, with a parapet and corridor for guards, strong buttresses and between twelve and fourteen towers, were built in the thirteenth century with such skill and solidity that as late as 1456 they could still be described as being 'in good condition'. The principal buildings that stood within these walls were the great church of the Temple, and two stone towers. The largest of these towers was known as the 'Great Tower' or the 'Donjon', while the smaller tower was called 'Caesar's Tower'.

In the 1140s, while the Templar house in Paris was still close to the Seine, a round church was constructed on the site of the future Enclos. In that original state it was a building some nineteen metres in diameter, with an umbrella vault which stood on intersecting arcades. These arcades in turn rested on pointed arches, which were developed from the dressed columns at ground level. No trace of this church remains, but the recorded dimensions and architectural detail suggest comparison with the original, round section of the surviving Temple church of Fleet Street, London (it may even have been the model for the later London church). Beside this round church was a free-standing belltower, a square Romanesque tower which was perhaps the oldest building in the Enclos and which survived until the Revolution. This tower tapered into a four-sided pyramid-shaped spire, supported by eight buttresses which were pinched into four points towards the spire. At the upper level there was a two-storeyed belfry. Later a sundial was placed on the first floor and this tower became known as the 'Clock Tower', but that was after 1310. Several chapels belonging to the church were also added later, although a chapel dedicated to the Holy Sepulchre beside the belltower may already have existed at the time of the trial.

Around 1217 a long narrow choir was added to the original round church. This choir, which was designed in such a way that it joined the belltower to the main building of the church, seems to have been a simple and relatively unadorned gallery, with a rib-vaulted apse at the eastern end. The entire structure, both the round church and the choir, was roofed with tiles. Once again, the London church seems to have followed the lead and may therefore provide some indication of the appearance of the lost Paris church: Heraclitus, the patriarch of Jerusalem, consecrated the round church just off Fleet Street in 1185, and then in 1240 a three-aisled choir was added to this primitive structure. There are two main differences: first, the London choir was shorter: and second, the Paris choir was built with an apse, a feature absent in London. But, both in its dimensions and in its transitional style between Romanesque and Gothic, the magnificent church of the Temple in London enables us to picture its lost predecessor in the Enclos. The last feature to be added to it, befitting the wealthiest moment of Templar history and architecture, was an elaborate porch built on to the west end towards the end of the thirteenth century to create an imposing entrance. This was decorated with fine sculpture, probably following the model of the recent and successful Sainte Chapelle built by St Louis in the royal palace – especially the elaborate windows of the chapel.

The Great Tower was a solid, keep-like fortress which survived until its demolition in 1810. A truly massive structure, it consisted of a central body constructed from squared limestone blocks. It was approximately fifty metres high, and thirteen by nineteen metres in plan. The walls were over two metres thick, and the base was strongly fortified and buttressed. When the enlarged walls of Paris were built at the end of the fourteenth century, one side of the Great Tower stood over the moat which encircled the city – as can be seen in prints of Paris made in the seventeenth and eighteenth centuries. At each corner of the main structure was a slender pointed tower some five-and-a-half metres in diameter. The interior consisted of four main floors. The most important of these appears to have been the second floor, which had vast and vaulted rooms, while the top floor consisted of a garret beneath the pitched roof. Between the towers on the upper floor there was a wooden walkway for passage of the guard: when necessary these walkways could be temporarily protected by a clay pugging which joined the corner towers. Beneath the ground floor cellars and wells had been dug, so that the fortress could withstand a siege (and could have held off Guillaume de Nogaret in October 1307 had the Templar garrison so wished).

This was the tower which later gained notoriety as a prison. It lingers in Parisian folk memory as the place where King Louis XVI and Queen Marie Antoinette were held in 1793 before their execution, together with the Dauphin Louis XVII and the remainder of the French royal family. We may also assume that it was the main building used by royal officers and the Inquisition for Templar prisoners during the trial. During the two months of hearings in 1310, which we shall shortly examine in detail, papal notaries record that seventy-four Templars were held in the Temple. This number included Jacques de Molay and other leading dignitaries, but it is likely that in the early phases of the trial the number was even greater.

The second, smaller town was known as Caesar's Tower as a result of its supposed antiquity. It was also sometimes known as the 'Dove-Cote Tower'. Less detailed information is available concerning this tower, but it is known to have stood to the north of the Great Tower, on the other side of the church, and to have had three storeys. It too was well fortified, again with a round tower at each of its corners. Such fortification was essential because Caesar's Tower served as the Treasury of the Temple in Paris – and thus for many years as the royal treasury.

Little evidence survives of other buildings. Certainly there was a cloister beside the church, with a chapter-room, a refectory, a dormitory, and other communal rooms around it – probably arranged on the south side of the choir according to the Cistercian model. Contemporary abbeys such as Fontenay, in Burgundy, provide some idea of the structure and layout of this main block. The English chronicler Matthew Paris, who visited the Temple in the middle of the thirteenth century, mentions a great hall, innumerable rooms for the Templars, and vast stables. To these must be added adequate kitchens and storage-space, work-rooms, lodgings for the many visitors to the Temple, and quarters for the leading officials of the Order. There were also other chapels. The trial transcripts distinguish between the 'large chapel' and the 'small chapel', and at one point in the hearings Jacques de Molay asks the papal commission to grant him his own chaplains and the right to pray *in his private chapel*.

The Enclos was therefore a formidable complex comparable to the great fortified abbeys and royal palaces of Europe. Even from this brief and hypothetical reconstruction of the number and dimensions of the buildings, we may imagine how Philip the Fair gazed on the walls and towers of the Enclos from his own palace and perceived it as a gigantic sore thumb in his own capital city. It was a presence which dominated the rising ground to the north of the Seine, and appears in most early representations of Paris. The strength of the Temple was such that it continued to play an important role in the history of Paris – and France – until its destruction during the Revolution.

The Templars' property did not end with the Enclos, huge as it was. Since their original house near the Seine had been founded, lands and houses had been donated to them throughout the city. A few examples will suffice. On the Ile de la Cité, the Templars owned the later-demolished monastery of Saint Eloi, on a site opposite the present Palais de Justice. In 1175 an agreement was made whereby the prior of Saint Eloi, in later years always the bishop of Paris, paid rent to the Temple – an arrangement which continued until 1789. This meant that from a technical point of view, Guillaume de Baufet, one of the accusers of the Order and compiler of the first instructions for inquisitors, was at the same time a Templar tenant. Another example of the close and inter-twined relations between the Templars and their accusers concerns the now-disappeared church of Saint Jean en Grève, which stood on a site opposite the present Hôtel de Ville. This church, which was built in 1212 with a fine chevet and cloister, and which possessed its own strand (i.e. *grève*), was donated to the Templars in 1258 by Philip the Fair's own father, Philip III, the Bold. Royal support also emerges from a dispute concerning a private slaughterhouse and butcher's shop which the Templars owned in rue des Bouchers. On the model of past disputes in the Holy Land concerning extra-diocesan churches, the Templars so antag-onised the Parisian guild of butchers that, on one occasion, Philip the Fair was forced to issue an act to settle a disagreement between the two parties. Neither was Templar property confined to the Right Bank: to the south of the Seine, on the still existing rue de la Parcheminerie, they owned houses which were rented to the scholars of the Sorbonne.

103

The greatest concentration of Templar properties was on and near the Grand Pont. As early as 1137 they owned one of the mills there, and documents show a steady increase in property until the time of their arrest. In 1141 King Louis VII made a gift to a doctor named Dulcisson who lived on the bridge in a house belonging to the Temple. Forty years later, in 1181, the Templars received the gift of another house there from Hebroin de Goumay, and in the following year the gift of one of the arches of the bridge on which they were to build a new house. In the 1230s they had a chapel on the bridge, and held a house and mill belonging to the Chapter of Notre Dame in mortmain. Finally, in 1293, Philip the Fair liquidated three mills on the bridge which belonged to the Templars. From these details, and given the fact that they also owned one of the mills on the Petit Pont, it is evident that the Knights Templars were amongst the greatest property owners in the largest city in Europe. From the point of view of the citizens of Paris, many of whom enjoyed some legal or commercial association with the Temple, this role as powerful landlords can only have heightened the drama of the trial. For them, the Templars were not the abstract power they often appear to be in chronicles, but a living, tangible entity in the heart of their own city with property to rent or sell and rights to cede, and the need to purchase a certain number of provisions, materials and animals from local merchants.

Moreover, the trial spilled over from the power-centre of the Enclos into churches, chapels, hostels and private houses throughout the city. For no single building was sufficient to hold the enormous number of Templars involved during trial proceedings – at one stage around 600 men. Neither could the prisons provide hospitality. In this two-month period in the spring of 1310, the trial of the Templars was a huge perambulating event, something like a travelling funfair which dominated the life, business, and gossip of Paris as a major conference does in a small town today. The passage of a group of papal notaries with escort and royal prison guards, or of a group of Templars on their way from prison to court, could not have failed to attract notice and excite gossip. News of each dramatic incident must have been discussed in colleges and markets alike.

The most important site for the investigations of the papal commission was the episcopal palace, or more precisely certain rooms and the garden within the complex of the bishop's palace. This complex used to stand on what is now an open space, known as square Jean XXIII, between the south wall of the cathedral of Notre Dame and the River Seine.

Construction was begun in 1165 by Bishop Maurice de Sully, who also projected Notre Dame, and developed throughout the thirteenth century. No trace survives today, since the entire palace was demolished in 1831. But eighteenth-century prints allow us to visualise a complex of buildings including a private chapel, the bishop's residence, a walled garden and orchard, and several other houses and outbuildings. The fortified southern wall formed the *quai* along the Seine from the Pont au Double to a line just beyond the last buttresses of the apse of Notre Dame. Then to the north-east of the cathedral were the cloister and orchards, with further buildings belonging to the chapter. In this cloister were the schools which antedated the foundation of the university, where in an earlier century Peter Abelard had taught. Beyond the apse were some oratories, while to the south of the line of the nave – towards the present quai de l'Archevêche – were fifteen or so houses built for the dean, chancellor, deacons, archdeacons, priests, and other staff of the cathedral.

The part reserved for the personal residence of the bishop of Paris, and later the archbishop, stood at right angles to the south transept of Notre Dame. It was a strongly fortified residence like those of many medieval bishops, with its full panoply of buttresses, keep, merlons and guard-houses. This made it the ideal place for the interrogations of the papal commission. Various rooms in the palace were used according, we may assume, to the number of persons present on any given day. Trial transcripts mention the main hall (*aula episcopi*) in which the first session took place, a smaller room behind this hall in which Jacques de Molay was interrogated (*camera existante post dictam aulam episcopalem*), and the chapel next to the hall (*capella adherente aule episcopali*) which is clearly visible in prints. Finally, when all of these spaces were deemed insufficient to receive a general hearing with over 500 Templars, the commissioners used what is described as a pleasure-garden 'behind the hall and episcopal palace' (*in viridario retro aulam et domum*). This may have been a private garden, but was more likely the orchard which can be seen in prints as stretching down to the Seine. But later in the trial it is also referred to as a *prato*, or meadow. Certainly, however, it was inside the complex of the bishop's palace.

Later, in some of the sessions of late April and May, probably because a provincial council of the Church then occupied the episcopal palace, the papal commissioners carried out their investigations in the chapel dedicated to Saint Eloi (*capella sancti Ellegii*) inside the royal abbey of Sainte Geneviève.

105

This was the most distinguished of Parisian abbeys, having been founded originally as the abbey of St Peter and St Paul by the Merovingian king Clovis in 508, the year after he made Paris the capital of his kingdom. Four years later Geneviève, the patron saint of Paris, died there and her body was placed in the crypt of the unfinished church. This austere saint saved Paris from Attila the Hun and has been credited with the original design of the church. She came to occupy it and the name was changed in her favour. A century later, around 630, St Eligius (i.e. Eloi) – who had trained as a goldsmith at Limoges in his youth – made a shrine adorned with gold and silver for her relics. Then in 890 a nave dedicated to Sainte Geneviève was added to the church of Saint Peter and Saint Paul. Finally, when it was completely rebuilt in 1180, the abbey and its church were dedicated to her. This was the magnificent Gothic-style church which existed at the time of the Templar trial. It is known to have consisted of three large aisles, a transept with two rose windows and a tall thin spire above it, and a tower placed at the west end of the nave. But the triangular façade which is visible in eighteenth-century prints was probably added later. In fact, in 1310 the abbey church of Sainte Geneviève was probably like a smaller version of Notre Dame, with equally fine stained-glass windows and soaring vault. Unfortunately, by the mid-eighteenth century it had fallen into such a bad state of repair that the decision was made to build a massive new church in the neo-classical style nearby. The new construction was begun in 1755 after designs by Jacques-Germaine Soufflot, but it never served as the church of the abbey. Instead, with a new function invented by Napoleon, it became known as the Panthéon. What was left of the Gothic church was then demolished in the years between 1801 and 1807. Today the Lycée Henri IV occupies the site of the abbey, which was at the beginning of rue Clovis where it opens from place Sainte Geneviève behind the Panthéon, to the south of Saint Etienne du Mont. But the tower of the abbey survives, together with traces of the library (not the Bibliothèque Sainte Geneviève along the road), the refectory, and a marble staircase, inside the Lycée.

In addition to these important buildings used in the trial in 1310 there are the thirty places where Templar prisoners were held in custody, which papal notaries visited and duly named in their transcripts in the period from 31 March to 6 April. This figure includes the Temple itself and the abbey of Sainte Geneviève, but the distribution of the remaining 'prisons' provides an insight into the difficulty of accommodating such a large number of prisoners even in such a city as Paris.

Among the other twenty-eight places named, several are monasteries or ecclesiastical residences. But some are secular homes or hostels. The transcript always uses the Latin denomination *domus*, meaning 'house' or 'home'. But in the single instance where a Latin designation is repeated in one of the few sections recorded in Old French, the *domum Johannis Roscelli* becomes *l'ostel Jehan Rossiau*. Other references mention payment from Templar funds, so it appears that when the Templars could not be housed in the Temple itself, or in other buildings belonging to the Church, they were farmed out on the basis of full board and lodgings. Thus the 537 Templars of all ranks whose names are given in the transcript in connection with a specific address were scattered all over Paris, and absorbed within the total population of 200,000. Logistics rather than legal considerations seems to have guided the choice of prison or hostel. But it also means that the atmosphere in Paris must have been more relaxed than sensationalist accounts of the trial would appear to suggest. For the conditions of imprisonment were by no means exclusively harsh. At least seven of the places mentioned, housing altogether seventy-two Templar prisoners, are described as 'next to' or 'near' one of the city gates. Thirteen of them actually resided outside the city walls, at the abbey of Saint Martin des Champs. Moreover, the numbers mentioned in one particular place often change, and new names crop up while others disappear. As the trial went on, fresh witnesses were brought into Paris from provincial tribunals; others died, were released from prison after absolution and reconciliation to the Church, or perhaps even escaped.

In the spring of 1310 the greater part of the 537 Templars were held or resided within the *Ville*, the same part of the city as their headquarters. Seventy-four brothers were held in the Temple itself, including Jacques de Molay and other dignitaries. The hostel belonging to Jean Rosselli, mentioned above, provided hospitality for twenty-eight brothers; it was situated near the church of St Jean in Gravia, or Grève, on the site of the present Hôtel de Ville. Seven brothers were held nearby in the Paris residence of the abbot of Tiron (the abbey itself was in the Perche, near Nogent le Retrou), and seven more in the house of a certain Jean de Chaminis. Both these houses were said to be in *vico de porta Bauderi*, rue de la porte Baudoyer, which can be approximately identified with the present place Baudoyer, off rue de Rivoli. Moving eastward along the ancient rue de St Antoine towards the Bastille (the full name of which was the 'Bastille St Antoine'), thirteen more brothers were held at the house of an otherwise unknown Blavot and nine at the hostel belonging to Guichard de Marsillac. This in itself is interesting because de Marsillac was not only a former *sénéschal* of Toulouse, and therefore a royal official, but he was later to figure in the trial as a witness against the men he was holding. Both these hostels were described as 'near the gate of St Antoine'. But turning left off the rue St Antoine before the gate, another forty-seven brothers were to be found at the hostel of Richard de Spolis, in rue du Temple, and eleven in the residence of the abbot of Latigny, which was right beside the Porte du Temple.

Still in the Ville, but towards the north and west, along the main roads leaving the city in that direction, there was another group of houses used to accommodate the Templars. Eleven brothers were held, as the trial transcripts state, in the *domum de Charavalle*, which was situated in rue St Martin. Further north, outside the city beyond St Martin's gate, thirteen brothers were held in the abbey of Saint Martin des Champs. Then, returning within the walls, another group of twelve was to be found in the tenth-century abbey of Saint Magloire: this abbey is long since demolished, but then stood on rue St Denis near the present junction with rue Rambuteau. Ten brothers were held in the hostel of Nicholas Hondrée in *vico predicatorum*, which became the present rue de Prêcheurs, just to the east of Les Halles. South of the site of the old market area, seven Templars were housed in the hostel of Robert Anudei. This was situated in 'vico platée near the pig market', meaning the old pig market which stood near the present Métro station, Les Halles. Further west, closer to Philip Augustus' walls and just beyond the extant church of St Eustache, thirty Templars were to be found in the house of Jean le Grant *prope ponctam sancti Heustachii*, or near the bridge of Saint Eustache. To a modern visitor to Paris this might appear a strange place to find a bridge. But it should be remembered that before the marshland beyond the city walls was drained, bridges were constructed over it to facilitate traffic. Precise records of the population of Paris in 1292 have been preserved in the *Book of the Poll-Tax of Paris* which was compiled in that year for Philip the Fair's administration. It is interesting to note that a certain 'Jehan le Grant' then lived near Porte Saint Eustache. His profession is given as fishmonger, and in that year he paid relatively high taxes of 30 *sous*. It is intriguing to speculate that the same Jehan prospered as a fishmonger and like many merchants and shopkeepers invested his profits in property, to the extent that by 1310 he possessed a hostel big enough to house thirty 'guests'.

Fewer Templars were held in the Cité. This is not surprising because the principal function of this area, today known as the Ile de la Cité, was administrative. It was the site of the royal palace, the *parlement*, the cathedral of Notre Dame, and the bishop of Paris' palace. Only two hostels there are recorded as housing Templar prisoners. The first one, referred to as the hostel of Ocrea, held thirteen brothers and is said to have been in rue St Christophe. Now the church of St Christophe was one of three that once stood in front of Notre Dame, on the site of the present Hôtel de Dieu and place du Parvis, and beside the ancient hospital for the poor dedicated to St Christopher which became the nucleus for the Hôtel de Dieu. It was demolished between 1745 and 1757, but we know that the street named for it ran beyond place du Parvis to the right of the church towards the royal palace. The second place in the Cité was the hostel of Guillaume de la Huce in rue Marché Palu, where eighteen Templars were held. This is described in the transcripts as being in the parish of Sainte Geneviève la Petite, a church which stood a stone's throw from St Christophe near the parking place at the west end of the present place du Parvis.

As far as the Université was concerned, twenty Templars were held inside the abbey of Sainte Geneviève. Just nearby, a further fourteen brothers were in the former house of the bishop of Amiens. This was situated next to Porte St Marcel, a gate which marked the end of rue Sainte Geneviève behind the present Lycée Henri IV. Also near Porte St Marcel was the Paris home of the count of Savoy, where eighteen Templars were held. Twenty-one further prisoners were held in the house of the bishop of Beauvais, on the street which led west from Sainte Geneviève to the convent of the Dominicans. This religious order, which figures prominently in the story of the trial, was – confusingly – known in Paris as the 'Giacobini' because this, their second Parisian monastery, was given to them by the University near the ancient chapel of St Jacques (now disappeared). The monastery stood on the area today enclosed by rue Soufflot, rue Cujas and rue St Jacques. Further south along the latter street the last six Templars in the *Université* were held in the hostel of a certain 'Coyssoine de Braybancia'.

Ten of the hostels or prisons mentioned in the transcripts are now hard to trace. But the meticulous working habits of the inquisitors make it possible to guess their location with some certainty. For example, we read that on Wednesday 1 April 1310 the papal commissioners visisted eleven Templars in the *domum de Leuragie* which was situated in *vico de*

Calino and may be identifiable with the present rue de la Calendre. But since this visit was made in the limited time available after lunch on that day, and between a visit to the house of the abbot of Latigny near the Temple Gate and that of Richard de Spolis in rue du Temple, we may safely assume that this hostel was to be found in the same area. Similar reasons suggest that the *Domum Guillelmi de Domonte*, where four brothers were held in *vico novo Beate Marie*, the house of the Abbot of Prulhaco in *vico de la Montelarie* with twenty-seven brothers, and the hostel of Penne Vayrie *in cimiterio vici de Lucumdella*, where twenty-three brothers were held, were all located in the area near the Grève and Porte Baudoyer. It is also likely that the *domum Serene* in *vico cithare*, which is said to have held twelve Templars, was near Sainte Geneviève. Finally, the hostel of a certain Guillaume de Latingi, who was possibly the man referred to in the *Book of the Poll-Tax of Paris* as Guillaume le Clerc living in the same street, described as housing four Templars in quarrefour Guillorille, was near the church of Saint Eustache.

To conclude this brief survey of the thirty sites, four hostels or residences are given in the transcripts with no address at all, rendering identification even more difficult: there were twenty-one Templars in the house of the Prior of Cornay, eleven in the *domum Rabiosse Sive de la Ragera*, seven in the house of 'Johannis de Calinis', and twelve held in that of 'Stephani le Bergonho de Serena'.

Other buildings and localities which feature in the story of the trial will be identified in the text as they occur. But this reconstructed itinerary of Paris in 1310, with twenty-six of the thirty 'prisons' identified and the other major buildings associated with the trial also mapped, should make the dramatic events of the months between February and May of that year more readily comprehensible.

7
THE FULL LIST OF ACCUSATIONS, 14 MARCH

The second hearing to be conducted by the papal commission was formally opened at the hour of Prime on Tuesday 3 February 1310, in the great hall of the episcopal palace. But once again, for two unrelated reasons, the opening session was a most inauspicious event.

The first reason was that the president of the commission, the archbishop of Narbonne, Gilles Aicelin, did not appear in the court with the other members. Neither did this absence have any normal or temporary cause such as ill health. Although he chaired the commission as the nominee of Pope Clement, and therefore formally represented the Church, Aicelin sent a message which announced that he was away from Paris on official business for Philip the Fair. Moreover, it sounded very much as though he was excusing himself in anticipation of many future occasions. The phrase he used, stressing that this single message would suffice for 'all other days on which he might be absent', suggested the disinclination of a man caught between two batteries of artillery. It is almost as if his intention were to avoid the trial of the Templars as much as possible. Since he was the only man on the commission with real political clout, given his Metropolitan status and royal connections, this disinclination augured badly for the Templar prisoners. For without a strong guiding hand, the trial could ramble on indefinitely.

The second reason was that no Templars turned up either, as the result of circumstances that must have made it look to superstitious minds as though the gods were against the trial. For just as preparations were being made for the hearing, the city was inundated by the flood waters of the Seine. This was a frequent occurrence in medieval Paris, and it was only when the first *quais* were constructed two years later that annual floods could be channelled safely through the city. Flood waters meant that the marshland and low-lying parts of the city became impassable; owing to the overcrowding on the two bridges, many of the prisoners should have arrived at the episcopal palace on ferries. These could not now operate. The commissioners waited alone in the vast and cold hall until they felt sure that no Templars would come. Then they went together to hear mass in the church of Sainte Marie. This church has since been demolished, like so many others in the story, but then stood midway between the north wall of Notre Dame and the Seine, near the present rue Chanoinesse. After the mass, the commissioners made arrangements to ensure that at least some prisoners would appear the next time they convened. Written invitations to attend the hearings were sent out to the prisons and hostels where the Templar brothers were being held. When this was completed, they returned to their lodgings, in the case of the three French bishops, probably within the palace itself.

That only the weather prevented Templars from coming to the episcopal palace is shown by the extraordinary events of the next few weeks.

Renewed optimism seems to have been instilled in the minds of the prisoners during the winter interval. After the hint of resistance perceptible in the testimony of Ponsard de Gizy the previous November, it is likely that the two lawyer-brothers whose names he put forward – Renaud de Provins and Pierre de Bologna – had managed to convince their fellow prisoners to stand up and be counted in defence of the Order of the Temple. While there had been only isolated instances of brothers denying the charges during Guillaume de Paris' 1307 inquisition, now the trickle of Templars willing to espouse the defence cause in public rapidly grew to flood proportions reminiscent of the inundations of the Seine. Three days after the inauspicious opening, on Friday 6 February, fifteen Templars of varying rank appeared before the commission to announce that they were prepared to defend their Order. On Saturday, a further group of thirty-four came forward, and the following Monday fifty-eight. Many were willing to defend the Order as a whole, while some were only prepared to speak for themselves. But the striking fact is that the similarity of replies made to the commissioners by over a hundred Templars suggests concerted action behind the scenes. Someone was hard at work instigating this rebellion against the charges, with a force of persuasion at least as effective as the torture and deprivation used by the prosecutors. In the light of later evidence, it must be assumed that this 'someone' was the two lawyers named above.

Neither did the momentum fail. On Tuesday 10 there were eighty-one Templars willing to make a defence, including the lawyer Pierre de Bologna himself. Then, after a day's pause in proceedings, thirty-eight

112

brothers came on Thursday 12, thirteen on Friday 13, and seventy-seven on Saturday 14. The laconic record of papal notaries provides a momentary aperture on the drama of the proceedings when we read about the demeanour of Jean de Chames, who had appeared in court on Saturday. This Jean, who came from the diocese of Amiens, was described as 'unrestrained' in his behaviour in court, and was said to have shouted before the commissioners that he was ready to defend the Order of the Temple 'to the death!'. From this single incident it is possible to imagine the tension in court as the gathering tide of defenders swelled and also to sense the unease of the commissioners – especially in the continuing absence of Gilles Aicelin.

One of the most curious features of the statements recorded in this ten-day period is that the Templars demonstrated a faith in Jacques de Molay as blind and unfounded as that of the Grand Master himself in Pope Clement. For the only real negative note came from the Grand Master himself when he appeared for the third time a fortnight later, on Monday 2 March.

His statement that day reads like a recorded message. Five hundred Templars, very close to the total number of brothers present in Paris, were now prepared to defend the Order *in his name*. But the Grand Master dithered. The commissioners asked him the same question they had been putting to all the prisoners: would he be prepared to defend his Order? Jacques de Molay's reply seems to be anchored in the tensions and fears of Poitiers nearly two years earlier, while around him the ferment of resistance must have been the gossip of the day both within the Temple and in the streets of Paris. He answered weakly that 'the pope was reserving his case in person, and for that reason he begged the commissioners to spare him on these matters until he were in the presence of the pope, adding that then he would say what he believed to be expedient'. Given the context, and the responsibilities of his rank, his words amounted to no more than a cop-out.

In fact the plea for a papal audience fell on deaf or unwilling ears. The commissioners observed that they had no desire to proceed against him as an individual, but were simply following their instructions in seeking to proceed against the Order of the Temple. Still Jacques de Molay persisted in his stance, demanding that the commissioners write a letter to the pope so that Clement V would then summon him to an audience. They eventually agreed to do so, and then terminated the hearings for that day.

113

The moment was lost. That Monday's court appearance would have been the ideal moment for Jacques de Molay to assert his personality as supreme commander of the rebelling Templars, and to impress his stamp on the trial. Instead, he wasted his time on what amounted to an irrelevant cavil, thus demonstrating both a lack of imagination and a failure to understand the ripeness of the moment. It must be said that his behaviour and inactivity during this period of ferment within the prisons of Paris is perhaps the greatest indictment against him. A strong personal statement, together with involvement of the other dignitaries of the Temple, might have been sufficient to wrest the initiative. But he failed.

Fortunately, however, no one seemed to heed the Grand Master's negative attitude.

The tide of defenders coming forward was such that on Friday 13 March the total number of Templars willing to stand up for their Order reached the grand total of 561. Templars of every rank, from serving-brothers to knights and preceptors – though not, it must be noted, the most senior officials of the Order – shifted to the new position, no doubt encouraged by the safety in numbers. Something akin to a bush telegraph operated between the abbeys and private hostels where prisoners were held, as the more literate and legally trained Templars prepared detailed and carefully reasoned defence statements. The dimensions of this defence movement made it impossible for the commissioners to ignore what was happening and, given Pope Clement's formal support for the hearings, they were obliged to hear and record the protest, in spite of the anger of royal lawyers. In a sense, the strangest aspect of this three-week period in which the defence movement gathered force is the absence of any counterploy by King Philip, or more especially by Guillaume de Nogaret and Guillaume de Plaisians. Earlier in the trial they had been willing enough to gatecrash private ecclesiastical hearings in order to make their presence tangible. That they should not see the dangers implicit in this near-revolt is at the very least singular. Perhaps they had been so confident in the success of the hearing that they were out of Paris, maybe even with the still absent Gilles Aicelin?

Whatever the case, by early March of 1310 it was evident that the prisoners would be allowed to present their defence case.

The real problem for the Templars was that no complete list of charges had yet been made available. In the absence of charges, the preparation of a detailed defence was impossible. To a modern observer it may seem outrageous, but two-and-a-half years after the arrest of the Templars in

France the information which they possessed concerning the charges was still vague.

A full list of 127 articles of accusation had in fact been drawn up in August 1308, at Poitiers. Now, on the morning of Saturday 14 March 1310, these charges were read out to a representative group of ninety Templars. They were first read in Latin, the language in which they had been compiled, for the benefit of the court; and then translated into French (or 'vulgar Gallic', as the transcript has it), so that everyone present would understand. The list of names of the ninety brothers present that morning reveals that Templars known to possess some scholarly learning had not been present. Ponsard de Gizy, the first openly to claim the right to a defence, was not there. Neither were the lawyers who seem to have been behind the increasing clamour for a concerted resistance, Renaud de Provins and Pierre de Bologna. Other brothers who were soon to make a spirited defence of the Order, such as Elias Aymerici and Jean de Montréal, were also significant absentees. It would have been reasonable to expect the presence of some of the leading dignitaries of the Order, representing the thousands of Templars elsewhere in Europe. But Jacques de Molay was not invited to the reading of the charges, and neither was Hugues de Pairaud, nor Geoffroi de Charney (who had not yet appeared in the trial at all). The evidence suggests that perhaps the only attempt to forestall the defence movement was in the careful selection of the ninety brothers who were to hear the reading of the charges.

Further information can be extrapolated from the list of names. Twenty-four brothers present that morning may be identified beyond the mere fact of name, and in this sub-group there were nine knights, eight priests, and seven serving-brothers. But the fact that eight of the knights and four of the priests appear in the first sixteen names of the list, after which few of the names are identifiable, suggests that it was compiled according to rank. If that were the case, then the total number of knights may be nine, and the total number of priests eight. That would leave seventy-three serving-brothers and other ranks – including the sergeant-brothers, who in active service often fulfilled the role of knights. The fact that this division tallies with the proportion of knights to other ranks estimated in chapter 1 as one to ten supports such a hypothesis, and may also serve as an indication that the brothers were chosen with care. Even more interesting is the revelation that the ninety brothers were drawn from several different prisons and hostels, as if a deliberate attempt were made to separate brothers who had found the courage to defend the

115

Order within peer groups that had formed in individual prisons. Divide and rule. It is noteworthy that *not a single brother* was chosen among the seventy-four known to have been in the Temple, which substantiates the view that great care was taken in the process of selection.

One further detail clinches the matter: of the ninety brothers who did appear, as many as a third – exactly twenty-eight – *never appear elsewhere in the trial transcripts*. It would have been hard to select a more anonymous, unimportant group. There were ninety Templars, but each had been singled out as a man who could be relied upon not to create a public commotion (a man such as Jean de Chames was obviously excluded).

Only three men seem to have escaped the net of the selectors. One, a certain Nicolas Versequi (elsewhere Versequin), described as from Tours but with no rank given, was later to be mentioned by the defender Jean de Montréal as one of the Templars whose advice he had sought as he prepared a written statement. But the remaining two are more interesting since they later formed part of the key group of four defenders of the Order, together with the lawyers Renaud de Provins and Pierre de Bologna. One, Guillaume de Chambonnet, of Limoges, was a knight who had been the preceptor of Blaudeix in Auvergne. He was a Templar of long standing who is also cited in the testimony of another brother as having been present in Cyprus. The other was Bertrand de Sartiges, from Clermont, who had been preceptor of Carlat in Rouerge. He too had seen service in the East and, in later evidence, is accused of having performed an illegitimate reception ceremony in the Templar house at Tortosa. De Chambonnet and de Sartiges were both housed in the royal abbey of Sainte Geneviève during the trial, and always appear in tandem, rather like twins. As we shall see below, they were part of a group of nine Templars led by Pierre de Bologna who presented a defence of the Order a few weeks later, on 7 April; and they were also also present at the last-ditch attempt at a defence on 10 May.

Yet Guillaume de Chambonnet and Bertrand de Sartiges never participated actively in the defence, and failed when things came to the crunch. For, in the third session of the papal commission, when Pierre de Bologna was said to have fled Paris and Renaud de Provins was forbidden to appear as a result of his loss of priestly status, the two knights appeared alone on 3 November 1310 and were offered the chance to grasp their moment of glory. But they declined, claiming, rather weakly in the circumstances, that they did not wish to present a defence without the presence of their legal colleagues. Their words, if ever they spoke during the trial, are recorded nowhere in the transcripts, so that they come across as cardboard cut-out figures. Perhaps they were simply trusted spies? In this sense, their presence at the reading of the accusations might mean that they could immediately pass on detailed information to Renaud de Provins and Pierre de Bologna.

That Saturday morning, 14 March, the charges against the Templars were made public, at last creating the possibility for arguments for a defence to be marshalled. The formal announcement began: 'These are the articles on which inquiry should be made against the Order of the Knights of the Temple'. The 127 articles which were dutifully and slowly read out in Latin and then in French mainly concerned the Templar rite of reception into the Order. For here was the essence of the supposed 'heretical depravity'. The articles are often repetitive, but can be readily divided into nine main categories:

1. That during the reception ceremony new brothers were required to deny Christ, God, the Virgin or the Saints on the command of those receiving them.
2. That the brothers committed various sacrilegious acts either on the cross or on an image of Christ.
3. That the receptors practised obscene kisses on new entrants, on the mouth, navel, or buttocks.
4. That the priests of the Order did not consecrate the host, and the brothers did not believe in the sacraments.
5. That the brothers practised idol worship, of a cat or a head.
6. That the brothers encouraged and permitted the practice of sodomy.
7. That the Grand Master, or other officials, absolved fellow Templars from their sins.
8. That the Templars held their reception ceremonies and chapter-meetings in secret and at night.
9. That the Templars abused the duties of charity and hospitality, and used illegal means to acquire property and increase their wealth.

That these accusations are not put forward without a strong basis in confessions is shown by the concluding paragraphs, where it is expressly stated that the Grand Master, the visitor, the preceptors of Cyprus, Normandy and Poitou, as well as other preceptors, knights, priests and lower ranking brothers, had confessed to many of the above errors whilst under oath.

117

But key phrases in the list reveal that the 'proof' is perhaps not as convincing as the tone of the accusations would suggest. For the meagre evidence is bolstered as much by the grandeur of the language as by the existence of any real 'crimes'. Argument is sustained by means of adverbial allusion, in scattered phrases like 'sometimes', 'generally held', and 'generally received'. Similar ambiguity appears in reference to the great scandals which have arisen 'in the hearts of elevated persons', and have been broadcast in 'public talk, general opinion and repute'. In the end the compilers of the accusations are forced to fall back on the slender grounds that there was 'vehement suspicion' against the Order of the Temple. Nothing more.

But this farrago of innuendo was sufficient. For, as we have seen, confession was all. Disregarding for a moment the means by which they had been obtained, there had been an abundance of confessions – from the dignitaries down to the humblest and most illiterate of serving-brothers. Yet even here, the language of the list of accusations was strangely cautious – almost as if the compilers themselves did not believe in the charges entirely. The document concludes with the rather watered-down observation that *some* brothers of the Order of the Temple 'have confessed the aforesaid *or a great part of* the said errors'. None had in effect confessed to all 127 charges, and few confessed to more than a small number. Once again, it is hard to resist the thought that had Jacques de Molay resisted torture and refused to confess, had he found the courage to make a forceful defence of himself and his Order on March 2, then the story of the trial might have taken a different turn.

Twelve days later, the Templar crimes and heresies had been clearly defined once and for all and the trial began to gather momentum.

Taken as a whole, the accusations consist of a shrewd mixture of charges with three main elements: a powerful suggestion of links with established heresies (especially that of the Cathars); clever use of the customs of the Temple based on a detailed knowledge of the Templar *Rule*; and an awareness of the tradition of criticism and suspicion against them. It is a heady mixture, skilfully concocted and resistant to objective analysis. Roughly speaking, the categories 1–5 mentioned above are those where links to Catharism are suggested, while categories 6–9 are those elaborated on the basis of the *Rule* and tradition.

Some brief considerations on the heresy of the Cathars will serve to illustrate why these links were so readily accepted by contemporary observers – and especially by the clergy. This sect, which first appeared in south-western France during the twelfth century, belonged to the dualist tradition. Adherents to this tradition, which ultimately derived from first century Gnosticism and Manichaenism, sought to explain the origin of evil by stating that it was beyond God, in the material world. The Cathar *perfectus*, an initiated priest, considered that his soul was of divine origin, while his body had been created by the Devil and was therefore evil. Thus he should avoid everything which enchances the imprisonment of his soul in this evil container, such as meat, sex and property – a radical stance which inspired non-heretical poverty movements, such as the Franciscans, and caused great embarrassment to the wealthy church as heresies such as Catharism took root in France and Northern Italy. The asceticism and purity of the pairs of *perfecti* who travelled through these areas stimulated veneration in the people, but fear in the clergy as its wealth and wordly power came under fire. Moreover the Cathar heresy facilitated the rapid development of other heresies and that of witchcraft in the thirteenth century. As a result of the Albigensian Crusade (preached by Innocent III in 1208), and the work of the Inquisition founded to combat the heresy, it was no longer at its peak. But in the minds of members of the Roman Church around 1300, the Cathars and their ramifications still represented a serious threat.

The Cathar heresy is thought to have been spread through Europe by missionaries sent westward by the Bogomils, or possibly by returning crusaders who had been converted while in the East. It first took firm root in in the area of Toulouse, Agen and Albi, and for this reason they became known as Albigensians. The perennial Christian dilemma of the existence of evil was resolved by the Cathars in their full acceptance of Satan. From the point of view of the Templar trial one of the most interesting aspects of the Cathar ritual was its total renunciation of the Christian sacraments in favour of its own. The most important of these Cathar sacraments was the *consolamentum*, during which the laying on of hands cleansed the postulant of all previous guilt and sin. An initiated priest who had undergone the *consolamentum* was called a *perfectus*, and the first of five basic ceremonies which a Cathar performed was to embrace and kiss the *perfectus* on meeting him. It was this kiss which in the popular imagination soon became transformed into an 'obscene' kiss. For instance, towards the end of the twelfth century, the English chronicler Walter Map wrote of secret ceremonies in which the participants – while 'enflamed with frenzy' – kissed a huge black cat under the tail. Even worse, from a Catholic point of view, was the consequence of

119

Cathar denial of the incarnation of God as man. According to them, Satan had created matter in order to trap the human soul in a cage, a view whose consequence was that all biblical characters and even the apostles were seen as demons. Only Christ himself remained a pure spirit, and as such it was impossible that he should have suffered physically on the cross. The notion of the incarnation of God on earth was entirely alien to the Cathars. The logical outcome of this belief was that there was no sense in venerating the cross, just as there was little point in the traditional sacraments.

Even this over-simplified account of the sect should be sufficient to indicate where Guillaume de Nogaret found the elements necessary to elaborate the supposed Templar heresy. The basic idea behind the charges was to paint the Temple as a *sect* rather than as a religious Order: a sect which met in great secrecy, and whose rites include desecration of the cross and the holy sacraments, together with the formal repudiation of Christ and his Church. Indeed, it is likely that within a vast and widespread organisation like the Order of the Temple there were some brothers who had embraced these heretical doctrines. To this heady mixture, it was only necessary for theologians to add devil worship and the obscene kiss to create the full-blown concept of witchcraft which was just about to appear throughout Europe. Some elements already appear in the Temple trial; others, such as the pact, the night-ride, orgies, and blood-sucking, were not yet part of the popular perception of witchcraft as it derived from the Cathars and other heretical sects.

The historian of witchcraft and heresy Jeffrey Burton Russell reports in his book *Witchcraft in the Middle Ages* the manuscript confessions of a German heretic named Lepzet, made towards the end of the thirteenth century, which may serve here as an example of received opinion concerning more or less 'catharist' heresies at the time of the Templar trial. The first step in the initiation ceremony which Lepzet confessed to having undergone was a formal renunciation of the holy sacraments, after which the postulant was required to kiss a man dressed in black who appeared before him. Next he was expected to kiss a huge frog with a gaping eye, after which he was considered to have been initiated. More pertinent still is his account of the place where the rites of this heretical sect were practised: in a secret cave beneath the master's cellar, where the master displayed his buttocks and members of the sect were required to kiss them. Then the members of the sect sat around a pillar while a large cat climbed up it. Once he had reached the top, the cat lifted its tail so that those present could kiss its anus.

The similarities between these rites and the accusations against the Templars are almost too obvious to require emphasis: the basic elements of each include the master, a secret and dark place for the ceremonies, a formal renunciation of the holy sacraments, two different kinds of obscene kiss, and even a cat. It is almost as though the compilers of the accusations worked with a copy of a confession similar to Lepzet's to hand.

A second, more indirect piece of evidence reinforces this hypothesis. For the monk of Saint Denis who was writing the *Les grandes chroniques de France* at the time of the trial adds further details to the charges which were rendered public on March 14. In his account, he enumerates eleven articles of accusation 'for which the Templars were burned, condemned and captured'. While for the most part these eleven articles follow the accusations made in the standard charges – the denial of Christ, the carrying out of part of the reception in a dark room, and the adoration of an idol – they also contain far more elaborate and damning charges. They were never published and sent to the inquisitors of all of Europe like the official accusations, and so the chronicler might have picked them up from rumours spread in Paris at the time for local consumption. Two charges in particular are horrific, and were clearly designed to suggest the link with the most abominable of heresies. Article VIII states that 'if a Templar who worships their idol dies in his error, sometimes they burn him and the powdered remains are given to novitiate Templars to eat, in order that they then hold their heretical beliefs and idolatry with greater firmness'. If this sounds appalling enough, Article X is perhaps even more explicitly related to traditional charges. It affirms that 'the new-born baby born from the union of a Templar and a virgin was roasted over a fire, and the fat was collected to anoint their idol'. These horrific practices are never mentioned in the offical trial records. That in itself is surprising, since the royal lawyers must at least have heard of them – if they were not responsible for fabricating and spreading the rumours – since they appear in what is a semi-official chronicle of the Capetian monarchy. Perhaps even they suspected that scholars, theologians and inquisitors might not be prepared to believe such charges, and reserved them for popular use. In any case, they provide a further indication of the lines along which the compilers of the formal accusations were working.

If we turn now to the first category of accusations, those regarding the reception ceremony and the denial of Christ, the parallel with Cathar doctrine is manifest. But it must be said that while some of the charges – those regarding cupidity and avarice, for instance – were simply elaborated on the basis of criticisms of the Order which had been in circulation for decades, nothing resembling those of the denial of Christ or the cross had ever surfaced before the trial. Furthermore the entire spirit and severity of the Templar *Rule* works against these accusations. The insistence on the title of 'knights of Christ' in the second paragraph of the *Primitive Rule* emphasises this.

There are, however, certain aspects of the *Rule* which could easily be twisted by a skilled lawyer such as those who compiled the charges. One such aspect concerns the discretionary power of the Master of the Temple regarding the reception of novitiates into the Order. Paragraph 97 states:

> The Master should not admit brothers without the consent of the chapter, but if he goes anywhere where he cannot find a chapter, and is beseeched by a worthy man to make him a brother for love of God, because he is so ill that it is believed he cannot escape death, then, with the consent of the brothers present, he may make him a brother providing he sees that he may rightly be a brother . . .

The existence of such power facilitates insinuations, and the ambiguity of phrases like 'a worthy man' which we have observed in the *Arrest Order* could equally well be applied here. Later in the *Rule*, during a brief outline of the reception process which appears in the section entitled 'Formulae of Profession', when the postulant has sworn to serve the Knights of Christ and promised obedience to the house he is ordered to 'lie (prostrate) across the altar' and pray. Once again, the insinuations of a skilled interrogator whose main task is to find answers to the questions in his formulary could read this as a suspicious action. Beside these potential mines of ambiguity in the *Rule*, however, there are continuous assertions of the importance of prayer, obedience, good faith, and an explicit recommendation that each brother of the Temple 'should know that he is not committed to anything so much as to serve God'.

Once the suggestion of parallels with the heretical practices of the Cathars is made, the charges in the second to fourth categories are a necessary consequence. Now we have established that the Templars were a kind of secret Cathar sect, the inquisitors could argue, it is obvious that they committed sacrilegious acts on the cross, practised obscene kisses on new entrants, and neglected to consecrate the host.

The insistence on desecration of the cross in the accusations provided an emotional link in the popular mind with Muslim behaviour in the crusading kingdoms and thus, by association, the notion that the Templars had been tainted by Muslim beliefs (when Jerusalem fell to Saladin, according to the chronicler Ibn al-Athir, the Sultan ordered that the al-Aqsa mosque which had been occupied by the Templars should be 'cleaned of all filth', meaning the crosses). In fact, the condemnation of the host is a perfectly logical consequence of the denial of material substances. This was no false testimony, but a straightforward transfer of Cathar doctrine to Templar practice. Actually, the *Rule* emphasises the importance of performing the entire religious service 'according to canonical law'. Prescribed practices of the Order included the reading of scriptures during meals, maintaining the complex rhythm of feast days and fasts (at least thirty-five days each year apart from Sundays, together with four major periods of fasting), the frequent repetition of paternosters, and the insistence that no brother may leave chapel until the canonical hours are completed. (The only excuses for absence were illness, having hands in pastry when the bell sounds, being at work in the forge, or preparing horses' feet for shoeing.) It also stresses the need 'to set a good example for secular people'. An entire section of the *Rule* comprising twenty-five paragraphs is dedicated to 'religious service'. But all this was irrelevant once the seed of the imaginative link between Templars and Cathars was sown.

And it was sown well. The fifth category of the accusations, concerning the worship of an idol, remains today the most controversial aspect of the Templar trial. The parallel with Cathar practices is evident, but it is a strange case where no unified reply was elicited by the Inquisition's formularies. The Templar idol was described as a head with one face, or two faces, sometimes bearded and sometimes not, made of silver or wood, a picture of a woman or a man, an embalmed head which glowed in the dark, or a demon. Yet in this variegated composite image of the idol – rather like a continuously shifting computer image – was later to be found the conclusive 'proof' of devil-worship, and evidence of the possession by the Templars of the Turin Shroud. Even more peculiar, given the strictures against idolatry as an unforgivable sin in the *Koran*, is the suggestion that the Templar idol, in its manifestation as the Baphomet figure, was proof of veneration for Mohammad and adoption of Muslim practices.

The sixth category of accusations, regarding charges connected with homosexuality, also remains controversial. That in an organisation of some 15,000 men often living in isolation and difficult circumstances there should be instances of homosexual relations must seem to a modern observer entirely plausible. It was then too. The Templar *Rule* includes a specific warning against what it terms 'acts against nature'. Paragraph 573 tells of an occasion at Castle Pilgrim, situated on an isolated promontory on the coast between Jaffa and Haifa, when 'there were brothers who practised sin and caressed each other in their chambers at night'. On hearing about this the Master decided that since 'the deed was so offensive' it should not even be discussed in a normal chapter. The offenders were taken to Acre, stripped of their Templar habits, and clapped into heavy irons. The 'sin' of sodomy was twice condemned in the statutes, in #418 and #572. On the former occasion, the very thought of it drives the compiler to heights of virulence which surpass that of any of the other 685 paragraphs. Listing the penances for various errors, it states in language vaguely reminiscent of the trial of Oscar Wilde that the fourth penance 'is if a brother is tainted with the filthy, stinking sin of sodomy, which is so filthy and so stinking and so repugnant that it should not be named'. This attitude is nothing if not clear, and may well lie behind the repeated threats against Templar brothers who sleep outside their house for more than one night (#462 and #621). Yet the evidence is there, in the incident at Castle Pilgrim, and certain rituals of the Templars could suggest further 'sins' if read with an inquisitorial eye bent on unearthing fresh 'evidence'. For example, #502 says that:

> ... when the Master or the one who has authority wished to put a brother on penance, he should say to him, 'Good brother, go and undress if you are well'. And if he is well, he should undress and afterwards come before the one who holds chapter, and should kneel.

After prayers have been said, the penitent brother was to be punished either with a whip or a belt.

Here again, the damning association is with 'heretical depravity', and in particular with the Cathars. For in the years from 1140, when it first emerged as a heretical sect, to around 1230, when the repressive action of the Church succeeded in diminishing its distribution, Catharism was the greatest influence on demonology and witchcraft. As we have seen, an obsession with Catharism informed the Inquisition and its manuals from the 1220s onwards. In this context the crucial point – and defect – was that the inquisitorial formularies themselves shaped the presumed

124

heresies and errors which they were designed to unearth. In the interrogations carried out by Guillaume de Paris immediately after the arrests, each question was necessarily a leading question. The formulae and the mental set of the inquisitors made identification with Catharism almost inevitable. Despite the vehemence of later retractions and attempts to defend the Order, the elements which emerged in those early confessions formed an emotional core of accusations against the Templars which could not easily be eliminated.

Another striking fact about these first six categories of accusations is that they concern a single, brief moment in the life and routine of the Templars: the reception ceremony. The implicit parallel is again with the secret Cathar rituals. Yet nothing appears so pure and severe as the Templar reception ceremony when viewed on its own terms. It is instructive to read the instructions in the *Rule* for carrying out an orthodox reception ceremony, which comprise the section from #657 to #686 – the concluding remarks of the whole document.

The Master or preceptor who was conducting the ceremony was, according to the *Rule*, to open with a statement which suggests that the discretionary powers mentioned above were rarely used: 'Fine brother knights, you see that the majority has agreed that this man should be made a brother', and immediately launched into a speech intended to discourage any postulant except those who were utterly certain about their vocation. The man who sought an easy life, the tangible rewards of illegal activity, or the spiritual benefits of heretical activity, would glimpse the reality of Templar life from the Master's words and perhaps change his mind:

> You see us with fine horses and fine harness, and eating well and drinking well, and possessing fine clothes, and it therefore appears to you that you will be much at your comfort. But you do not know of the harsh commandments which obtain here within: for it is a hard thing that you, who are master of yourself, should become the serf of another. For with great difficulty will you ever do what you wish to do: for if you wish to be on land this side of the sea, you will be sent to the other side; if you wish to be at Acre, you will be sent to Tripoli, or Antioch, or Armenia ... And if you wish to sleep, you will be awoken.

Templars of a lesser rank than knight, who represented the vast majority, would suffer even greater humiliation by being obliged to work at the

125

oven or in the kitchen, to tend camels, or to muck out a pigsty – like any military indoctrination. The key questions, based on a feudal and hier-archical picture of the world, were as follows: 'Do you wish to be, all the days of your life henceforth, a serf and slave of the house?', and 'Do you wish to leave behind your own will all the remaining days of your life in order to do what your commander orders?'

Far from being conducted to a secret room at this point of the cere-mony, the postulant was asked to leave the chapter-room while the other brothers were asked whether they knew of anything which should pre-vent him from becoming a Templar. Having passed this stage, the postulant returned and requested admission to the Order: 'Sire,' he was to ask, 'I come before God and before you and before the brothers, and ask and request you for love of God and Our Lady to welcome me into your company and into the favours of the house, spiritual and temporal, as one who wishes to be a serf and slave of the house all the remaining days of his life.' Are you sure? the Master would ask. 'Sire, yes, if it please God,' was the correct reply. Then, after prayers and paternosters, the postulant was taken through a series of oaths and promises regarding conduct, and the errors for which he could be expelled from the Order. Next he was given the Templar mantle, which was placed round the neck with laces fastened. After a reading of their favourite psalm, Psalm 133 ('Behold, how good and pleasant it is when brothers dwell in unity . . .'), and yet more paternosters, came the only point of the ceremony which could provide the slightest suspicion: 'And the one who makes him a brother should raise him up and kiss him on the mouth; and it is cus-tomary for the chaplain brother to kiss him also'.

Last of all, after further admonitions and a reading of the rules for everyday conduct, the ceremony reached its conclusion with the follow-ing words: 'Now that we have told you the things you should do and of what you must beware, and those that cause loss of the house, and those that cause loss of the habit, and of other rules; and if we have not told you everything that we should tell you, then you may ask it. And God permit you to speak well and do well.' It was surely an austere and beautiful ceremony, confirmed as such in many trial depositions. The kiss is indeed there, but a single one and on the mouth. Only a perverse reading of this ceremony, which appears to have been used in this form right up to the end of the Order's history, could distort it into something as hideous as the rites described by Templar prisoners after torture.

Next in the list of accusations against the Order follow two sets of

126

charges which could also be derived from a perverse reading of the *Rule*, those regarding absolution and the secret reception ceremonies and chapters. The matter of absolution echoes criticism of the Order in the early years of its history. For the bull *Omne Datum Optimum*, which has been discussed earlier, had long been a bone of contention. The need for the privileges it contained as expressed in the bull itself – that it was 'indecent and perilous for the soul that professed brothers, on their way to church, should have to mix with the rabble of sinners and those who associate with women' – was hardly calculated to increase the popularity of the Templars. The same privileges and autonomy of diocesan control which helped make the Templars so powerful brought upon them the jealousy of both ecclesiastical and secular rulers. The right for the Master to absolve members of his own Order was one of the most controversial matters. Yet it was encapsulated in the Primitive *Rule* written under the aegis of St Bernard. Paragraph 45, 'On Faults', orders any brother who commits a slight sin to make it known to the Master in order 'to make amends with a pure heart'. If the sin is more serious, then he 'should sumbit to the mercy and judgment of the Master and brothers, that he may be saved on the Day of Judgment'.

In fact, in this case the real problem was one of changing customs rather than Templar 'guilt'. In the early twelfth century it was entirely legitimate and normal practice for the head of a monastic order to administer the rites of confession and absolution, so absolution within the Templar chapter was acceptable to the popes who created the privilege. The difficulty was that in the intervening period public confession and absolution in chapters had gradually been replaced with private absolution by chaplains and preceptors, while at the same time Church doctrine on these matters had been modified. In other words, it was simply the antiquity of the Order and its *Rule* which caused the difficulty. What was valid in 1128 was no longer so in 1307: until the arrests nobody bothered – or had the authority – to complain about this long-established tradition; after the arrests, it became one of the few genuine 'errors' of the Temple on which its accusers could get good purchase.

This is shown by the fact that #272 and #273, which provide the instructions for conduct for the chaplain-brothers, actually list the particular offences which they may *not* absolve. These are the killing of a fellow Christian, causing blood to flow from a wound in another brother, laying hands on members of any other religious order or ordained priest and, entering the Order when already in holy orders or through simony.

127

The absolution for these things, the latter paragraph sustains, has been reserved by the pope for the Church of Rome, so that only 'the patriarch or the archbishop of bishop of the country where they are' may absolve Templar brothers of them. But this of course implies that many sins *may* be absolved by the chaplain-brothers, and thus also by the Master. It is a matter which hardly needed further proof.

On the secrecy of the Templar chapters the *Rule* is also quite specific. There seems almost to have been a collective obsession with keeping Templar matters from the eyes and ears of non-Templars. From the point of view of a Guillaume de Nogaret, or an inquisitor trained to read Catharism into the slightest hint of secret ceremonies, some of the paragraphs must have amounted to a self-condemnation.

The section devoted to 'Penances', for example (#224–#278), which has been dated to around 1165, provides an instructive case in point. It opens with a list of the 'things for which a brother of the house of the Temple may be expelled from the house'. The first and foremost of these was simony, which was then considered a heresy and had been a major preoccupation of ecclesiastical reformers in the eleventh and twelfth centuries. But the second, indicating its importance for the compilers of the *Rule*, concerned the revealing of matters discussed in Templar chapters both to non-Templars and absent brothers. According to #225, a brother who 'discloses the affairs of his chapter to any brother of the Temple who was not there, or to any other man', was to be expelled from the Order. Yet this early emphasis on the need for maintaining secrecy was clearly not sufficient. For the same strictures are repeated in #418, probably dating from the late-twelfth century, and again in #550, written between 1257 and 1268. Both the continual reiteration of the penance and its extreme severity indicate the difficulties of keeping the secrets of chapters within the Order.

The obsession permeates the entire *Rule*, which was itself considered a secret document. The categorial tone of #326 makes this evident:

> No brother should have the *retrais* or the Rule, unless he has them with the permission of the convent, for by the convent they have been and were forbidden to be kept by the brothers, because the squires found them once and read them, and disclosed them to secular men, which could have been harmful to our Order.

Similarly, the section of the *Rule* on 'The Holding of Ordinary Chapters' emphasises yet again the need for concealing Templar business from outsiders. In the words of #387, the brothers 'should take care that no one who is not a brother of the Temple may listen when they hold their chapter'. Then, in an interesting passage concerning the process whereby a brother who believes that he has sinned should present himself spontaneously to his commander in chapter, #391 provides a final instance of this concern:

And when the brothers have communally given their advice, as they see fit, and the commander has heard what the majority agrees, he should have the brother return before him, and he should indicate the fault to him and relate how it is serious and how the brothers hold him to have failed; and he should command him to do what the brothers have judged, and should relate to him the judgment of the brothers; but he should not say, 'such-and-such a brother gave such-and-such a judgment' or 'he agreed to that', for he would disclose the dealings of his chapter.

In the context of the trial, this is indeed self-condemnation.

At least on two charges, the Order therefore stood condemned. How could the Templar lawyers possibly defend themselves against the charges that 'they held these receptions secretly' or that during the receptions 'there was no one present except the brothers of the said Order' (accusations 38 and 39)? Moreover, things are much worse than this apparently random choice of two charges from a list of 127 might appear. The damning accusation which follows states that 'on account of *this*, vehement suspicion had, for a long time, worked against the said Order' (accusation 40). Since many discussions of Templar guilt in the end turn to this concept of 'vehement suspicion', we can see that in a sense the heart of the Templar 'crimes' was this matter of secrecy.

Yet the Templar *Rule* explicitly commands the very secrecy for which they were under accusation. Quite simply, there was no way out!

This episode provides us with perhaps the best example of the skill of the royal lawyers. For on this matter the articles of accusation forge a strange but convincing alloy from overt Templar practice and so-called 'heretical depravity', since the implicit association between secrecy and heresy – and later witchcraft – was by 1310 an accepted fact in most people's minds. Early Christians themselves used the secrecy and darkness of catacombs, and at least since a Synod held at Rome in 743 secret meetings had been linked in popular imagination to witchcraft. One of the earliest documents on witchcraft, the *Canon Episcopi*, which was addressed to bishops around 900 so that they would 'uproot ... the pernicious art of sorcery', set the seal by placing the work of demons 'in the hours of the night'. It needed little for an expert propagandist like Guillaume de Nogaret to insinuate the link between Templar secrecy and the nocturnal meetings of the Cathars.

The last category of charges, those concerning charity, hospitality, and the illegal acquisition of property and wealth, falls within an established tradition of accusations. The original purpose of the Order of the Temple was without taint, for the second paragraph of the *Rule* stresses that the new knighthood was to reverse the old values of plunder, despoiling and killing in favour of defending the poor, widows, orphans and churches. The giving of alms and charity had always been considered to be amongst their primary functions. Later paragraphs of the *Rule* specify that the Master should allow five paupers to eat at a Templar house every day that he is in residence there; and that on Maundy Thursday, wherever he happened to be, he 'should wash the feet of thirteen paupers, and should give to each of them shirt and breeches, two loaves of bread, two deniers and a pair of shoes'.

But the noble purpose of these exhortations was from the beginning tainted by accusations of avarice. Within the lifetime of Bernard of Clairvaux, it was possible for William of Tyre to accuse the then Master, Bernard de Tremelay, of allowing no other men but the Templars through a breach in the walls of Ascalon so that they could 'obtain the greater and richer portion of the spoils and plunder' for themselves.

At the same time the Templars began to come under fire for the tax concessions allowed to them, and for exemptions from customs duties which enabled them to import from the Holy Land at low cost luxury goods like silk, dyes and spices. They were envied for their great wealth and property, for the right to keep for themselves the spoils of war, for the number of benefactors who increased their riches, for their highly visible financial operations, and – especially in the kingdom of Aragon – for their role as moneylenders. The Third Lateran Council in 1179 reprimanded them for improperly receiving churches from lay people; Pope Innocent III berated them for their avarice and, among the accusations in Gregory IX's bull *On Templar Pride*, was the charge that they usurped other people's domains by placing their crosses on houses which did not belong to them. Within living memory at the time of the trial, Boniface VIII had admonished the Order of the Temple for granting rights and revenues to lay persons – which amounted to obtaining profit from benefactions made in religious spirit.

A striking condemnation of illegal appropriation of land and consequent avarice appeared in the Templar trial in Scotland. Adam of Wedale, a monk from Newbotle and a witness at the trial, made the following allegations: 'The Order is defamed in manifold ways by unjust acquisitions, for it seeks to appropriate the goods and property of its neighbours justly and unjustly with equal indifference, and does not cultivate hospitality except towards the rich and powerful, for fear of dispersing its possessions in alms'. Here, if we may accept this testimony at face value, the Templars had reached a point diametrically opposite to their point of departure nearly 200 years earlier. This and many other examples of Templar cupidity and avarice ensured that this last group of the articles of accusation would be readily accepted. Once again, the skill of Guillaume de Nogaret as a publicist can be seen at work, mixing the plausible with the absurd in just the right doses to pass off the whole farrago as believable to his contemporaries.

For this brief review of the main charges illustrates above all the extraordinary acumen of the legal minds which compiled them, most likely de Nogaret himself, together with the assistance of Guillaume de Paris and Guillaume de Plaisians. Overall, they consist of an astonishing mishmash of inventions, fantasies, suggestive links, half-truths and truths. The blend is as perfect as that of a convincing dish whose separate ingredients are not readily discernible. Taken as a whole, they could never be disproved to the satisfaction of a court. *All* Templars who obeyed their own *Rule* were necessarily guilty of some of the charges; most of the prisoners confessed to at least a few of the others. Regardless of how these confessions were obtained, their existence in transcripts made under oath represented a formidable obstacle to establishing innocence.

But the Templars did not desist, and this coming together of several hundred brothers to defend the Order in March 1310 is a salient fact in an understanding of the trial. Fear of the consequences now that the charges had been made explicit seems to have rubbed against genuine outrage at them, with the result of creating an explosive spark. Far from forcing the Templars to cover or submission, then, it appears to have been the public reading of the accusations itself which convinced many of them to come out into the open and declare their positions. The jungle drums which had operated between the prisons in Paris now managed to send news of the defence movement far beyond the city walls.

When the papal commission resumed its hearings on Friday 27 March, thirty-two Templars from the diocese of Bourges – including one knight

– came forward declaring their willingness to defend the Order. On the same day a further group of four from Tarbes joined them, again with one knight named. At that stage, the total number of Templars willing to support the defence reached its maximum of 597.

Such a number of prisoners, whether in isolation or with a certain amount of freedom, would have created logistical problems in any medieval city. For this reason they were dispersed in the thirty sites throughout Paris listed above. But it was equally evident that none of the great halls available for the commission's use, such as that in the episcopal palace, would be sufficient to contain such a vast body of men with the guards, clerics and servants necessary to keep order. Yet the president of the commission, the archbishop of Narbonne, who was now in Paris, wished to address them together. For this reason, on the morning of Saturday 28 March, two weeks after the original reading of the charges, the prisoners were summoned to a great gathering in the bishop of Paris' garden. The transcript refers to 'the garden behind the hall and house of the said bishop of Paris', which presumably means the garden or orchard which is visible in later prints between the main hall of the palace and the Seine. Notable absences in this crowd of 546 Templars included Jacques de Molay, Hugues de Pairaud, and Geoffroi de Charney, who never appeared amongst those who were prepared to defend the Order and were left in their cells within the Temple. On the other hand, Gilles Aicelin *was* very much present, a fact which may indicate the concern of Philip the Fair that a concerted defence against the accusations could further delay the condemnation he sought.

In the garden that morning a 'full and perfect' Latin reading of the 127 accusations was made before a shifting, nervous and shivering crowd of men who must nevertheless have drawn fresh courage from the presence of so many fellow Templars. When the reading had been completed, the commissioners explained that they wished to complete the apostolic mandate which they had been given in the best possible manner, but that this would be difficult amidst the confusion and noise of so many prisoners. They therefore requested, reasonably enough considering the circumstances, that the Templars present would choose 'six, eight, ten or even more brothers' to present the case for the defence. The brothers chosen would be given every chance of speaking on behalf of the Order during the hearings. Having made this pronouncement, Gilles Aicelin and the other commissioners stepped aside for a moment to allow the Templars to discuss this proposal.

It was that morning that Renaud de Provins and Pierre de Bologna, the lawyers who had been named earlier by Ponsard de Gizy, stepped into the limelight.

Renaud de Provins was introduced in the transcript as the preceptor of Orléans, while Pierre de Bologna was described as the 'procurator of the said Order at the Roman curia'. Both were said to be literate men, although this affirmation was rendered superfluous by the cautious statement which they had prepared before coming to the bishop's garden. Their main point at present was not to offer a defence of the Order against the accusations, but to complain about the conditions and treatment reserved for the Templars in prison. It is interesting to note that their demands and priorities are perfectly in accord with the strictures of the *Rule*. Although they naturally bemoan the fact of being imprisoned in chains, their first thoughts concern the fact that the prisoners have been deprived of the Templar habit and denied the sacraments of the Church. They are equally concerned about 'all the brothers' – it would be interesting to know just how many – who had died in prison outside Paris, and had been buried in unconsecrated ground like heretics. That is to say, without the last sacrament – a fact which would be perceived by a man of the time as certain passport to eternal damnation. Deprivation of other possessions and the harsh regime of diet, which we might expect to be primary concerns, fall into second place.

After this preamble of complaints, the two lawyers came to the specific issues in hand. Once again, loyalty to the Templar *Rule* and the strictly hierarchical organisation of the Order is the most striking aspect of their observations. Renaud de Provins and Pierre de Bologna could not see how it was possible for them to present a defence of the Order without the consent of the Grand Master. They wished to have a chance to discuss this question of procurators who were to represent the Order both with the Master himself and with the senior Preceptors. For, they argued, the advice of such prudent and wise men was essential for the majority of Templars, who were 'illiterate and simple' men. Failing such consultation, they concluded, it would be impossible for them to present an adequate defence.

This in itself must have been a good reason for Gilles Aicelin to deny permission.

In fact, his actions demonstrate beyond doubt that the archbishop of Narbonne was impatient with the delays and procrastinations which were prolonging the trial. When another of the commissioners had informed the Templars with evident pleasure that their Grand Master had already refused to defend them, and repeated that they would be ready to listen to the chosen procurators, Gilles Aicelin himself addressed the restricted group. The words he used not only betray his personal annoyance, but suggest the irritation of Philip the Fair as the potential defenders gathered force. 'Brothers,' he said, 'you have heard what has been said by myself and my fellow commissioners. Make up your minds today, while you are here. This matter needs to be dealt with quickly, since the date set for the general council is drawing near.' The irregularity of this procedure, and the strange experience of being in an enclosed garden with over 500 restless and noisy Templars must have unnerved the archbishop – and, only a stone's throw away from the garden, his master the king. Anger, fear, dissatisfaction with prison conditions and sheer disgust at the whole affair, must have been palpable in the crowd before him to an intelligent and sensitive man. Such gatherings were manifestly dangerous, he must have thought, and the Templars would have to accelerate their discussions and make up their minds. He may have decided there and then that this would be the last time they were allowed to meet in such large numbers. His concluding words left no room for doubt: 'You must know that we do not intend to allow you to come together like this again,' he said, 'but we intend to go on with the proceedings in the established manner.'

This impatience was reinforced by Bishop Guillaume Bonnet, a royal nominee to the bishopric of Bayeux who had been absent from the commission on royal business almost as much as Gilles Aicelin. 'Brothers,' this second prelate announced even more bluntly, 'it would be fitting that you do as has been suggested. Tomorrow is Sunday, and we shall not continue with the proceedings; neither will there be a hearing on Monday. We shall meet on Tuesday, and at that time go on with the said matter . . .'. A scarcely veiled threat rests between the lines of the bishop's words: get back to your prisons, and make up your mind about how you wish to present your defence by Tuesday at the latest.

In substance, the procurators chosen to represent the 546 Templars gathered in the garden had three days to prepare their defence.

8

A MOBILE COURT: DEFENCES AND VISITS, 31 MARCH–6 APRIL

The trial of the Templars in Paris now entered its strangest phase, as a kind of itinerant court. For a full week, a team of perambulating papal notaries criss-crossed the city gathering the statements of defence which were made by the thirty groups of brothers in their respective prisons and lodgings.

The core of this team consisted of five notaries, but the number increased and decreased throughout the week according to need, sometimes varying between morning and afternoon sessions.

The five-man team made its first visit on the morning of Tuesday 31 March, to the hostel of Guillaume de la Huce, near the Temple, where there were eighteen brothers of unknown rank. From the commissioners' point of view this might have seemed a promising group to begin with, since it included seven of the brothers chosen amongst the ninety who heard the first reading of the list of accusations against the Order. But whether out of fear, uncertainty or simple ignorance, this sub-group of seven indulged in exactly the sort of procrastination which Gilles Aicelin had lamented. First they claimed that the provost of Paris, Jean de Jamville, had promised them the previous Saturday that Pierre de Bologna and the other brothers charged with the defence would be allowed to visit each of the houses where the Templars were detained, to discuss the charges. But this, they protested, had not been allowed. Then they argued that if the commissioners wished to proceed on the basis of the articles of accusation which had been read out to them the previous Saturday, then the prisoners would require a copy of the list in order to be able to prepare a reasoned defence for some future date. Given the admonitions of Gilles Aicelin and Guillaume Bonnet to use the intervening period of three days to formulate a defence, these protests sound feeble. Surely, after the drama of the reading, they could recall the substance of the most shocking of the accusations? On the whole, it was an inconclusive first visit.

135

From Guillaume de la Huce's hostel the investigators rode beyond the city walls to the nearby Temple, where two more notaries joined them for the much greater task of questioning the seventy-five Templars held there. Although neither Jacques de Molay nor the other dignitaries appeared in this phase of the trial (and were not amongst the seventy-five brothers named in the transcript), this second visit was of crucial significance because Pierre de Bologna was amongst the brothers interrogated at the Temple. For while he too protested that the procurators could not be chosen without the Grand Master's consent, it was during this visit that the first real attempt at a concerted statement of defence was made. Pierre de Bologna emerged as a shrewd, intelligent and powerful personality, with a legal mind subtle enough both to absorb and to counter the charges made against the Templars.

Even in the cool notarial transcript, Pierre de Bologna's words that morning read as an impassioned speech, perhaps incomplete as a defence but effective as a statement of position. He was a Templar of some standing, having been received into the Order twenty-five years earlier by the preceptor of Lombardy, Guillaume de Novis. During his interrogation of 7 November 1307, he had been described as a priest of about forty-four years old but, as we shall see below, this does not reveal the full story. In the role of procurator, his language was as vivid as that of his arch-accuser Guillaume de Nogaret and echoed the rhetoric which had instigated the trial. Just as the alleged crimes of the Templars were 'detestable, execrable, abominable and wholly inhuman' so, for brother Pierre, the articles of accusation were 'shameful, wicked and detestable'; just as the world order had been imperilled by 'recourse to the sensuality of irrational beasts', so, for him, were the articles of the papal bull 'irrational' and 'iniquitous'. There had never been, he argued, the slightest trace of the heresies with which they were accused in the entire history of the Templars, and their Order was to be considered 'pure and immaculate'. The accusations made against them were simply false charges, invented with no basis in fact by rivals and enemies – who, in a neat reversal, were themselves shown to be 'infidels and heretics' in daring to challenge such a Christian military order. For this reason, he believed that all the Templar prisoners should be totally and irrevocably freed, so that they could then prepare a strong defence and attend the forthcoming Council of Vienne as free men.

But the most interesting position taken by Pierre de Bologna concerns the acceptability of confessions which had been made during or after torture. He was himself an expert in such matters on two counts: first, as a lawyer who had presumably come across the use of torture in his career; and second, because he had been amongst the original Templar prisoners who had been tortured by the Inquisition and then interrogated by Guillaume de Paris. Although the standard formula asserts that he had then confessed 'freely and without torture', there can be little doubt given his later stance that his 1307 confession of spitting on the cross, and being kissed on the mouth, navel and a 'vile inferior part' had been made as the consequence of torture. He had, however, even in that first interrogation, denied the more serious charge of having carnal relations with other brothers. This unusual combination of direct experience and legal expertise resulted in an argument against accepting confessions made under torture which was as lucid and powerful as any modern advocate could make it:

> For all the Templars who say that these lies or some of them are true are liars themselves and speak falsely. Nevertheless they were not deceived, because they spoke them in the fear of death. Neither should they prejudice the order or its members, because it is known that these things were said in the fear of death and the terrible tortures the confessors had suffered. And even if some of them were not tortured they were in any case terrified by the fear of torture, seeing others who were tortured, and so they said what the torturers wanted them to say. So these (confessions) should not be taken into account, because the punishment of one is the fear of many.

He then made the intriguing assertion that many Templars were cajoled into confession by 'entreaty, blandishments or generous promises'. This may remind us of the 'pauper' Templars, Jean de Melot and Pierre de Sornay, who came to the Paris hearings in hope of financial gain. It would be interesting to know how many of the original depositions in Paris were influenced by such blandishments and promises, or – in blunter terms – how many men sold themselves to King Philip?

Details culled from the transcripts of the various stages of the trial allow us to formulate some hypotheses on this question.

According to the testimony of Ponsard de Gizy, some thirty-six of the 138 Templars arrested and interrogated by Guillaume de Paris died within the first three months of imprisonment. As many as thirty-seven of the survivors were among the 546 defendants who appeared in the bishop's garden two-and-a-half years later, suggesting that they were far from broken men after such a long spell in prison. A further twenty-five of them appear elsewhere in the later trial transcripts, although they were not present in the garden. The first inclination is to include this second group among the prisoners who refused for one reason or another to defend the Order in March. But closer examination suggests otherwise, for this smaller group contains a disproportionate number of high-ranking Templars: four knights, three priests, one preceptor, and the priest, treasurer and preceptor of the Paris Temple. It would appear plausible that these twenty-five brothers were imprisoned in isolation, perhaps in the Great Tower, with Jacques de Molay, Hugues de Pairaud, and Geoffroi de Charney. For the dignitaries also appear in the original list, but never amongst the named groups of defenders.

Taken together, therefore, these sixty-two Templars from the original 138 represent a hard core of prisoners whose refusal to buckle amply justified Pierre de Bologna's protestations of innocence. But that still leaves forty of the original prisoners. They do not appear in the grand total of 597 Templars which represents the maximum number of defendants recorded at any one time (itself a fascinating statistic, since it allows us to calculate at 535 the number of Templars brought in to Paris from provincial prisons, which tallies roughly with Gilmour-Bryson's total of 424 Templars in trials and provincial councils outside Paris). In other words, forty Templar brothers of indeterminable rank disappeared between the arrests in 1307 and the second papal hearings in 1310. Could this mean that as many as forty – less the dignitaries and a few more who might have died in prison between February 1308 and March 1310 – in fact confessed and betrayed the Order of the Temple for financial reward? If so, it would seem to indicate that recruiting policies and general morale were so lax that anyone could join, and anything could happen. Worse still, if Templars were prepared to betray their Order for cash, then why could they not believe in some heretical doctrine?

Pierre de Bologna did not of course suggest anything like this. But the presence of corruptible brothers appears from his words to be as certain as the fact that torture was used to extract confessions. All these things, he says, are 'publicly known and notorious'. He concluded his speech with a prayer invoking the mercy of God to obtain justice in their case. The Templars were, he insisted, good and faithful Christians who did not deserve to have been held in such bad conditions for so long.

The notaries must have been taken aback by the prisoner's eloquence, for a note of scepticism and perhaps even sarcasm creeps into the transcript. They observe with blatant incredulity that Pierre claims to be 'nothing less than the procurator general of the said Order of the Temple at the Roman curia.' As we shall see, independent evidence gathered at Penne, in Central Italy, during a trial which took place in April of the same year, shows that their incredulity was unfounded. Besides, brother Pierre's rhetorical skills suggest an excellent preparation, and the very fact of his designation both as a priest and as 'de Bologna' suggests a link with the university most famous, together with Paris, in the late-thirteenth century for legal studies. Legal training also transpires from his words, as even the brief passages quoted above are sufficient to illustrate – especially if they are compared with the muddled statements of his fellow prisoners. Moreover, the evidence of his dominant role in this crucial phase of the trial suggests that he was speaking the truth, for leading officials of the Order were more than willing to leave the defence of the Order in his hands. In the next few days, Pierre de Bologna revealed himself to be an extremely intelligent man and a shrewd legal tactician; if the odds were not stacked against him by his position as a prisoner, he would have been a match for any of Philip the Fair's lawyers. Whatever the commissioners thought about him, his statement that morning was the catalyst which soon brought the Paris trial to its climax.

After this cold shower the notaries rode across the short stretch of open countryside in front of the Temple, probably on a track which followed the line of the present rue des Fontaines du Temple, to visit the brothers held in the abbey of Saint Martin des Champs (today the Musée National des Techniques). Here too they met a vociferous group of prisoners including one knight and two priests, thirteen men in all. None of them had appeared in the earlier groups wishing to make a statement of defence, but now they all seemed anxious to protest against the conditions in which they are being held and to defend their 'good and holy' Order. They assured the notaries that they themselves were good and faithful Christians. Moreover, they asserted that the Grand Master and other leaders of the Order were 'good, just, upright and lawful', and that the Order itself was totally free from all error. The accusations made against them were false and mendacious. Not only were they themselves innocent of all the charges, but they had never even heard of the crimes with which the Order was imputed until the day they had been arrested.

The notaries must have been disheartened by these robust assertions of innocence as they rode back towards the bishop's palace. Since the next group of houses visited that day was in the extreme south of Paris, beyond the Seine in the area near Sainte Geneviève, we may reasonably assume that these first visits were made on Tuesday morning and that the notaries now paused for lunch and prayers. Their news and reports can hardly have been reassuring to the commissioners, who had met for a brief session that morning. Three days of reflection had increased the willingness of the Templars to defend their Order. Even though the promise of allowing access to the procurators had not been kept the spirit of defence seemed somehow to filter from prison to prison.

In the afternoon the notaries first went to the former residence of the bishop of Amiens, next to Porte St Marcel. This was the gate just south of Sainte Geneviève, where the street named after the abbey passed through the walls near the present junction of rue Descartes and rue Thouin. This may well have been a deliberate choice after the events of the morning, since Pierre de Bologna's main partner in the defence was amongst this group of prisoners. It was in fact Renaud de Provins who now spoke on behalf of the other thirteen brothers who were held there. When asked if they had discussed the choice of procurators to represent the Order, he replied that 'for himself and the other brothers he would come before the commissioners tomorrow, and then he would publicly defend the Order'. This brief appearance of Renaud de Provins, while it indicates his explicit desire to speak on behalf of the Order, does not reveal the passion and eloquence of his friend and colleague Pierre de Bologna. There is just one show of his character when he asserts that he will be prepared to present his defence not only tomorrow, but 'the day after tomorrow, and other days, at the appropriate place and time'. Renaud de Provins remains throughout the trial very much the second string, even though he and Pierre are always mentioned henceforth in tandem.

Next they moved on to the home of the count of Savoy, also next to Porte St Marcel, where eighteen Templars were being held. Here another interesting problem arose in the observations of the knight Raymond Guillaume de Boncé, or Bence. His words suggest a difficulty which may have been common in the Order of the Temple:

Brother Raymond replied that for the moment they could not make any deliberation on the above accusations, since they had been and still were together with other Templars who wished to defend the Order separately. He added that if they were allowed to meet to-

140

gether in the same place with other Templars, especially if they were brothers who spoke Occitan, they would be able to discuss the above charges in such a way as to provide full answers to these and other questions to the above-named lord commissioners. They particularly asked to be allowed to meet with others, especially with those who spoke Occitan.

This is a curious statement from a knight member of an international crusading order: for it suggests, as might reasonably be supposed that, apart from the problem of the less-educated and illiterate prisoners, many others had difficulty in discussing the charges and preparing a suitable defence in a language that was not their own (it should in fairness be added that there is no trace of the language problem in the only other reference to Raymond, when he is cited in the testimony of Bernard Bonhomme as having been present at his reception ceremony some twenty years earlier).

What of the others, we may ask: the English, Hungarians, or Portuguese? Today it is easy to imagine, or at least to accept implicitly, that in everyday Templar life and in battle there was a universal language. Presumably this was Latin, or, given the strongly Burgundian influence on the foundation of the Order, perhaps even French. Evidence shows that few of the Templars had a good grasp of Latin, so that the articles of accusation had also to be read out in French. Yet many – even those born within the area of modern France – must have been uncomfortable in French as they spoke Occitan as a first language. If we accept the Pope Clement's estimate of 2,000 Templars in France at the time of the arrests, and Lea's estimate of a total membership of the Order as around 15,000, how did the other 13,000 communicate in everyday life? Raymond de Boncé, as a knight, was a high-ranking member of the Order, and even he seems to have had difficulty in discussing the defence with his fellow Templars. His case begs the question of what was happening in the other prisons throughout France, and beyond the kingdom. Unfortunately, this intriguing problem cannot be resolved by a study of the trial documents, and even the brothers imprisoned with Raymond seem to be unbothered by it.

The last visit on Tuesday was to the residence of the bishop of Beauvais, which stood midway between Sainte Geneviève and the Dominican convent, on a site opposite the present Panthéon. Here an undistinguished group of twenty-one Templars, including two priests but no knights, replied to the notaries' demands that they were unwilling to appoint procurators for the defence of the Order. All in all, especially given the eloquence of Pierre de Bologna's defence and the spark of resistance in Renaud de Provins' words, Tuesday must have been a disappointing day from the point of view of the papal commission. Certainly it was a long and tiring day's work for the notaries.

Wednesday was even busier. The notaries were already at work before Prime, inside the royal abbey of Sainte Geneviève where twenty-seven Templars were held – including the knights Guillaume de Chambonnet and Bertrand de Sartiges. They visited two further hostels in the course of the morning, and then returned to the episcopal palace to listen to a general defence of the Order articulated by Pierre de Bologna and Renaud de Provins. Then, after lunch – and in this case there is no hypothesis, since the transcript indicates the break – they visited three more hostels.

At Sainte Geneviève one of the prisoners, a certain Elias Aymerici of Limoges, provided the most idiosyncratic attempt at a defence of the Templars in the form of a prayer. It was written on a parchment, which he took from the pocket of his tunic and read aloud to the notaries. Beginning with a moving invocation to God, Christ, the Holy Spirit and the Virgin Mary, this long prayer (some 1,200 words, or four printed pages) constituted a repetitive appeal to the humility, clemency and mercy of God. As it gathered power, Elias managed to bring the good name of St Bernard into his appeal, to flatter King Philip by referring to him as 'the grandson of the Blessed Louis', and to request the 'intercession on their behalf of angels, archangels, prophets, evangelists, apostles, martyrs, and confessors'. These disparate ideas, concocted in desperation, of an intercession was then extended to the Virgin, who is not mentioned in the opening paragraphs of the *Rule* but was now presented as the person 'in whose honour our Order was made and founded', to the Templars' patron St George, and – we almost want to say – anyone else who happened to come to his mind as he wrote the text. Brother Elias makes no real attempt to defend the Order, or to demonstrate their innocence of the charges. A prayer was not the best form in which to make a legal argument. Yet Elias' repeated insistence on the falsity of the accusations and the suffering the Templars have undergone in prison renders it nonetheless a dramatic document. The exalted language and recurrent pleas serve to indicate the absolute despondency into which the imprisoned Templars had fallen nearly three years after their arrest.

But the notaries were unmoved. Like pedantic schoolmasters reading an essay, and without the slightest sign of compassion or interest for Elias' plea, they ignored the subject-matter and observed instead that there were several grammatical mistakes in the Latin of the prayer. Naturally, these pedants then took the trouble to correct the errors (Shakespeare's Holofernes comes to mind). The content went unheeded.

From Sainte Geneviève the notaries went to two more houses, one belonging to the prior of Cornay and the other to a certain Serene, which we may assume to have been in the vicinity of the abbey since afterwards they returned directly to the bishop's palace. In both these houses, which held twenty-one and twelve prisoners respectively, but no one of rank in the Order or note in the trial, the brothers replied to the standard question about whether they wanted to defend their Order with the now equally standard answer that they could not do so without the authority of the Grand Master. They were sworn to obedience of the Master, they argued, and were therefore unable to act without his consent. But they also pointed up a contradiction – or the presence of a loose tongue? – in the procedures. They affirmed that the provost of Paris, their official jailor, had promised them that they would be able to consult with the Master before appointing procurators for the defence. The fact that the same affirmation had been heard from the Templars in Guillaume de la Huce's hostel suggests that there was some truth in it. But Jean de Jamville's promise had been an empty one, made with no authority.

After these fruitless visits the notaries returned to the episcopal palace, where the commissioners were waiting in the chapel next to the main hall. With them was a representative group of five Templars: Pierre de Bologna, Renaud Provins (who had come to fulfil his promise of the previous day), Guillaume de Chambonnet, Bertrand de Sartiges, and the serving-brother Robert Vigier of Clermont. The latter, who now appears for the first time in a prominent role in the proceedings (although he had been among the 546 in the bishop's garden), was described as being about sixty. He had been received into the Order at the Templar house of Mont Ferrand twenty years earlier, and seems to have been present as a representative of the serving-brothers. In fact this group of defenders was well balanced, with two Templar priests, two knights, and one serving-brother. Vigier himself was to play no further role in the defence of the Templars, and was never condemned. Later in the trial, he was absolved and reconciled to the Church.

That morning, Wednesday 1 April, it was Renaud de Provins who

143

spoke. The Templar priest drew a prepared statement from a pocket in his tunic and began to read. The precise legal language and confident tone of his statement confirm that he had been working on it for some time.

He began with explicit reverence for the commissioners and great care in his choice of words. For a safe path through the mire of accusations and confessions required exceptional delicacy of step. Thus brother Renaud began by covering himself, in terms which indicate that he had given a lot of thought to the problem. He first requested that anything he said which might be perceived as open contestation should not be allowed to prejudice him or his fellow defenders. Since he had neither the necessary advice – implying the superior counsel of Jacques de Molay – nor the funds for a defence, such contestation was not his intention. Neither did he wish to say anything which might be construed as directly against 'the holiest father, the supreme pope of the holy Roman Church, nor against the episcopal see, nor against the most excellent princely person of the king of France, nor against his sons'. That more or less created a bridge over the most treacherous ground, providing a kind of advance exculpation for what he was about to say.

The next move was to repeat the assertion of Pierre de Bologna, and several other prisoners that, without the Grand Master's explicit consent, it was impossible for them to appoint procurators for the defence. But Renaud de Provins went further. In order for the Templars to conduct a proper defence, he argued, it was imperative that the Master and the preceptors of France, Aquitaine, Cyprus and Normandy be released from the custody of royal officials and placed 'in the hands of the Church'. He observed shrewdly that if these dignitaries were to remain in the royal custody, then false confessions would persist for as long as the case would last. Following the official line of defence which had been ineffective in the case of Jacques de Molay, he insisted that his case too could only be judged by Pope Clement in person.

After this long preamble, the Templar priest and lawyer moved on to the legal part of his argument, which fell into two distinct parts.

The first concerned a list of demands. He requested that funds be provided to pay for procurators and advocates in the defence, and for such expenses as were necessary to carry it out. He also requested that the same procurators and advocates be assured the safety which was necessary to conduct their work. These demands might have seemed reasonable enough to a commission which was going to such lengths to gather statements of willingness to defend the Order from prisoners scattered all over Paris. But the next two entreaties were equally certain to provoke the ire of royal ministers. De Provins asked that all brothers who had spoken badly of the Order in their confessions should be placed in the hands of the Church, so that it would be possible to distinguish between truth and falsity in their assertions. More interestingly, he asked for an inquiry to be set up to obtain from priests, or others who had been present at the time, the death-bed confessions of Templars who had died after confessing to the inquisitorial or papal commissions. It would then be possible to ascertain on the one hand whether, in their last words, the dying brothers had repeated the original confessions; or, on the other, whether, at the moment of death, they had retracted them and spoken well of the Order of the Temple.

This last request appears for the first time in the trial, and is therefore most likely to have been an original idea of Renaud de Provins. It provides a keen example of the intelligence behind his defence strategy, since a confession made at the moment of the last rites would generally have been accepted as the truth. It might also have evoked a sympathetic response in the less biased members of the commission. Yet there is little evidence of the few commissioners not subject to direct French influence having any power of decision. So it was perhaps naïve of brother Renaud to expect such a provocative request to be granted. Could the aim simply have been to insinuate doubt in the minds of the clergy present?

The second part of Renaud de Provins' legal argument concerned procedure. This was the real thrust of his prepared statement, a closely reasoned case far from the emotional protests of such as Elias de Aymerici in both tone and content. Like his colleague Pierre de Bologna, brother Renaud responded to Guillaume de Nogaret on his own terms and in his own language. He concluded that morning as follows, with precise procedural objections worthy of a medieval Perry Mason:

I say, reverend fathers, that you may only proceed legally against the Order in three ways, or in any one of them, that is by accusation, by denunciation, or by the authority of a judge; whence I derive the fact that if it is by accusation, then the accuser should appear, and he should be subject to a financial penalty and also pay the costs of the case if it is found to be unjust.

Likewise, if the intention is to process by denunciation, then the denunciator should not be heard, because before the denunciation he should have warned our fraternity of the corruption, which he did not do.

Likewise, if the intention is to proceed by the authority of a judge, then I reserve to myself and my followers reasons and defences to be proposed in the ordained proceedings, not being restricted at all on those things which are conceded to myself and the Order.

To a modern reader these procedural objections will appear solid enough, and the courts in which Perry Mason appeared would have been obliged to deal with such publicly raised and legal issues. But, however much this speech must have helped the morale of the four other brothers present at the reading, its juridical consequences were minimal. Renaud de Provins' words were received in a respectful and probably chilly silence and transcribed without comment. Nothing happened. After so much care in preparation, the speech fizzled out like a damp squib. The notarial record moves relentlessly on, without changing, like the proverbial tortoise.

That morning a second letter was read out to the tribunal, this time a protest composed in French by the thirteen vociferous prisoners held in Saint Martin des Champs. When the reading was completed, the commission adjourned the hearing until the following Friday, in the same chapel. There is no sign of perturbation in the court record, but the commissioners must have gone to the refectory of the episcopal palace for prayer and lunch with disappointment and perhaps even anger. For the defence they had heard from Renaud de Provins was framed in their own language, and employed legitimate legal objections to the methods used in the trial. As we have seen in the section on the procedures of the Inquisition, these legal clerics were nothing if not meticulous in their application of the rules.

After lunch, the notaries continued their perambulations, visiting three more prison sites that afternoon. First they went north to the Seine to the house of the Abbot of Latigny, which was near the Temple gate. Like others before them, the eleven Templars held there replied to the notaries' questions that they neither wished nor could choose procurators to act on their behalf since their loyalty and obedience was due to their superiors in the Order. Nevertheless, in the privacy of their house arrest, these Templars had discussed the matter and were clearly worried about the consequences of the trial. They said that they

... were ready, and wished to choose amongst themselves procurators who would speak in their defence, or whoever in his own right

146

be ready and willing to defend the said Order in such a way as might appear useful to him, asking that any individual be allowed to make a defence in his own right if the procurators, whom they themselves had chosen, were not allowed to defend the above-mentioned Order. They all asked to receive the holy sacraments, saying that none of them had confessed anything as a result of torture or promises made to them, and neither had they confessed anything beyond the errors attributed to the said Order.

This was the first occurrence of a request to receive the holy sacraments, which now began to appear frequently. It was presumably intended to emphasise the Templars' distance from heretical sects which denied the sacraments, and to curry favour with the commissioners. The frequency suggests that it was part of the concerted defence strategy.

Following these observations, the eleven Templars proposed four of the brothers present to prepare a common defence: these were to be Jean Lozon, Pierre de Landres from Reims, Laurent de Provins from Sens, and Bernard de Saint Paul. They then asked for ink and paper to make a written copy of their defence, and also requested that the document should be consigned to the commissioners by the procurators they had chosen. But at the same time they were cautious, and unwilling to put themselves out on a limb. Terror lurked behind each affirmation. Rather like timid schoolboys, they argued that, although they had chosen their own representatives, they did not wish them to appear formally in their defence unless the other Templar brothers in custody also chose procurators. It was very much a case of 'you jump first, and I'll follow'. Thus, after an initial show of bravado, the four men chosen retreated behind a smokescreen of words. This attempted defence disappeared without trace; and so did the four Templars.

Strangely, given the courage they displayed that Wednesday afternoon, neither Jean Lozon nor Bernard de Saint Paul had been listed as present for the reading of the articles of accusation in the bishop's garden on 28 March. Neither do they appear elsewhere in the trial transcripts. Similarly, the spark of defiance in Pierre de Landres and Laurent de Provins – both of whom *had* been in the garden – was shortlived, for their names never appear again. Perhaps all four were among the fifty-four Templars chosen to be burned in Paris a few weeks later?

Next the notaries visited a further group of eleven prisoners in the house of Leuragie. Since they came from a house near the Temple gate, and the next visit was to a house in the street where the Temple stood, we may assume that this hostel was also nearby. Here, too, the brothers seemed afraid to come forward without the support of those imprisoned elsewhere: Philip the Fair's strategy of divide and destroy was working well. The words they used reflect the characteristic blend of piety, certainty in the wholesomeness of their Order, and fear of speaking out, which mark Templar statements during this period of the trial. Their voices ring down the centuries as those of honest but frightened men, in desperate need of the leadership which never emerged. These eleven men were presumably led by Mathieu de Cresson Essart, who was to become a prominent figure in later defences and in the last collective defence. He was a younger man, around thirty-nine years old in 1310, from the diocese of Beauvais. Although he was by rank only a serving-brother, his pedigree as a Templar was impeccable. For he had been received into the Order at the Temple in Paris in 1289 following a chapter-general presided over by no less a person than the visitor for France, Hugues de Pairaud. In spite of his non-knightly status, at the time of his arrest brother Mathieu had risen to become preceptor of the Templar house at Belleville in the diocese of Amiens. Like many of his fellow brothers he had confessed to some of the charges during the 1307 interrogation. But in the early months of 1310 he had been amongst the protesters and had figured in the noisy crowd which heard the accusations read out in the bishop's garden on 28 March.

Mathieu replied as follows to the notaries' questions:

> they had not chosen procurators and neither did they wish to do so without the advice of other brothers, saying in defence of the Order, that they saw nothing in it but good and that they wished to live and die in the same Order, holding it to be good and holy and legal and for this reason entrusted to them, and they had preserved it as such while they were members of the Order and intended to preserve it as long as they were part of the same, requesting as good and faithful Christians, so they said, to receive the holy sacraments, and they asked to have the advice of other brothers and their superiors of the above-mentioned Order.

Once again, the fear for their future which animated many of the Templar prisoners transpires between the lines.

Wednesday's last visit was to the hostel of Richard de Spolis, in rue du Temple. It is of special interest because the spokesman for the large

148

group of forty-seven Templars held there was Jean de Montréal. This Jean was an articulate serving-brother from the diocese of Carcassonne who until now had only appeared in the trial as one of the 546 Templars in the bishop's garden. Now he was to emerge as the last defender of note to be added to the ranks of Pierre de Bologna, Renaud de Provins, their silent sidekicks Guillaume de Chambonnet and Bertrand de Sartiges, the equally silent serving-brother Robert Vigier, and – to a lesser extent – Elias Aymerici. On being interrogated by the notaries, Jean de Montréal's reply was recorded as follows:

> Regarding the fact that they have not chosen any procurator, they neither could not nor wished to make such a choice without the permission of their superiors; they request nevertheless the advice of some expert and wise man to whom they might dictate and arrange those things which appear to them necessary for the defence of their Order, things which one or two of them will take to the above-mentioned lord commissioners, [Archbishop Narbonne and the other judges of the court] and also ask for the holy sacraments. In the same way they request that if all of them or one of them should die, they should be buried in holy ground as faithful Christians.

Here, amongst the confidence and certainly of purpose, the Templar fears are made explicit. The prospect of imminent death, whether from judicial execution or as a result of prison conditions, was at this stage foremost in their minds. It was almost as if they had good reason to believe that, after two-and-a-half years, word of forthcoming execution was in the air. For, as we have seen, the terror of eternal damnation was very real for a Christian living around 1300. To avoid such a destiny, burial in holy ground was as crucial as the receiving of holy sacraments; to be condemned on the charges made against their Order would deny it.

Yet again, there was no formal reply. Information was passed on to the royal lawyers and prelates operating behind the scenes, and the notaries continued their perambulations.

On Thursday 2 April they managed a real *tour de force*, visiting eleven houses and hostels and interrogating a total of 164 Templars. They began with the twelve brothers who were in the abbey of St Magloire, which stood on rue St Denis near the present intersection with rue Rambuteau. Then they went to the hostel of Nicholas Hondrée in the nearby – and still-existing – rue des Précheurs, just behind Les Halles. Here the replies of the ten Templars were so close to those of their fellows in the hostels visited by the notaries the day before that they constitute good circumstantial evidence for the existence of a centrally organised defence. First, they said that they were unable to choose procurators without the permission of the Grand Master. They then asserted that the Order of the Temple had been approved and confirmed by the Holy See as good and just and affirmed, like their brethren in the other hostels, that they were good Christians who received the holy sacraments. Somone – possibly, Pierre de Bologna or Renaud de Provins – had succeeded in conveying secret messages to each prison and hostel, instructing the Templars in preparation for the visits.

The testimony of this group is interesting because it went beyond the concerted defence. In an almost tangible show of pride, the Templars affirmed in no uncertain terms that they 'had believed in their Order, believed in it now, and would believe in it until death'. Furthermore, anyone who suggested that the Order was heretical was not a true Templar. Here at last we can hear between the lines of the impersonal transcript the tone of authentic protest from a group of honest, if not high-ranking Templars. For among them a single priest is recorded – together with the magnificently named Adam de Inferno and Jean Fort de Vin.

The wave of protest increased as the notaries moved west to the hostel of Jean le Grant, near the present headquarters of the Banque de France. Seven of the thirty Templars held there came forward to state that they had not been present in the bishop's garden last Saturday during the reading of the articles of accusation, but would now like to be counted amongst the defendants.

Next they visited the nearby hostel called Ocrea, where twelve Templars were held, and thence moved on to Robert Anudei's hostel near the pig market on the south side of Les Halles. Here, too, the seven brothers refuted the 'falsity and mendacity' of the 127 articles, but a new protester emerged in the figure of Raoul de Thauvenay. In the interrogations of Guillaume de Paris, Raoul had been described as a man aged fifty-six who had been received into the Temple in the diocese of Meaux in 1279 and had served as preceptor of two houses in the intervening years. In this capacity, he said, he had received many brothers into the Order (a fact corroborated later in the trial, when he is cited by one Pierre de Cercellis as having been present at a reception around 1303). That morning, in order to illustrate the holiness of the Order, he repeated to the notaries the words he claimed he had always used during receptions: 'I, in the name of the Holy Trinity, Father, Son, and Holy Ghost, and the Blessed Mary and all the saints, do receive you and give the habit of the Temple ...'. In his implicit denial that any secret ceremony took place, the authenticity of tone reflects a faith and honesty in the Order quite different from the protests and legal arguments. Yet that is not to say that brother Raoul and his eleven companions rejected the official line of defence. Quite the contrary. They begged to be allowed to confer with Renaud de Provins.

Here a break in the itinerary suggests that the notaries returned to the episcopal palace, perhaps to report on the morning's work or perhaps for lunch.

In the afternoon they began work again on the opposite side of the city, with the thirteen Templars lodged at Blavot's hostel near Porte St Antoine, which stood on the present rue St Antoine where it joins place de la Bastille. From there, gathering further protests and further demands to confer with Renaud de Provins as they progressed, they called on the nine Templars held in the hostel of Guichard de Marsillac, also near Porte St Antoine, and the fifteen held between the hostel of Jean de Chaminis and the house of the abbot of Tiron, both situated in the rue de Porte Baudoyer, near the present place Baudoyer. They then visited twenty-seven Templars in the residence of the abbot of Prulhaco, which must have been very near since the next visit was also a stone's throw from place Baudoyer. The last call made on Thursday afternoon was to Jean Rosselli's hostel near the church of St Jean en Grève. Here an individual named Aymo de Pratim made one of the most singular protests of the entire trial, seeking a private and egoistic escape from the dilemma which faced all the French Templars. After an undisclosed preamble, he went on to say that:

he could not defend the above-mentioned Order against the Lord Pope and the Lord King since he was a poor and simple man, and that he was not a heretic and had never committed any of the errors of which the aforesaid Order was accused, neither, since joining the Order had he heard or seen that such errors existed in the above-mentioned Order. He then said that he was not interested in the advice of the other aforesaid brothers who were in the same house concerning the choice of procurators for the defence of the said Order, or concerning the arranging and discussing and things to be

151

done with them for the defence of the Order, but asked that he may
be given permission to leave the said Order of the Temple and
return to the secular life or enter into some other religious order,
since he did not like that to which he belonged – without saying
why he did not like it.

This unique testimony, like that of Raymond de Bonce, serves to point
up what might be defined as the variety of response of the Templars on
trial. In the absence of strong leadership from above, the attempt at a
concerted defence was fraught with difficulty. Secret messages, or whispered suggestions between prisoners as they crossed paths going to and
from the commission, might have been sufficient to provide the hint of
coordination we have observed. But many brothers, either in stubborn-
ness or without commands from above, struck out on their own. In the
end, these authentic voices, and often egoistic and idiosyncratic demands,
undermine any attempt to generalise about the Templars and their innocence or guilt.

After Thursday's *tour de force*, the procedure changed. The notaries
were spared their constant criss-crossing of Paris, and the hearing returned to the episcopal palace. Fourteen Templars had been chosen to
represent their Order and, on Friday morning, appeared before the papal
commission in the chapel.

It is not clear who had done the choosing but, on the evidence of the
previous day's testimony, there was a fairly representative group. Yet the
leading advocates for the Order were not included. Neither was each
prison or hostel represented by the fourteen: the Temple itself is conspicuously absent from the list. The knight Guillaume de Sornay had
been chosen to represent the brothers in Blavot's hostel, Raoul de Compendio and Jean de Fontaineville those in Ocrea's hostel, Raoul de
Thauvenay those in Robert Anudei's hostel, Nicholas de Romanis and
Dominique de Verdun those in Guichard de Marsillac's hostel, Adam de
Inferno those in Nicholas Hondrée's hostel, Jean de Valbelant those in
Jean Chaminis' hostel, and Gilles de Parbona and Nicholas Versequin
the brothers in St Magloire, while the knight Guillaume de Fuxo, together with Jean de Montréal, Bernard Charneri and Jean de Bellafaya
represented the large group of forty-seven Templars in Richard Spolis'
hostel.

This time Jean de Montréal stepped into centre stage, with an elaborate argument for the defence which he read out in French in the presence

of the commissioners. It was a document redolent of the garbled defences on the grounds of honour and antiquity which Jacques de Molay had made in his *Memoir* concerning the union of the crusading orders to Clement V before the arrests, and in his second deposition before the papal commission the previous November. There was nothing of the legal elegance and precision of Renaud de Provins' statement. Nevertheless it offers an intriguing insight into the way the Templars viewed their own history and role.

In language which echoes the tone and content of the Templar *Rule*, he indirectly denies the articles of the accusation by providing counter-examples. Sometimes his examples are so close to the *Rule* that we may assume he was one of the few brothers who had studied it. He begins by asserting that the Order of the Temple was founded and approved in olden times, and that all the brothers who entered the Order from that time until the present day did so 'well and honestly, and without sin, according to the Roman Catholic faith'. To illustrate this last point he stresses the importance of ritual for the Templars. They made frequent fasts and kept two Lents each year. They confessed and took communion with the required regularity. In addition, they were scrupulous in carrying out the the last rites for dead brothers, in reciting paternosters for the souls of the dead, and in veneration of the cross on Good Friday. All these rituals and rites, far from being carried out in private or in secret, were performed 'in the presence of the people' – that is, he stresses after each example, 'secular' people, those not belonging to any religious order. Such was their devotion that when a chaplain-brother was not available for the thrice annual confessions at Christmas, Easter and Pentecost, then the brothers went 'to another priest in a secular chapel'. In short, according to Jean de Montréal, the Order was a model of faith and rigour: the chapters were carried out as 'well and honestly' as the receptions, according to the faith of Rome and without the slightest hint of sin; alms were given to the poor daily, or more generously three times a week; each Sunday they heard mass, whether in their houses or elsewhere; last of all, they organised great and public processions on important feast days, thus participating in the lives of the communities in or near which their houses were situated.

As far as heresies or evil practices were concerned, the enormous number and social range of people who came into close contact with the Order and never suspected the slightest misdoings were, brother Jean felt, sufficient testimony to the purity of its activities: '... canons, monks,

153

Dominicans, Franciscans, Carmelites and friars of the Most Holy Trinity, have left their orders and come into the Order of the Temple, and they would not have come if they knew of the slightest hint of sin'. Moreover, the king of France and other kings had used the services of the Templars as treasurers and almoners without suspecting sins or errors, as had archbishops, bishops, counts and barons. Similarly, such noblemen had requested to join the Order, or as a result of their devotion had asked to become Templar brothers on their death-beds. All this would never have been possible were there a hint of sin.

Having established the purity of the Order, Jean de Montréal went on to provide historical evidence of its propriety and devotion to the faith. He informed the commissioners of Templar services during the crusade of St Louis, Philip the Fair's grandfather and, on the seventh crusade of Edward I. He reminded them of the heroic death of Guillaume de Beaujeu, then Grand Master, at Acre, and of the fact that they bore the cross against the Saracens in Castille and Aragon as well as in the Holy Land. In nearly 200 years of existence, he argued, more than 20,000 Templars had died for the faith in the Holy Land. If they had not sacrificed their lives and the Order had been guilty of the accusations made against it, then the Temple would not have been able to accumulate such a collection of holy relics. Neither would the miracles associated with them have occurred. As an example, brother Jean first cites the crown of thorns which Jesus wore, which had flowered in the hands of the chaplain-brothers on Good Friday. Then he told the story of the arrival of the heart of St Euphemia at Castle Pilgrim, in the Holy Land, and the consequent miracles which occurred. All this was to his eyes clear evidence for the purity of the Order.

After this crescendo of protestation and example, Jean de Montréal concluded with an extraordinary challenge which would have been worthy of the atmosphere of a tournament rather than the severe Gothic chapel of the bishop of Paris. No other moment in the trial matches it for the audacity of his proposal. It was almost as if he had forgotten that he was a prisoner of the king in a hostel in the street *outside* the Temple. 'Last of all, if any man wishes to assert that evil things were done in the Order of the Temple, then the brothers are ready to meet such a man in combat . . .' It must remain a moot point whether the issuing of such a challenge to a commission of bishops provoked anger or hilarity. But even at this high point of his rhetoric, brother Jean is as cautious as his predecessors in the defence: that is, he adds, any man except 'our lord

154

King and our lord Pope'. How could he even postulate Philip the Fair or the cancer-ridden pope in arms against him? We may wonder with what nostalgia and memories of great battles in the Holy Land a sincere and combative man like Jean de Montréal looked out from his prison on the massive walls and towers opposite.

There was just one brief postscript. A note on the back of Jean de Montréal's statement, written in Latin, specified that if the commissioners should wish to propose anything 'we request a transcript and a day on which it can be discussed'. As ever, there was no reply.

After this, another brief statement written by the eleven Templars held in Leuragie's hostel, in French, was read out to the commissioners. After the by now customary paragraph on the origins of the Order, these brothers presented another new argument. 'We have', they protested in simple yet poignant language, 'suffered much from the torment of irons, prisons and chains, and spent a long time on a diet of bread and water, as the result of which some of our brothers have died; and no one would have suffered such torments unless our Order was good and we maintained the truth, and if it was not for the world outside free of the errors which have been attributed without reason'. They then addressed a plea to the commissioners to be able to consult Renaud de Provins, Pierre de Bologna and other leaders of the defence movement, and offered to send Mathieu de Cresson Essart and André le Mortoier as representatives to assist in the defence.

In a sense, the really surprising fact at this stage of the trial is that no firm action had already been taken by the royal lawyers or Gilles Aicelin against this increasing groundswell of protest. Neither had any effort been made to stem the growing willingness of the prisoners to come forward in spite of past tortures and to defend their Order in public. That Mathieu de Cresson Essart should now do so suggests that news still travelled easily and rapidly between one prison and another, perhaps by way of the guards or perhaps even by means of off-the-record comments or threats of the notaries. However news was transmitted, the tide of protest now risked flooding the entire proceedings and putting into jeopardy years of punctilious legal work, not to mention Philip the Fair's credibility. The commissioners themselves seemed to have serious misgivings. For they ordered the notaries to go back once again to the hostels and prisons where the Templars were held, in order to check whether the chosen procurators *really* spoke for the brothers they claimed to represent. This process was reinforced by a fairly explicit threat designed to speed up the proceedings. Patience, both their own and that of the royal court, was obviously stretched to the limit: the instructions stress that 'the said commissioners did not intend to wait any longer before going on with the trial'. The net was closing. That afternoon, the notaries informed the Templars who visited that the commissioners wished to resume the full trial the following Wednesday.

For the moment, however, the hearings were suspended. The fourteen rebel Templars returned to their previous anonymity, while the papal notaries resumed their rounds through Paris.

After lunch on the same Friday they visited eleven prisoners held in Rabiosse's hostel. They then returned to Richard de Spolis' hostel in the street of the Temple where Jean de Montréal was held, and completed their rounds at Guichard de Marsillac's hostel. On Saturday they visited six places, and found that the Templars in four of them demanded to be able to speak either to Renaud de Provins or to Pierre de Bologna. There was no sign of the tide receding. Moreover, a further visit to the abbot of Tiron's house produced an original complaint which indicates how strong – and almost impertinent – the movement for defence had become. Under the cover of such a widespread umbrella of protest, voices which had remained silent for nearly three years now found the courage to speak.

The seven Templars held in the abbot Tiron's house, all of whom had previously stated that they wished to defend the Order, now complained about the cost of residence there. With fascinating detail, they explain why the twelve *deniers* assigned to them for daily expenditure were simply not enough to survive. So low was it, that the guard in their hostel had left two of their number, who were unable to meet the charges made on them, to sleep in a dark and dirty ditch every night. They provide a breakdown of their expenses. This offers a glimpse into the conditions of the Templars held in the prisons and hostels of Paris:

Daily cost per bed:	3 *deniers*
Rent of kitchen and linen (weekly):	2 *sous*, 6 *deniers*
Unfettering and rechaining:	2 *sous*
Laundry (every 15 days):	18 *deniers*
Daily cost of firewood & candles:	4 *deniers*
Ferry from the Island of Notre Dame 'to the other side of the water':	16 *deniers*

156

It may reasonably be assumed that this daily allowance of twelve *deniers* was standard throughout Paris. Since these sums were paid from the sequestered treasury of the Temple, we may reflect on the incredible depletion of Templar wealth if they are multiplied by the numbers of prisoners held in Paris and elsewhere over such a long period. In view of the cost of wars, the heavy financial losses suffered at Acre, a decrease in donations and gifts since then, and the total halt in income since 1307, serious doubts must be raised about the real size of the Templar treasury in the spring of 1310. The trial was costing *them*, literally, a fortune.

But such a daily allowance was still insufficient. One *sou* consisted of twelve *deniers*, so one week of expenses including half the laundry cost for fifteen days came to eighty-one *deniers*. This had to be met from a weekly allowance of eighty-four *deniers*. So far, so good. There may even have been a slight surplus. But this calculation excludes the cost of unfettering chains and paying the fares for ferries. In a week which involved a hearing in the bishop's palace, it was clearly impossible for these Templars to cover costs. No extra money was of course available to them so, when the hearings of the papal commission became more frequent in March 1310, they could do nothing but fall behind on payments. The consequence of not meeting the bills, in this case, was deprivation of a bed – which saved them 3 *deniers* daily.

The costs which presumably caused the problem – unfettering and ferrying – are in themselves remarkable. No modern court would dream of charging prisoners for transport under guard from prison to a court hearing. On being summoned by Gilles Aicelin, these seven brothers first had to pay a blacksmith to unchain them, and then pay a boatman to ferry them from Notre Dame Island (today known as the Ile St Louis) to the Ile de la Cité (since there was no bridge between the islands). When the session was over, the whole procedure had to be repeated in reverse. They had to pay the boatman for the return trip, and then pay the blacksmith to *have themselves put back into chains*.

Two further facts emerge from this singular testimony. First of all, it throws light on the conditions in which the Templar prisoners were held. For the term 'hostel' might easily lead us to imagine them housed in something akin to a boarding-house, with all the freedom that implies. But even though they were in hostels and official residences rather than real prisons, on the evidence of the prisoners in the abbot of Tiron's house – and there is no reason to postulate different conditions elsewhere – the Templars were permanently chained. This in itself explains why no

157

Templar managed to evade custody at this stage of the trial: royal guards commanded by Jean de Jamville, the royal gaoler, brought them to the commissioners and then returned them to their chains. The second fact is equally interesting. For the presence of items such as the cost of a kitchen and fuel suggest that the days of a bread and water diet were over. Clean bed linen, heating and lighting also appear to have been available. Above all, the complaints introduce a rare human note into the trial proceedings. For even in the midst of a trial for heresy whose drama would echo down the ages, one of the main concerns of these seven brothers – like prisoners of any epoch – was the satisfaction of basic needs.

The financial arrangements revealed in this complaint to the court also suggest why so many private hostels and religious houses were willing to offer hospitality to the Templar prisoners. Obviously there were good profits to be made from the twelve *deniers* daily allowance, especially for a man such as Richard de Spolis with room for forty-seven Templars. After months and in many cases years of imprisonment, these payments represented in practice a wholesale transfer of Templar funds to the merchant classes and clergy of Paris. For many of them, the Templar trial must have been a kind of manna.

Once again, however, the complaints passed without comment.

Fresh urgency in the proceedings meant that this time the notaries continued their work even on Sunday, for the first time since the papal commission began its work. In each of the four places visited they found that the Templars now generally agreed that Renaud de Provins and Pierre de Bologna, together with Bernard de Sartiges and Guillaume de Chambonnet, should be allowed to appear on behalf of all the imprisoned Templars. The only reservation was that these four representatives should not be appointed as official procurators, presumably because Jacques de Molay's consent could not be obtained. Monday 6 April saw another *tour de force* by the notaries. Organised in three separate groups, they made a total of twenty-four methodical but short visits. They even returned to some of the 'prisons' for a second visit, checking the replies against their previous notes with almost fanatical precision.

Then, on the morning of Tuesday 7, after three brief visits to hostels where the Templars were held, the exhausted notaries returned to the chapel in the episcopal palace. The information had been gathered, and it was time to press on. In fact the commissioners usually began work at

Prime, and had planned to recommence at that hour on Wednesday morning. But urgency pressed them to open proceedings at once. The stage was set for what was to be the major collective statement of defence ever made by the Templars.

9

A MAJOR STATEMENT OF DEFENCE: 7 APRIL

Archbishop Gilles Aicelin chaired the full commission in person on Tuesday 7 April, in the chapel next to Bishop Guillaume de Baufet's main hall, where nine Templar brothers were brought before the commissioners around mid-morning.

Renaud de Provins and Pierre de Bologna were by this time generally recognised as the leaders of the defence movement; Bertrand de Sartiges and Guillaume de Chambonnet had been accepted by the commissioners as their right-hand men; Jean de Montréal had also now asserted himself as one of the leading defenders, after his forthright speech on the previous Friday.

To this core group was now added Mathieu de Cresson Essart. His appearance in this restricted group of nine is of special interest. For if he were to deny that there was anything amiss in his own reception ceremony, his denial would imply that the Visitor for France was innocent of the charges made against him. For Hugues de Pairaud, like Jacques de Molay and Geoffroi de Charney, was never given the chance to defend himself in court.

The seventh member of the group was Guillaume de Fuxo, or de Fugo, a knight who had earlier been chosen to represent the forty-seven prisoners in Richard de Spolis' hostel together with Jean de Montréal. He had not been amongst the Templars arrested in Paris, but had been brought to the capital later by the *sénéschal* of Carcassonne – where presumably he had been arrested in 1307 and then held in custody. On arrival in Paris he had stated that he wished to defend the Order, and he had also been been present in the bishop's garden. It is possible that he came under the influence of Jean de Montréal in the hostel, and that he had collaborated with him on the statement presented to the court the previous Friday.

The last two Templars present that morning, Jean de Saint Leonard and Guillaume de Givry, are more mysterious; their participation remains unexplained. They had never previously appeared among the various groups of defenders, not even amongst the 546 in the bishop's garden. Neither do they figure again later in the trial. Jean de Saint Leonard is only mentioned in the trial transcripts as having been one of the prisoners in the Paris house of the Cistercians, in rue St Martin. Guillaume de Givry does not appear at all elsewhere, unless he is to be identified with the 'Guillaume de Gisiaco Bisuntinensis', that is Guillaume de Gisiaco (Gisy? Givry?) from the diocese of Besançon, who also makes a single – and equally undistinguished – appearance earlier in the proceedings.

In fact this group represents an unexpected choice of defenders. Jean de Saint Leonard and Guillaume de Givry seem to be names picked at random. For other more suitable candidates had already come forward, and could have been included in the group. What had happened to Bernard Charneri and Jean de Bellfaya, who had represented the Spolis hostel prisoners with Jean de Montréal and Guillaume de Fuxo? Or André le Mortoier, who had defended the brothers in Leuragie's hostel with Mathieu de Cresson Essart? Where was the courageous Elias Aymerici, or the serving-brother Robert Vigier who had briefly appeared earlier with the four leading defenders? Unfortunately, these questions must remain unanswered. In fact, as so often in the course of the trial, the papal commissioners combine the obvious with the unexpected. They always seem to be able to conjure a Templar out of nothing when required. It was as if they had special stocks at hand in some Parisian warehouse, or in a prison somewhere in the provinces. Likewise, when these Templars no longer serve any purpose, they simply disappear from the records. And presumably from life.

These nine Templar brothers, the transcript affirms, had come before the lord commissioners 'both on their own behalf and on behalf of all the aforesaid brothers who had offered to defend the Order'. Once they had taken their places in the court, they once again produced a written memorandum to be read before the commission.

On this occasion, their argument was developed through a preliminary statement and four main stages: the first of these stages consisted of a renewed declaration that the confessions of the 1307 interrogations had been obtained by means of torture, fear and various kinds of persuasion; the second was a fresh assertion of the purity of the Order; the third was a direct attack on the articles of accusation; and the fourth consisted of a criticism of the method of proceedings, reasserting the fact that all evidence against the Order had been obtained falsely. The whole statement was reported by the notaries in the third person plural, representing all nine Templars present. But it was Pierre de Bologna who read it aloud before the papal commission.

He began with what was by now the customary caution and a loyal reference to Jacques de Molay. 'In your presence, reverend fathers and commissioners,' he read solemnly, 'appointed by the lord pope to inquire into the statutes of the Order of the Temple concerning certain horrible articles of accusation made against the Order of the Temple, the undersigned brothers of the said order propose and state, not with the intention of contesting the trial, but simply in reply, that they cannot, must not and do not even wish to appoint procurators in such an important case without the presence, advice and consent of the Master and Chapter . . .' For this reason he and the other eight brothers were appearing before the commission to defend the Order as individuals, and begged to be allowed to attend the forthcoming General Council of Vienne in person and to be present at all times when the statutes of the Order were under discussion. For this purpose they had designated Pierre himself, together with Renaud de Provins, Bertrand de Sartiges, and Guillaume de Chambonnet to present their case.

At this point we – and the commissioners – might legitimately ask: designated by whom? For they had only just asserted the impossibility of choosing procurators without the consent of Jacques de Molay, and now to all intents and purposes set themselves up as procurators. Why, moreover, not include in this list the other five brothers present that morning? These apparent contradictions did not seem to trouble Pierre de Bologna as he moved into the first phase of his argument, and they remain unexplained later.

On the matter of the use of torture and other coercive measures, Pierre de Bologna flipped the coin of complaint to reveal another side which favoured the defence. 'It is not at all surprising,' he argued brilliantly, 'that there are those who have lied, but rather that there are some who have sustained the truth, given the tribulations and distress which those who tell the truth endure, and the threats, outrages and other ills which they suffer daily.' From this it followed that it was for everybody 'an admirable and even astonishing fact that greater credence is accorded to corrupted liars who provide such testimony for the sakes of their bodies, rather than those who died from their tortures like the martyrs of Christ with the martyr's palm in order to maintain the truth'. In a statement which reveals that torture had not ended with the initial interrogations of Guillaume de Paris, he affirms that those Templars who had maintained the truth and were still alive in prisons within the kingdom of France continued to endure daily tortures and punishments. Elsewhere, he added – in 'all the lands of the world' – not a single Templar will be found to repeat the 'lies' which have been fabricated against the Order. It is evident, he concluded, that those who have spoken against the Order in France did so because 'they were corrupted by fear, by prayers, or by money'.

This elegant and eloquent reasoning is a development of Pierre de Bologna's previous, personal statement of defence. It is as lucid and perceptive as any modern assessment of the Templar predicament. He was well aware of the problem of royal corruption. He and the other defenders seem also to have been in contact with – or at least to have received messages from – the many Templar prisoners beyond the kingdom of France. Moreover, this memorandum is striking for the clarity with which this group of Templars appears to have understood the real crux of their problem: the existence of damning confessions obtained by Guillaume de Paris in the autumn of 1307. Sworn under oath, signed, and faithfully recorded, they now stood as official documents which the court could not ignore. The circumstances of their making did not tarnish their factual value. They existed. This is why, at that point in the proceedings, the only way to establish innocence was to discredit the earlier confessions.

The remaining three stages of Pierre de Bologna's statement took on this near-hopeless task. The job was done with legal acumen. Rather than provide a long and emotional plea based on the purity of the Order's foundation and history, as Jean de Montréal had done, he glossed over the historical facts of the Order of the Temple's foundation and purpose. With a precision worthy of his contemporary William Occam (of the proverbial razor), he sliced through extraneous argument to the issue which was at the heart of both the confessions and the articles of accusation: the reception ceremony.

The reception ceremony was for him an entirely legitimate and religious element of the Order. In perhaps the clearest ever summary of its purpose, Pierre de Bologna said that:

> Whoever enters the said Order makes four essential promises, namely obedience, chastity, poverty, and to devote his entire

163

strength to the service of the Holy Land, that is to conquer the Holy Land of Jerusalem if God grants the grace to do so, and to maintain, guard and defend it to the best of his ability.

It was true that the engagement of this promise entailed a kiss, but it was far from the 'obscene' or 'Cathar' kiss elaborated by zealous inquisitors. Once the neophyte Templars has made his four promises, he explained, 'he is admitted to the honest kiss of peace, and when he has received the cross which they wear perpetually displayed on their breast' he is instructed in the *Rule* and customs of the Order. After this reaffirmation of the devoutness of the Order of the Temple, and the purity of its rituals and ceremonies, brother Pierre then offered his conclusion about the reception with indignation equal to his clarity:

And that is the only profession of faith of all the brothers of the Temple, which has been maintained throughout the world by all brothers of the said Order from its foundation up to the present day. And whoever says or believes otherwise errs totally, commits a mortal sin, and deviates completely from the truth.

In a fine barristerial crescendo he next engaged in a direct attack on the 'disgraceful, horrible, dreadful, detestable, impossible and foul' articles of accusation. They were no more than lies and falsehoods invented by false Christians, heretics and detractors of the Church. In an implicit admission that there were *some* Templar brothers guilty of similar crimes, who had for that reason been expelled from the Order as their *Rule* prescribes, he argued that these false accusers were 'moved by the zeal of cupidity and the ardour of envy . . . to seek out apostates and others who had been thrown out of the congregation of brothers, as sick sheep are thrown out of the fold, because of their crimes'. Here we may detect a reference to Esquin de Floyran and the other two 'traitors' – or 'worthy men', depending on the point of view – who had been the catalysts for the original arrests. For the crimes and lies attributed to the Templars were 'invented and concocted' together with these apostates and fugitives, until it was possible to take a full dossier to the king and his council. In words which illustrate a perfect understanding of the way in which the formularies of inquisitorial manuals guided interrogations by a series of leading questions, he explains that in this way 'prisoners brought from different parts of the world were induced by bribery or otherwise to make the same depositions concerning these crimes'. All the

164

hardships, dangers, tortures, murders and violence which the Templars had suffered derived from this treachery and trickery. In a passage which probably comes as close to the truth as anything stated in all the seven years of the extended proceedings, Pierre de Bologna and his fellow-defenders again show their technical understanding of the situation: the Templars 'were forced to confess these crimes because the said lord king, in this way beguiled by these seducers, informed the lord pope of the above, and in this way both the lord pope and the lord king were deceived by false advice'. Here, from the commissioners' point of view too, he must have been uncomfortably close to an accurate reading of the history of the trial. But he could not make the next move.

The unsurmountable difficulty was of course that a prisoner under royal guard could never openly accuse Philip the Fair or even his legal counsellors. In fact, the opposite was required to ensure personal safety: brother Pierre needed to exculpate the king. In this, his strategy was equally subtle. He asserted that it had been by the above devious means that 'the soul of the lord king and those of his council were led to believe in these crimes'. Yet in a sense it was worse still, since King Philip had been more than willing to be 'deceived'. The seed sown by the traitor Esquin de Floyran could not have fallen on more fertile ground.

The problem now, in mid-trial and with the confessions as tangible as tombstones placed solidly over the field of elegant script in the inquisitorial records, was to halt the rot. The only hope, as Pierre de Bologna perceived, was to seek out loopholes and flaws in procedure. He began this final stage of the argument by repeating Renaud de Provins' argument that the commissioners could not proceed *ex officio*: first of all, because there had been no trace of any such accusations before the arrests of 1307; and second, because there had been no movement of opinion against the Order. Next he moved on to the injustice of the fact that the Templars were held in custody by their chief accuser, a state of affairs which could not guarantee their personal safety. In fact, he stated, many of the prisoners would now be prepared to retract the confession they had made to Guillaume de Paris after torture. The only reason they fail to retract is that every day the royal guards threaten them with the stake if they do so. That this was a very real anxiety is shown by Pierre de Bologna's concluding words: 'In consequence,' he said, 'they request that during their audiences they will be granted sufficient safety, so that in the absence of fear they will be able to return to the truth'. But it was, in view of imminent events, a vain request.

Harsh reality rendered it vain. The defenders had presented an excellent case, and there were many lawyers and clerics in Paris ready to give them the benefit of the doubt. But that would be tantamount to accusing King Philip, or expecting him to admit that he had been wrong to believe the stories of brother Esquin and to ask the Templars' forgiveness. Nearly three years of diplomatic pressure, personal conviction, legal proceedings, and the expenses involved, obviously could not be thrown to the wind. The pride and honour of Philip the Fair were on the line. Such a rational and lucid defence could do nothing but fan the royal ire.

When Pierre de Bologna had taken his place amongst the other Templar representatives, Jean de Montréal was allowed to add a shorter statement to his earlier defence. While the lawyer's plea had been read in Latin, the serving-brother spoke in French. He too complained about the use of torture to extract confessions, which in any case were to be considered invalid. For the Templars were directly reponsible to the Holy See, and possessed special privileges which exempted them from appearing before any other judge, whether ecclesiastical or secular. Only the Pope in person, and the Grand Master of the Temple, could pass judgment upon them. In consequence, Jean de Montréal demanded in the name of the prisoners in Richard Spolis' hostel that the false confessions made by Jacques de Molay and other individual Templars be annulled by Pope Clement.

In contrast to the precise legal language of the Latin memorandum, he furnished his argument with picturesque examples drawn from the recent history of the Order.

The first one was adduced to illustrate the unique power of the pope to pass ultimate judgment on individual Templars but, in passing, provides rare details about the severity of the Order. It concerned a French knight of the Temple, referred to by brother Jean as 'P. de Sencio', who had been expelled from the Order for unspecified misdoings during the pontificate of Boniface VIII (between 1294 and 1303). This knight, we may assume, had been guilty of one of the nine offences mentioned above which were to be punished by expulsion (simony, revealing information about the chapter, killing a Christian, theft, leaving a castle except by the gate, conspiracy, fleeing to the Saracens, heresy, leaving the banner during battle, and fleeing from the Saracens in battle). On this occasion, the French knight had appealed to Pope Boniface and his cardinals, asking them to write a letter to the Master in his favour. This had been done, and the knight had been readmitted to the Order, after undergoing the prescribed punishment of eating on the ground for a year and a day. This penance narrows the field: in the *Rule* there are two groups of sanctions which refer to penances of a year and a day: the first group comprises #262 and #263; the second, #462, #463, #467, and #469. In fact, #462 seems to fit the bill best of all. It concerns a Templar who has remained outside the house and taken things which he should not have taken:

> ... But if he sleeps two nights outside without permission, and has returned in their entirety the things he should return, and has taken away nothing he should not, he may recover his habit when he has done penance for a year and a day ... But if he takes away anything he should not, and sleeps two nights outside, and that without permission, he is lost to the house for ever.

The papal letter of recommendation had been necessary because even the Grand Master had no power to waive the penances specified in the Templar *Rule*. And this penance was severe. The *Rule* specifies that in this case the penitent brother 'should work with the slaves, and when he eats he should sit on the ground before the household and eat of their food, and always he should wear a cope without a cross'. To be forced to eat on the floor in the presence of fellow brothers at table was obviously demeaning; exclusion from the table, and from communal bread, was almost as harsh as the Muslim punishment of cutting off the eating hand (etymologically, those who eat bread together – *cum panis* – are companions; others are outsiders). He would also have been required to keep a fast every Monday, Wednesday and Friday during this year of penance. Such, according to brother Jean, was the rigidity of Templar practice a decade before the arrest. This in itself might have been taken by the commissioners as evidence of the rectitude of the Templars. But the real point was that ultimate authority in all aspects of Templar life had rested with Pope Boniface (if he survived, then brother P. de Sencio was doubly lucky, since he does not appear amongst the arrested Templars either). So, Jean de Montréal argued, should it in this case rest with Pope Clement.

His second example was evidently chosen with care to counter the notion of Templars denying Christ. When the Templar castle of Safed in the Holy Land had been taken, he said, eighty Templars were brought before the Sultan, who threatened to cut off their heads if they refused to deny Christ. They naturally refused, and were immediately decapitated.

167

'For this reason the Templars say', Jean de Montréal added, 'that if the brothers had been as they are said to be, they would have been delivered from such an end.' This example refers to the capture of Safed, from which the Templars controlled Galilee, by the Mameluke Sultan Baibars in July 1266. After three separate assaults had been repulsed by the garrison of the heavily defended castle, the Sultan offered an amnesty to non-Templars who were fighting beside the knights. Soon the Templars realised that they could no longer hold Safed, and their offer of surrender was countered with a promise of safe conduct to Acre. Naturally, once the castle was in his hands, Sultan Baibars reneged on his promise. The Templars' decapitated heads were displayed on the castle, while Baibars himself advanced on Acre with the Baucent or Templar banner. For Jean de Montréal, it was yet another example of Templar courage and faith: had they denied Christ, they would have saved their lives. Why should others have done so, he argued rationally enough, when their lives were not even at stake?

As might be expected at this stage, brother Jean's historical excursions made little impact on a man of Gilles Aicelin's mettle.

When he had finished, and no doubt rejoined his fellow Templars with at least a glow of satisfaction and hope, the commissioners replied. It was a reply which managed to be at the same time precise and evasive. First they demolished Pierre de Bologna's complex defence statement step-by-step, and then they worked over Jean de Montréal's more personal appeal. In essence, their reasoning was a classic case of passing the buck. There was absolutely no question of their releasing the prisoners or returning confiscated property, they argued, since they themselves had neither arrested the Templars nor sequestered their property in the first place. Both, they added with more than a dose of sophistry – and close to blatant mendacity – were now in the custody of Pope Clement and the Church. To this buck-passing was added a medieval Catch-22: they could not credit the argument that the defamation of the Templars was itself based on false premises, since they had it on the authority of a series of papal bulls that there was evidence of such defamation. There could be no higher authority for a papal commission! As for the claim that Guillaume de Paris had no authority to make an inquiry against the Templars, the commissioners replied that this too was untrue since apostolic authority had been given to the inquisitors to proceed wherever there was a suspicion of heresy.

On the specific matters of legal procedure, and the other detailed arguments of Pierre de Bologna, they again passed the buck in what could be described as a Wittgensteinian move. Anything too close to the bone was rejected as being out of their power: they would simply pass on the information to those who did have the authority. Most irritating to the modern reader of the transcripts is their reference here to points 'both written and not written' in the arguments, implying an oral discussion off the record which there is no possibility of reconstructing. The same may be said of the mention of unspecified 'other matters'.

Thus the gathering defence seems to have made no impact at all on the stern commissioners. The certainty which derived from dogma and papal authority – and which had been bolstered by the royal will – was not corroded by the two-pronged attack they had heard that Tuesday morning: the first on a legal and procedural level, and the second on a more emotional and historical level. It was their firm intention to go ahead with their inquiry into the truth of the articles of accusation. The legal gauntlet had been thrown down by the Templar procurators, but the commissioners were more than ready to take it up.

Off-stage, King Philip was also ready to act.

10

THE RESPONSE: 24 PICKED WITNESSES, 11 APRIL–10 MAY

At this stage in the proceedings, the primary need of Philip the Fair and his lawyers was to replenish the armoury of the prosecution with fresh evidence.

The nine Templar defenders led by Pierre de Bologna had taken on the papal commission on legal terms, contrasting both the legalistic trimmings of Guillaume de Nogaret's accusations and the rhetoric of Guillaume de Plaisians with protests about the methods used for obtaining confessions, with refutation of the charges, and with criticism of the procedures. The mouse was now playing the cat at its own game, suscitating a degree of protest and defiance amongst the imprisoned Templars that the royal lawyers would not previously have imagined possible. Now, from their point of view, such a firm defence required an even firmer response.

That entailed obtaining supplementary confessions as damning as those obtained by Guillaume de Paris. Perhaps it is for this reason that the commissioners did not meet on Wednesday, Thursday or Friday of that week. For the royal conjurors needed to produce more Templars from their top hats. This almost certainly meant bringing in prisoners from towns near Paris, with consequent delays owing to travelling time.

It was in fact on Saturday 11 April, the day before Palm Sunday, that the commissioners met again in the same chapel under the chairmanship of Archbishop Gilles Aicelin. The first business on the agenda that morning suggests that Aicelin had also taken advantage of the break to consult his legal colleagues at the royal court. For they began by a discussion of whether or not Pierre de Bologna, Renaud de Provins, Bertrand de Sartiges and Guillaume de Chambonnet should be allowed to represent the Templars formally before the court as procurators. To judge from the convoluted summary in the transcript, the discussion must have been long and complex, dwelling on the legal and technical difficulties involved in admitting the four Templars to the court hearings. The commissioners accepted that the procurators had been freely chosen by the other Templars, and agreed that they were 'more suitable than the others to watch witnesses on oath' – presumably a reference to the legal training of Pierre de Bologna and Renaud de Provins. At the same time, however, they had no intention of allowing the procurators more freedom as defenders and lawyers than they were obliged to by law.

At first sight, these concessions are quite remarkable. They appear to be a striking success, even with their limitations. Who amongst the Templars could have imagined the acquisition of a right to defence after the way they had been arrested, summarily thrown into prison, and then tortured without the slightest chance of protest in October 1307? Now it appeared that they were to have formally recognised procurators present at all audiences of the papal commission. We may imagine a growing sense of optimism in the prisons and hostels of Paris as spring blossomed and Palm Sunday approached. Easter, with its liturgical message of resurrection after betrayal, was at hand.

But the counter-moves of the prosecution soon dampened Templar hopes.

As soon as these consultations were completed, and the decision announced, a fresh group of witnesses comprising twenty Templars and four non-Templars was brought before the commission. The four-day job of assembling these witnesses, carried out by the Provost of Paris and the royal jailor Jean de Jamville, presumably on the indication of royal puppet-masters pulling the strings behind them, was exemplary from the point of view of Philip the Fair. Rarely can such a biased group of witnesses have entered a court of law. The very oath-taking formula was extraordinary, as if anticipating the certainty that each of the twenty-four would provide negative evidence. For they were required to swear on the Bible that 'they would tell the whole, full, and pure truth as much against the same Order as in defence of the same Order'.

The bias of the key witness was breathtaking in its blatancy. For Raoul de Presles was not only one of the few non-Templar witnesses to appear during the Paris trial: he was a full-time royal official described in the transcript as an 'advocate at the court of the king'.

The other three non-Templar witnesses who appeared were, at least in prospect, equally biased. The first was Nicolas Symon, described as a secular squire from the diocese of Sens. In fact he seems more than anything else to have been the right-hand man of Raoul de Presles. Next came Guichard de Marsillac, described as over fifty years old at the time of the hearing. Although he was now retired, Guichard had once been an important royal official as sénéschal of Toulouse – one of the largest of the *sénéchausée*, with one *viguerie* and ninety-six *baillis* in its control. Now Guichard was a resident of Paris, which would not count against him were it not for the fact that he held nine of the Templar prisoners in his hostel 'near the gate of St Antoine'. The last non-Templar witness was a knight called Jean de Vassegio. But, although he came to the bishop's palace that morning, he never actually gave evidence.

Neither did most of the Templars: in the end, only five of the twenty eventually appeared as witnesses. With one exception, they constituted as anonymous a bunch of Templars as the royal lawyers could have hoped to find. Moreover, fifteen of them had already confessed freely in the session staged by Philip the Fair for the benefit of Pope Clement at Poitiers in June 1308. The other five appear to have been conjured out of a top hat, and appear nowhere else in the trial. Only one of the twenty had ever come forward to defend the Order of the Temple. This was the chaplain-brother called Jean de Sivry. He had, it is true, been amongst the confessors at Poitiers. But he had then appeared as a potential defender of the Order before the papal commission in Paris on Friday 13 February 1310, as part of a group of prisoners brought into the city from St Denis. But even brother Jean had not been among the 546 brothers in the bishop's garden.

The exception to this almost total anonymity was another chaplain-brother, Jean de Folliaco, who had been received into the Order at Paris three years before the arrests by the Treasurer of the Temple, Jean de Tour. He was about as negative a witness from within the Order as the royal officials could have chosen. For this was the same Jean de Folliaco who had been interrogated by Guillaume de Paris as the first witness back in 1307, and whose 'spontaneous and free' confession on the morning of 19 October had got the whole trial off to a good start. Having proved himself to be a star witness and a guaranteed performer for the prosecution, he had then been taken to repeat his confessions in even more dramatic form at Poitiers in 1308 – affirming there that during his reception ceremony he had been held by the scruff of the neck and threatened until he agreed to deny God. Now that reliably hostile Templar witnesses were needed, Jean de Folliaco was wheeled out to perform once again.

Only three of the other fourteen Templars who had been in Poitiers

172

appear elsewhere in the trial: Jean de Juvenis was a serving-brother received into the Order in 1300; Jean de Capricordio is cited as the preceptor of Oysimont; and Nicholas de Capella, fifty-five years old in 1310, is mentioned as having been received into the Order in 1285 by Jean de Tour, the Treasurer of Paris, and having earlier confessed to denying Christ and spitting on the cross. The remaining eleven seem to have had no other function than that of make-weight names on the list presented to the commissioners that morning. For none of this group of Poitiers 'veterans' were actually brought before the court, on the grounds that they had already appeared before Pope Clement.

The other five Templars, each of whom made his sole apparition during the trial in these hearings, did give evidence: the knight Gérard de Pasagio, from the region of Metz, who claimed to have left the Order just two years before the general arrest as a result of the depravities he had encountered; Jean Taylafer de Gene, a serving-brother from the diocese of Langres; the serving-brother Jean de Hinquemeta, otherwise referred to as 'the Englishman', from the diocese of London, probably arrested in France; Geoffroi de Thatan from Tours; and Hugues de Buris, from Langogne. One can only ask: where had they been kept since the autumn of 1307?

That Saturday morning, April 11, Gilles Aicelin was absent once again on royal business, and the commission seems to have been under the joint chairmanship of the bishop of Bayeux and the bishop of Limoges. When the preliminaries had been dealt with, they began the hearing with the non-Templar witnesses. First of all, as might be expected in the circumstances, was the royal advocate.

Raoul de Presles' claim to appear in the trial is based on the fact that while he was living in Laon a few years earlier he had become 'very friendly' with the then preceptor of the Templar house there, a certain Gervais de Beauvais (who does not figure in the trial documents). At one stage, brother Gervais sought the royal lawyer's recommendation for the purpose of promotion within the Temple – a fact which, if true, offers an indication of Raoul de Presles' power in Laon. Despite this status, however, his statement is a mishmash of hearsay. As an outsider he is unable to reply when the commissioners question him in detail about the articles of accusation. But one aspect of his testimony is important, especially in view of later Templar legends: his introduction of new and more elaborate features concerning the secrecy of Templar chapters. While de Presles made no mention of the most prominent and salacious elements of the trial to date, he did in part prepare the ground for the later discovery of occult practices in the Temple.

The advocate was not one to beat about the bush. He immediately recounted how the preceptor of Laon had spoken to him of a certain point in Templar practice which was 'so extraordinary and so well concealed that the same Gervais would rather have his head cut off than see this point revealed'. Then, having whetted the appetite both of the commissioners and of the modern reader of the transcripts, he went on in even more stunning terms to cite a yet more secret point in the general chapter. Indeed, this second point was 'secret to such an extent that if the same Master Raoul, or even the king of France, were by some misfortune to see this point, in spite of the punishment they would incur, those present at the chapter would do everything possible to kill them, bowing to the authority of no one in doing so'. Naturally, he is not in a position to reveal the precise nature of these 'points', but his words were sufficient to fan the flames of suspicion.

Worse still was the evidence that the Templars presumed themselves to be above all authority save that of the Holy See. For the mere suggestion that Philip the Fair would have to be *murdered* if he came into the possession of this secret 'point' could only be interpreted as a public affront to the throne.

But the most damning accusation made by Raoul de Presles was that the Templars possessed a book of secret statutes. Once again it was brother Gervais who had supposedly supplied the information, which is of enormous significance as the source for all future accounts of a secret *Rule*. First the preceptor had informed his lawyer friend that he possessed a small book of statutes which he would be able to show him. This in itself, if true, would provide rare details concerning the distribution of the *Rule*: that a relatively unimportant preceptory such as Laon should possess a copy, and that the preceptor should be assumed sufficiently literate to understand it and to employ it in his everyday duties. But Gervais went further. He told his friend that he also possessed 'another, secret book which he would not be able to show him for all the world'. The implication is that he would have been prepared to kill Master Raoul or King Philip for this too. The contents of such a secret book must have been of world-shattering importance. Hence the legend.

The real problem with this, however, is that for all its apparent authenticity Raoul de Presles' testimony reeks of fabrication. It is as though his statement represented an attempt by the same shrewd lawyers who compiled the original accusations to elaborate them into something so shocking that the arguments of the defence movement would be rendered innocuous. No attempt was made by the commission to obtain further information concerning these totally new allegations. As a matter of fact, no questions were asked at all; not even the usual leading questions. Unlike the Templar prisoners, Raoul de Presles walked into the chapel as a free man with no taint of suspicion. Once there, he simply read aloud what sounds like a well-rehearsed speech.

The long-term impact of this speech was little short of astonishing. Yet external evidence suggests that this significant testimony was one of the most blatant royal attempts at corrupting the course of justice in the long story of the trial of the Templars. For Raoul de Presles' life story was as romantic as that of Cinderella, as we can see from the biographical evidence assembled from notarial and other official archives by the modern scholar Franklin J. Pegues.

Raoul was born around 1270 in the village of Presles, in the valley of the River Aisne near Laon, which was then in the county of Champagne. He was the son of a man who may have been some sort of minor local official; his mother was a serf. This meant that he too had the status of a serf. From these humble social origins he seems to have become a clerk around 1285, with the sponsorship of a local abbot. In that position he must have demonstrated considerable ability and intelligence, for it seems he was given the opportunity to study law. Around 1300, he received his manumission from serfdom and, as a free man, became an advocate in the *bailliage* of Vermandois, possibly with the patronage of the counts of Champagne. It was in this capacity that he went to live in Laon, where, as a royal official, nothing would be more natural than for him to make the acquaintance of the Templars and their local preceptor. His influence with the *bailli* of Laon could have induced Gervais de Beauvais to seek a recommendation in view of promotion. Then, however, at some time between 1300 and 1310, Raoul seems to have moved to Paris, where he worked as an anonymous advocate or pleader at the *parlement*.

Then came the quantum leap. On 11 April 1310, Raoul de Presles gave decisive evidence at the Templar trial. From that moment his career took off, and his wealth multiplied as if by miracle.

In the summer of 1310 a number of royal rents were made over to him, together with a house and revenues at Courdemaine and a manor called La Royère near Filain. In December of the same year he received by royal grant the *prévoté* of Courdemaine, which, even after rents he paid to the king, remained what Pegues describes as 'an island of seigneurial privilege'. The revenues from this *prévoté* in fact proved to be enormous. Shortly afterwards, he even sold some of them to the dean and chapter of Laon – a fine reversal for the son of a serf within the diocese. But Raoul's sudden rise to wealth was not over: in January of 1311 he somehow raised the huge sum of cash required to purchase a fief. Then he became known as Master Raoul de Presles, seigneur of Lizy, clerk and counsellor to the king, owning extensive lands in Vailly, Filain, Condé-sur-Aisne and Presles. Within two more years, he had become the largest landowner in the lower valley of the Aisne, with land, mills, several villages, and forests which formed a continuous estate for about seven miles along the river, together with the ownership of an important bridge.

One endearing trait in Raoul de Presles as he moved up the social and economic ladder was that he always acknowledged the start which learning had provided for him. As a result, in 1314 he founded a school in Presles, and co-founded a 'College of Laon and Soissons' in the capital to enable poor students from those dioceses to study at the University of Paris – a fact which could intimate that he himself had studied law there. At about the same time he built a substantial house for himself in Paris, in the still-existing impasse du Boeuf, off rue St Merri.

From anonymous advocate in royal service to landowner and benefactor in four years flat, such was the success story of Raoul de Presles: sudden, and rapid once it had begun in the summer of 1310. It is for this reason that Franklin J. Pegues believes the source of his wealth to be the testimony made before the papal commissioners that spring. Master Raoul was the only royal official to appear as a witness in the trial, together with his sidekick Nicholas Symon. He did so at a crucial moment, when it was feared that the defence movement would gain the upper hand, and with notable success. Afterwards, he was rewarded with grants of land, and large cash sums – which can only remind us of the earlier hints of bribery of witnesses, and of the ragged ex-Templars who appeared before the Inquisition in the hope of financial gain. In the present situation of stall, Philip the Fair needed to force the issue, at any cost.

Nicholas Symon appeared before the court next. He was described as around forty years old, a secular squire, and literate. It is likely that he was a junior lawyer or official working under de Presles. But his performance was less smooth than that of his superior. He stated under oath that he knew nothing concerning the truth of the articles of accusation, but that he suspected that the Order of the Temple 'was not good'. What, the commissioners asked, were the reasons behind this suspicion? His answers were at best flimsy. First of all, he said that about twenty-five years before a maternal uncle called Jean who had been 'nurtured' in the Order of the Temple had come from Aragon with another Templar knight and had tried to convince him to join the Order. Then, in an extraordinary leap from this adolescent experience, he offered a garbled version of the same story the commissioners had just heard from Raoul de Presles. For he too had heard in Laon that

> a certain Templar named Gervais, about whom Master Raoul de Presles had given evidence, had a certain book containing many statutes of the above-mentioned order which seemed to this witness to be good, at which Gervais had spoken to the same witness as follows: 'There are other statutes in our Order, different from these'.

The story of Gervais' fears if he were to make these secrets known was also repeated, but without the telling detail of having to murder the king of France. According to his sworn evidence, Nicholas had learned of these things about two years before the capture of the Templars in France. He had heard Gervais repeat them several times, both in the presence of Raoul de Presles and while he was alone with the preceptor. At best, this makes Gervais de Beauvais sound like a gossip.

It is curious to note, however, that, even on his own account, knowledge of these secret statutes – whose existence alone would have been enough to warrant a charge of heresy – did not appear to have prejudiced Nicholas Symon against the Temple. For he adds that when his wife had died about four years earlier, only a year before the arrest of the Templars, he himself had attempted to join the Order through the good offices of brother Gervais. He had assumed that the fact that he was fairly wealthy would make him a worthy candidate, but perhaps he was too ambitious in asking to enter a Templar house near his own home. For Gervais had replied, with a touch of authentic-sounding French dialogue amidst the Latin of the notarial record, that it would be hard to arrange (*Ha! Ha! Il i auraye trop à faire*). It is impossible to check the veracity of Nicholas' affirmations. But that the court would accept as plausible the fact that in 1306 a house-owning lawyer, moreover with connections with a man like Raoul de Presles, could contemplate joining the Order is in itself a confirmation of lack of suspicions about Templar

177

probity. Indeed, if this story were true, then Nicholas Symon acted in a manner which contradicted his own evidence: first he harboured doubts about the Order, then he tried to join it. All in all, it may be concluded that Nicholas Symon was a primed but ultimately confused witness.

After the usual break in the hearings for Sunday, on the morning of Monday 13 April the commissioners began their work by going to a nearby infirmary to visit a bedridden Templar, the preceptor Jean de Saint-Benedict from the diocese of Tours. Whether this visit was made for humanitarian reasons, or because they hoped that a death-bed testimony would provide credible evidence, is not specified. They interrogated brother Jean on the main articles of accusation, and then returned to the episcopal chapel to hear Guichard de Marsillac.

The *ex-sénéschal* also seems to have been well prepared for his audience. He drove straight to the heart of the matter by referring to the most insidious of the articles of accusation: those concerning the obscene kiss (Articles 33–35). It is almost as if each of these secular witnesses had been charged with assaulting one weak point in the defence created by Pierre de Bologna and the other procurators. Guichard de Marsillac speaks of the kiss as if it were common knowledge. Starting from the dubious assertion that he had first learned of the fact that Templars practised a kiss on the anus as long as forty years ago, when he must have been in his early teens, he claimed that he had then heard about it in various places, and from various sources. When the commissioners pressed to find out where and how often Guichard had heard about the kiss, he replied that it was over 500 times – which would mean about once a month for the whole of his adult life. The places he mentioned were Lyon, Paris, Apulia, Aragon and, of course, Toulouse. Naturally a man who had been *sénéschal* in the area of greatest concentration of Cathars would be familiar with their rituals, and in the course of his career would have seen many trials concerning obscene kisses. He may even have been in service in the autumn of 1307, and in that case would know the contents of the original *Arrest Order*. From the prosecution's point of view he was another ideal witness.

Guichard's next assault was against the secret reception ceremony. Once again it is interesting to see from his evidence that such an important royal official had a relative who joined the Order of the Temple, as though each extended family of some social position in late-thirteenth century France counted at least one Templar. In this case the relative, a certain Hugues de Marchant of the diocese of Lyon, had been received into the Temple as a knight at the relatively late age of forty as a result of having studied law for many years previously. The story of his reception and his brief period as a Templar represents a curious interlude in the trial proceedings, rather than constituting crucial evidence. But it is worth repeating for the unusual light it throws on the Order and, as an illustration of the variety of experiences in an organisation we too often assume to have been monolithic.

Hugues de Marchant had been received into the Temple at Toulouse around 1300, in the great hall of the Templar house, by the then preceptor of the province Guigo de Ademar (who appears in several other testimonies). On his account, Guichard de Marsillac was himself present at the formal part of the ceremony, dressed in the robes of a secular knight. When this part was over, the brothers of the Order took Hugues into another room where Guichard was not allowed to follow. As he relates the story, the security and secrecy were obsessive: Hugues was taken into an alcove within the room to keep him even further out of view, while a curtain was hung over the inside of the door to make sure no one could spy on the proceedings through cracks in the wood. There was nothing to do but wait outside. When Hugues appeared again in the habit of a Templar knight his face had been 'pale, almost perturbed and shocked'. Guichard was much surprised by this, since his relative had been pleased to become a Templar and more than willing to enter this room. In fact, as he did so, his face had been 'happy, bold and firm'. The dramatic change naturally aroused Guichard de Marsillac's curiosity, so the next day he expressed his own astonishment and asked his relative what had happened. He explained to the commissioners that

> after this (Hugues) could never be happy or at peace with his own heart, and although then and many other times the same witness had asked him with insistence to explain the reason for the above-mentioned perturbation and his being stupified, he had never wished to tell him, neither after that time did he ever see him happy or with a pleasant expression on his face, even though before that he had been happy enough.

This in itself might sound bad enough, but next the story took a strange, and unique twist. Guichard discovered from a friend that his relative had caused a seal to be made with these curious words inscribed on it: *Sigillum Hugonis Perditi*, 'the Seal of the Lost Hugues'. Guichard tried to obtain this seal, whose existence and inscription smack of melodrama, in order to destroy it. But this had proved impossible, and he had only been able to get a wax impression made for him by Hugues. The story ended sadly, rather like modern tales of people who become involved in religious sects which are accused by relatives of kidnapping them – as in Jonestown or Waco. Guichard ended by saying that

> after the same Brother Hugues had been in the Order for nearly two months, as he believed although he did not remember exactly, he returned home to the same witness and other members of his family, and after nearly a year and a half amongst them he died of an illness in the city of Lyon; during this illness he had confessed to the Friars Minor, who were brought to him by the same witness and, when he had received the ecclesiastical sacraments with great devotion, or so it appeared from the outside, he ended his last day.

This important detail not only shows that Hugues died as a good Christian and free from all heresy, but would have reassured the inquisitors that Guichard himself had not been tainted. For, as we have seen, to know a heretic or be the relative of a known heretic, was itself tantamount to heresy.

This strange account of Hugues' seal, together, we may presume, with the commissioners' questions and discussion, took so long that Monday's session of the hearings finished later than usual. Guichard had to return on Tuesday morning to complete his testimony before a commission further depleted by absences, for now the bishop of Bayeux was also away from Paris. The commissioners asked Guichard what he thought his relative had meant by the word 'lost', and whether he believed that Hugues used this word because he had lost his soul or because he had left the secular world. Guichard gave two replies, each quite odd in relation to the desperate situation of his relative Hugues as he tells it, for the making of such a seal must be read as the act of an extremely miserable or damned man.

First he suggested that it had been because of all the things said against the Order of the Temple. This was decidedly prescient, given that Hugues was received into the Order some years before the arrests when there was no hint of misdoings amongst the Templars; that is, unless we accept Guichard's own, unsubstantiated, claim that they had been public knowledge for decades. Yet on Guichard's own admission, *he* had instructed Hugues as a knight and had himself arranged for him to join the Order with the intention of 'magnifying' or extolling him through membership.

Why, if the so-called errors of the Templars were already known, should the *sénéschal* have sent his relative to attain glory with them? In any case, this explanation is completely unsatisfactory. It is as if the accusations of abominable crimes made in 1307 were enough to *kill* a knight in two months flat seven years earlier.

Even less plausible is Guichard's second explanation, that Hugues believed his soul to have been lost as a result of the 'austerity' which the brothers and Order of the Temple then believed to be necessary. This, from a knight living in 1310, is an astounding affirmation. It is true that other witnesses speak of the horror of Templar prisons and of the conditions for miscreant brothers, but there was nothing in them that was not prescribed by the *Rule* – or for that matter commonplace in secular prisons of the time. As we have seen in the case of the complaining Templars on the island of Notre Dame, conditions could be as bad even outside the prisons. That an *ex-sénéschal* from a region pullulating with presumed heretics and inquisitorial prisons should speak of harsh conditions of life, even if only claiming to relate what he had been told, smacks of the ridiculous. While in their time the Templars were accused of cupidity, pride and arrogance, there is not a single trace of lament in the chronicles about hardship. On the contrary, they had often been accused of living too well: hence the emphasis in the *Rule* on the difficulty of Templar life, that prospective entrants should not be beguiled by the fine horses and mantles that they see. But although Master and Preceptors sought to emphasise the difficulties of life in the Order, the living conditions, dormitories, beds, food and other essentials seem to have been adequate. Theoderich's breathless description of the Temple headquarters in Jerusalem is sufficient testimony to the grandeur of much Templar life, as are many surviving ruins, although it is true that the life of agricultural serving-brothers in rural granges cannot have been much different from that of secular peasants. Yet here we are discussing a knight of a powerful family which furnished a *sénéschal* to royal service and several priests to the Church. The whole account of Hugues and his seal sounds like a hastily concocted story which broke down under the questions of the commissioners. If Guichard's testimony on Monday was at least a little convincing, then on Tuesday he threw his credibility to the wind with implausible explanations for the use of the word 'lost'.

It sounds as though the story was cleverly conceived behind the scenes, but that the teller was not sufficiently rehearsed to answer questions. When the commissioners pressed for details, for example in asking who had read the letters on the seal or the names of the Friars Minor, Guichard could not remember. In the end, the story suffers from the weaknesses which may be found in many a badly constructed alibi. But it is an excellent example of the kind of 'evidence' adduced in an attempt to convict the Templars.

Guichard was followed by the first of the Templar witnesses in this hand-picked group, Jean Taylafer de Gene, who was a serving-brother from the diocese of Langres. He was younger than many previous witnesses, at that time about twenty-five, and had only entered the Order three years before the arrests. He had now shaved off his beard, and appeared before the court in plain clothes made of grey wool. He told the commissioners that he had been received by a chaplain-brother called Stephen in the Templar house of Mormant, in the same diocese of Langres. The interesting thing here is that he refers to this house as 'recently acquired', which shows that in spite of the loss of Acre and the Holy Land in the 1290s, holdings of Templar property could at least in one area of France continue to increase. But it also suggests the limitations of the Order in 1304, when both castles and *raison d'être* in the East had been lost, and perhaps even a miscalculation by the royal officials who summoned to testify a young and inexperienced serving-brother who had never seen service beyond France. For, in his brief period as a Templar brother, Jean had been in two other Templar houses in the same diocese: the grange known as 'Bellus Visus' and a house called 'Biena', where he had been arrested and made prisoner. He could not have known much about the Order beyond these limited horizons.

The commissioners took this young Templar through the 127 articles of accusation one by one, requiring an answer to each single charge. It was the first sign of a new tactic possibly designed to break down the resistance of the prisoners. In this case, the serving-brother presented himself as an innocent obliged by the Templars to perform actions against his will: on the first accusation, that of denying Christ in a reception ceremony which took place in the gloom of early morning, he claimed that he had denied Christ in his words but not in his heart; on the accusations of spitting on the cross he affirmed that he had been ordered to spit on an old painted wooden cross but had been careful 'to spit near the cross, not on the cross, because of his reverence for the cross'. Even though there had been no other Templars received with him, and he had never been present at another reception ceremony, he stated with confidence that he believed all other reception ceremonies to have been the same as his. And so he went on, denying this, pretending ignorance of that, and admitting such things as could be attributed to the coercive practices of the Order but not seen as sins committed personally by him. It was very much a case of 'they did these things and tried to make me do them, but I refused and am therefore innocent'.

The two other main areas of accusation also appeared in his testimony: the obscene kiss, and the worship of an idol. But even here, brother Jean was a little modest, claiming for instance that he had received the kiss on the mouth, navel 'and the small of his back'. The head he was required to worship was also rendered ambiguous in his answers. He claimed that he never went close enough to be able to describe it now, and he seemed to know little about its purpose. In the end, Jean Taylafer de Gene professed complete ignorance of eighty-four of the accusations; but for many of the remaining forty-three he indicated with no real commitment that there may have been some truth in them. The charges he actually confessed to were those the commissioners – or the royal lawyers – wanted to hear. Besides, they were mainly those charges which the *Rule* of the Templar prescribed – concerning secrecy and absolution.

Once again, leading questions put to a docile and selected witness produced the required answers. When Jean Taylafer complains towards the end of his testimony about his long imprisonment, there is something in his words which suggests plea-bargaining: he will provide the necessary evidence in exchange for absolution and release from prison. Certainly, he never appears again in the trial.

On the next day, 15 April, which as Easter now approached was Holy Wednesday, Jean de Hinquemeta appeared before the commission. Like Jean Taylafer, he had shaved off his beard and now wore grey woollen clothes. He was about thirty-six, and had been received about ten years earlier in what he described as an unorthodox ceremony by the preceptor of Picardy. He too had denied Christ and spat on the cross, and had then received an unusual form of kiss on the chest and between the shoulder-blades. The commissioners questioned him on the religious observances of the Order, and then began to run through the articles of accusation. But in this case they only reached article seventy-three because, by that time, it was late in the day and they decided that the 'witness would be unable to complete what he had to say'. Easter impended, so they postponed the hearing until Thursday of the following week, when Jean de Hinquemeta should return to complete his testimony.

183

This problem of the time available, which emerges constantly in this phase of the hearings as the commissioners work meticulously through the articles of accusation one-by-one, affords an insight into the extreme precision of the trial. The transcripts themselves do not record each question in full, neither do they report discussions, interjections, comments by the commissioners, or other interruptions. But they do give the prisoners' replies in full, itself a painstaking task. The notaries worked slowly and carefully: in this case of the interrogation of Jean de Hinquemeta, a relatively unimportant testimony, even the printed summary and transcript consists of five closely printed pages. Indeed, it was with an almost audible sigh of relief that the apostolic notary, Floriamonte Dondedei, eventually brought his huge job to its conclusion by citing the 220 folios each with forty lines that he had written with his own hand. With so many prisoners to question, and now also the defenders to hear, it was hardly surprising that even the apparently distant date set for the Council of Vienne by Pope Clement had to be postponed.

The work of the commissioners was nothing less than remorseless. Now, with their customary punctuality, they began the hearings again on the morning of Thursday 23 April as planned, minus the bishop of Bayeux – who had excused himself for the next month since he had to attend a provincial council of the Church at Rouen. Even here, a week's break in the hearings is passed over seamlessly in the transcripts as Jean de Hinquemeta appears before the commission to answer questions on the remaining articles of accusation. But there were no significant additions to his testimony.

When brother Jean had been sent away, Pierre de Bologna, Renaud de Provins, Guillaume de Chambonnet and Bertrand de Sartiges were brought into the chapel. Pierre de Bologna once again read a prepared statement on their behalf. This time he began with a virulent attack on the unjustness of the proceedings against the Order, addressed to the commissioners in language which bears little of the caution and circumspect approach he had previously adopted. The whole business of the arrest, he says, had been rapid, violent and unjust. All the Templars in the kingdom of France had been led to their suffering, torture and harsh prison conditions in a way little different from that in which sheep are led to their slaughter. Once this preliminary attack was over, he provided what are presented as counter examples to the confessions, beginning with the now familiar lament that many of the previous confessions had been obtained either by threats or by royal bribes. For this reason, whatever such witnesses have said against the Order of the Temple must necessarily be false. Moreover, he went on, no one could be 'foolish and insane' enough to wish to join an Order in which the accusations had some basis in truth. Similarly, many noble, good and honest men had become Templars in the zeal of the faith, and would never have done so if there were the slightest hint of heresy or blasphemy.

Next, as was his custom, Pierre de Bologna moved on to points of legal procedure, making a series of specific complaints which to a modern reader again sound reasonable. He demanded that witnesses who had already deposed should be kept separate from those who have yet to depose and that, once their testimony had been obtained, it should be kept secret. He then repeated the request that inquiries be made into the evidence of Templar brothers who had died in prison, and added the new idea that those who had not wished to join the defence movement should be asked their reasons for not doing so.

Already these demands, had they been granted, would have undermined the case for the prosecution. But Pierre de Bologna and the other three procurators now went a step further. In order, we may assume, to prepare a much more detailed defence to present to the commissioners, they asked to be given a complete set of the documents which the commissioners had acquired, including copies of all sworn testimony. But, again, reading between the lines, it is the novelty of the audacious tone which strikes the modern reader. There was little completely new in the complaints and observations which Pierre de Bologna made that morning, but they had been delivered with a force and eloquence which indicated a new level of optimism amongst the defenders. Having been granted some of their requests twelve days earlier, the Templars were pushing for purchase on the next rung towards 'freedom'. Yet the kind of defence such an eloquent lawyer would be able to construct with a complete set both of the accusations and of the evidence, must have been a daunting prospect for the commissioners.

It is in fact possible that these requests, and the confidence behind them, were the origin of the dramatic events which were about to alter for ever the course of the trial.

For the time being the hearings went on as though none of this had happened. The next day, Friday 24 April, Hugues de Buris appeared before the commission and was taken through the full list of accusations; and then, after a weekend of respite, on Monday he was followed through the ritual by the fifty-year-old Gérard de Pasagio – a more

185

experienced man who had been received into the Order in Cyprus seventeen years earlier and had spent some years in the East. Perhaps as a result of his long service, Gérard replied at greater length and with more anecdotal detail than the younger Templar brethren. One full day of interrogation was barely sufficient for the commissioners to reach the thirteenth article of accusation. This illustrates further the extreme meticulousness of the commissioners. For there could be no doubt about brother Hugues' position: he claimed at once that he had left the Order five years before the arrests, 'as a result of the depravities' which he had seen.

On Tuesday 28 April, after nearly six months of regular sessions in various parts of the episcopal palace, the audiences were suddenly moved to the chapel dedicated to St Eloi inside the royal abbey of Sainte-Geneviève. No reason was given, although it was soon to become apparent. The hearings went on as before, but a strange uneasiness seemed to accompany the proceedings. It was in St Eloi that Gérard de Pasagio's testimony was completed, with a detailed consideration of the remaining articles. He was followed on Wednesday by Geoffroi de Thatan, the commission still dutifully plodding through each of the 127 accusations. But nothing new was emerging from these incredibly detailed interrogations; neither for the prosecution, nor for the defence. Then on the morning of Thursday 30 April the serving-brother Jean de Juvignac, aged fifty-four and – uniquely – still wearing his Templar habit, appeared before the court. The commissioners asked him whether he had already been interrogated during the trial of the Templars and, when he answered that he had been questioned by the pope at Poitiers, they decided not to go ahead. No one else was summoned that day. It feels almost as if the commissioners themselves were glad of the respite.

At the same time, during these moments of stall which may have resulted from the continued absence of Archbishop Gilles Aicelin and the bishop of Bayeux, the defence movement seemed to gather new strength. For supporters began to arrive in the capital from provincial prisons. On Saturday 2 May, for instance, twenty-five Templars from Périgord came to St Eloi, where their spokesman, the knight Consolinus de Sancto Jorio, announced that they wished to defend the Order. There is no evidence concerning how or why this group of Templars managed to travel from the Périgord to Paris in apparent freedom at such a late stage of the trial. But there can be little doubt that their appearance was embarrassing for the commissioners, who sorely lacked the authority of their president. It must also have encouraged a fresh spurt of resistance among the Templar prisoners and defenders in Paris. For Pierre de Bologna and the other procurators were now authorised to be present during the hearings, and presumably had the chance to confer with the new arrivals.

In the following week, from Monday 4 May to Saturday 9 May, on the part of the commissioners the sense of stall prevailed. On Monday no witnesses were heard, while on Tuesday the entire day was taken up by procedural matters. Then, for the rest of the week, the commission resumed its soporific rhythm, examining just one witness a day on each of the 127 articles of accusation. 'Item, asked about articles V to VIII above, he said that . . . item, asked about articles IX to XIII, he said . . . item, asked about article XIV, he replied . . .' The voices droned on, and the answers were carefully recorded: word after word, page after page, the evidence continued to accumulate. It must have seemed to the prisoners as the week ended that these hearings would drag on for ever.

But elsewhere events were taking a dramatic turn.

11

THE LAST DEFENCE: 10 MAY

The news that filtered through the usual clandestine channels to the Templar prisoners at the end of that first week of May was such as to chill them. On Monday 11 May a provincial council of the Church, summoned by the newly installed archbishop of Sens, Philippe de Marigny, was due to open in Paris and was scheduled to last until 26 May. The new archbishop was very much a royal man, as brother to Philip the Fair's counsellor Enguerrand de Marigny, who was by that time virtually the king's right-hand man. That spelled trouble for the Templars, since the diocese of Paris fell under the jurisdiction of Sens. In fact, while the hearings of the papal commission trundled on, and the Council of Vienne destined to pass judgment on the Order as a whole was still a distant threat, the word was that this new provincial council would be able to pass judgment on individual Templars at once.

Pierre de Bologna and the other procurators understood the implications of this perfectly. That is why on the morning of Sunday 10 May they let it be known that they urgently requested an audience with the papal commissioners.

The audience was granted, and they went before the commissioners in the chapel of St Eloi at Sainte Geneviève. That day, Archbishop Gilles Aicelin was present to chair the commission in person. Bishop Guillaume Bonnet was still absent, but Guillaume Durant (the bishop of Mende) and Renaud de la Porte (the bishop of Limoges) were present, as were the apostolic notary Matthew of Naples and Jean de Mantua, the archdeacon of Trent. The fact that the audience was granted on a Sunday, usually a day of repose for the commissioners, was itself ominous. The menace of the impending council must have been almost tangible. Even the presence of the archbishop of Narbonne was significant: in the past twelve days he had only appeared once during the hearings, and that had been on a day during which no interrogations were heard. Now royal duties had been lifted from his shoulders so that he could preside over the court. He and the other commissioners must have been very much aware of the pressure which Philip the Fair was beginning to exert.

So was Pierre de Bologna. Templar fears were made explicit as never before in the two prepared statements which he read before the commission. Speaking on behalf of the procurators and 'all the brothers of the Order of the Knighthood of the Temple and their adherents now and in the future', that Sunday morning he drove straight to the crux of the issue:

> The priests Pierre de Bologna and Renaud de Provins and the knights Bertrand de Sartiges and Guillaume de Chambonnet ... fear on the basis of conjecture and plausible supposition, and gravely suspect, that the trial will go on according to *de facto* procedures with the Lord Archbishop of Sens and his suffragans and with other archbishops and prelates of the kingdom of France, since they cannot proceed *de iure* while your inquisition or trial against them and other brothers is pending ...

In other words, to translate his observations into non-legal language, he protested to Gilles Aicelin that it would be illegal for the imminent provincial council to pass judgment while the Order was still technically being tried by the papal commission. But why, we might ask, such pressing consternation about the archbishop of Sens? What was there to fear? The simple answer is: everything.

Since 1292 the archbishopric of Sens had been held by Etienne Bécard, who was a distinguished Master of the University of Paris as well as a renowned scholar of canon law. A man of his distinction and power could afford to be independent of mind, and in fact it seems that for years he had been entirely impervious to Philip the Fair's pressures concerning the Order of the Temple. It may have been for this reason that the episcopal commission in Paris had not yet achieved much, and that even the papal commission – operating within the jurisdiction of Sens – had reached what amounted to a stalemate. But Archbishop Bécard died on 29 March 1309 and, although the chapter of Sens expressed its desire to appoint his successor, the influence exerted by the French king on Pope Clement made that impossible. For some time King Philip had been pressing – no doubt himself pushed by his counsellor and master of finances Enguerrand de Marigny – to achieve promotion for Philippe. For the younger de Marigny brother was as loyal a royal servant as

Enguerrand himself. He had been both a secretary and a counsellor at the royal court and, at the time of Archbishop Bécard's death, was bishop of the lesser diocese of Cambrai as a royal appointee (the bishop of Cambrai was one of eight suffragans of the Metropolitan area of Reims, which was at that time virtually a royal fief).

Thus the new vacancy had presented King Philip with an ideal opportunity both to satisfy his finance minister, and to bring Sens under complete royal domination. Once the chapter of Sens had been dominated, and Pope Clement also persuaded, Philippe de Marigny was duly appointed. He was consecrated archbishop of Sens on Passion Sunday of 1310, which fell that year on Sunday 5 April – just over a month before Pierre de Bologna's last-ditch petition.

At that time Sens was one of the twelve great ecclesiastical provinces of France which had existed since Merovingian times, known since the fourth century as the *Quatrième Lyonnaise*. The jurisdiction of its Metropolitan covered a vast area comprising the dioceses of Auxerre, Chartres, Meaux, Nevers, Orléans, Paris and Troyes. Thus, while Paris was capital of the kingdom of France, in ecclesiastical terms the bishop of Paris was a suffragan of the archbishop of Sens (Paris only became a Metropolitan diocese in 1622, when it absorbed half the previous territory of the diocese of Sens). If Bishop Guillaume de Baufet of Paris had succeeded in maintaining some control over the hearings of the papal commission, and the archbishop of Narbonne had been powerful and impartial enough to resist the most blatant illegalities of his own secular patron thanks to the position of the previous archbishop of Sens (and *his* loyalty to Pope Clement), the new situation meant that Philip the Fair had the Metropolitan in his pocket.

In fact, the new appointee wasted no time. One of his first actions as archbishop had been to convene this Council of the Province of Sens, with the sole purpose of passing judgment on the Templars in Paris. The solemnity of the occasion would be guaranteed by the presence of Philippe de Marigny himself, and his seven suffragan bishops. Given the time necessary to assume his new position, organise such a council, inform the participants, and then give them the chance to prepare themselves and travel to Paris, the May 11 opening was probably the first date which was materially feasible. It is almost certain that the hearings of the papal commission were shifted from the episcopal palace to the chapel of St Eloi to facilitate preparations for the Council.

As the bishops closed in on Paris, so did Philip the Fair. For most of

April, probably since his last recorded official function on 28 March, the records of his itinerary – the *Philippi Quarti Mansiones et Itinera* – show that the king had been away from his capital, at Pontoise and other nearby abbeys. He returned to Paris on the evening of Monday 27 April, and it may be that the date and other details of the forthcoming Council were decided then in conference with Philippe de Marigny and the royal lawyers. For it was on the following morning that the papal hearings were suddenly switched to St Eloi. There were also two other signs that the decision was made in a meeting on 27 April: first, it was from that date that the commissioners seem to have engaged automatic pilot and the hearings began to drag, as if they understood that their work was to a certain extent superfluous in view of the coming Council; and, second, Gilles Aicelin dropped out of sight again for twelve days, as if he too were engaged with other royal counsellors in preparing the terrain.

The Church Council to be held in Paris was not the only move in the decisive new strategy of Philip the Fair. At the same time, a parallel provincial Council was announced for Senlis.

Once again, as always in these royal pincer movements, the choice of site was not casual. Senlis was only forty kilometres north of the palace of the bishop of Paris (distances in France were and are measured from place du Parvis, just in front of the site of the palace). It was also the nearest diocese of the Metropolitan area of Reims, which included Amiens and Cambrai and reached to the English Channel. More important still, there were strong royal links with the great cathedral of Reims. At that time, the archbishop of Reims was Robert de Courtenay, who was the scion of a great family of Champagne and a cousin to Philip the Fair. The archbishopric was almost a family affair. For Robert de Courtenay's uncle, Jean de Courtenay, after serving as archdeacon of the diocese of Paris during the reign of Philip's grandfather Louis IX, had been appointed archbishop of Reims in 1266 under the saintly king's patronage. King Philip himself had been crowned at Reims in 1285, and it is likely that the young Robert de Courtenay was present at the coronation. Certainly, throughout his career he benefited from royal patronage to increase his princely control of the diocese. In a sense, he was a match for Pope Clement. For, as archbishop, he managed to introduce as many as three Courtenay nephews into the chapter of Reims. With such blatant royal links and influence, the Council at Senlis was destined to produce results identical to those of the Paris Council.

It is now clear that Pierre de Bologna and the other procurators had good reason to fear the new developments, and to request an urgent meeting that Sunday.

The Temple had been a truly international Order, but Philip the Fair's initiative had focused it down to the limits of his own kingdom. Now, the next morning, in buildings no more than 800 metres apart as the crow flies – and neither of them much further from the royal palace – two separate commissions would be sitting in judgment on the Templars. Worse still, while the commission chaired by Gilles Aicelin had been scrupulous in following legitimate procedures and sifting the evidence, the new Council set up by the archbishop of Sens would be likely to skip these niceties and move straight to condemnation. The Templars, symbolically trapped within the triangle formed by royal palace, episcopal palace and St Eloi would have no chance of escaping the heavy cross-fire emanating from the three points.

Ironically, however, the first person to be caught by this cross-fire was Gilles Aicelin, the archbishop of Narbonne. Up to this stage, he had managed a superlative balancing act between the interests of the king and those of the pope. His presence more than any other had guaranteed the aura of legality which surrounded the trial of the Templars in Paris. But now that events were accelerating, he was forced out on a limb.

He had probably been present at consultations between King Philip and Philippe de Marigny, and was aware of their strategy; he also possessed the legal training necessary to understand the problems which were now emerging. So the subtle argument which Pierre de Bologna expounded that Sunday morning must have caused him considerable unease. The heart of brother Pierre's argument concerned the injustice of proceeding *de facto*, that is, of the archbishop of Sens' attempt to override the legal process. He and the other procurators fully recognised the dire threat implicit in the provincial council to be opened the next day. For this reason, Pierre de Bologna argued,

> having found the remedy of a petition for appeal to mitigate the suffering of those unjustly oppressed, so that no execution be carried out against themselves and their persons, or that unlawful acts are not carried out against them by the above-mentioned archbishops and prelates of the kingdom, such as would certainly be – if they were indeed carried out – against God and justice, and would cause severe disturbance to your inquisition, for these reasons they apply and appeal to the Lord Pope and the Apostolic See,

both in spoken words and in writing, placing themselves and all the rights appertaining to them and their Order under the protection of the Apostolic See . . .

It was a desperate petition. For Pope Clement had never moved to support the Templars in the last three years, and neither the 1307 Inquisition nor the papal commission had agreed to allow the Templars access to the pope. Only profound terror could have driven them to appeal once more on the same grounds, *and on a Sunday morning.* Given the knowledge of what was to happen in just two days' time, it seems almost certain that the procurators had got wind of the archbishop of Sens' precise intentions. Gilles Aicelin must have known them too.

The desperation of the Templars is apparent in a recurrent emphasis on prayer which the normally cool Pierre de Bologna had never employed in his legal presentations. Suddenly, as if he were breaking down under the pressure, the lawyer burst into a rather pathetic plea reminiscent of the rambling prayer of Elias Aymerici over a month before. The procurators, he insists, '. . . pray to the apostles, and again pray and pray with the greatest possible insistence . . .'. He himself seemed equally suddenly to have lost faith in his own ability to present a defence of the Order. Reason had deserted him. Like a delirious man who had forgotten the urgency behind the request for an extraordinary audience on Sunday, he first repeated the call for a Council of wise men to make corrections to their appeal if that should be necessary, and then requested that funds be made available for the defence from the property of their Order. At the same time, he demanded to be sent – or taken under guarantees of safety – into the presence of Pope Clement as soon as possible in order to pursue the matter of the appeal.

In essence, it was an appeal to higher authority: in the first place to Gilles Aicelin, and then to Pope Clement himself. It seems to have been based on the vain belief that the archbishop of Narbonne, as a Metropolitan of long-standing and as chairman of the commission by papal command, would have the power to overrule decisions made by his newly elected peer at Sens.

Returning to his normal lucid style of reasoning, Pierre de Bologna insisted on the intention of the Templar procurators to adhere to legal procedure. He rather cheekily reminded the commissioners of the duty to complete *their* inquisition, and therefore to prevent the archbishop of Sens and his suffragans from introducing any dangerous novelty into the proceedings. A poignant awareness of the trap the Templars found themselves in emerged from his next request: he asked for Gilles Aicelin's assistance to obtain an audience with the archbishop of Sens. In doing so, he specified that 'one or two of your notaries or scribes' be sent with them to the audience, because *they were unable to find a notary willing to accompany them.* This in itself illustrates the dire predicament in which they now found themselves. The problem was that no one would dare to accompany a group of men on the verge of condemnation: as far as the available notaries were concerned, the Templars must have looked like the walking dead. But to the end, it is fascinating to observe, they had faith in the procedures and in the need for an honest written record of the audience which they sought. But did they really believe there was a chance of such an audience being granted? Probably not, as Pierre de Bologna's concluding demand makes clear. The last words the Templar lawyer spoke in the trial on behalf of the procurators once more emphasise his desperation: 'At the same time they beg that you make this appeal known to all the archbishops of the kingdom of France at the expense of the said Order, since they themselves cannot do so as they are imprisoned . . .'. Surely, he seems to argue, *somebody* will come to our aid.

But no one would. In fact, the consequence of this short speech was so unpredictable as to be astonishing. From a pragmatic point of view, Pierre de Bologna's words represented the hopeless plea of a group of men clutching for straws. But from a strictly legal point of view, the objections raised were impeccable. The onus fell fairly and squarely on the shoulders of the archbishop of Narbonne. For him, it was an impossible dilemma: the idea of setting up an audience between the Templar procurators and the archbishop of Sens, with a public notarial record of the encounter, would be certain to exacerbate the rage of Philip the Fair; blunt refusal of such requests would be equally certain to anger Pope Clement.

At last, after nearly six months of hearings, it looked as though Gilles Aicelin would be obliged to take sides. To whom was his ultimate loyalty due: pope or king? There must have been many both in the royal court and in the Church who waited with morbid curiosity to see which way he turned. In the event, his reaction to the dilemma must have stunned both camps. For the accomplished diplomat found a way out, even though it was hardly diplomatic. One of the most curious passages of the trial transcript records in the usual dry and technical language of the papal notaries that after listening to Pierre de Bologna's statement 'the aforesaid archbishop said that he either had to celebrate mass or to hear mass, and went out'.

In other words, he simply walked out of the court!

Just like that. There was no formal statement, and no announcement at the end of that day's session – as was usually the case. He simply gathered his robes, stood up, and left the chapel. The experienced negotiator was apparently so shocked or confused by the dilemma in which Pierre de Bologna's words had placed him that he did not even have time to invent a decent excuse. The reason he did give, if the notaries maintained their usual accuracy that morning, falls little short of being totally unbelievable: was it possible that a high-ranking cleric after more than forty years of life in the Church could not tell the difference between celebrating a mass and attending one? At best, on the surface this sentence betrays a serious state of confusion.

For he must have been as despondent as the Templars themselves in search of a loophole which would enable him to avoid making a clear decision. Recently, his power in the royal court had increased significantly. On 27 February 1310, he had been entrusted with the royal seal, and since then had been heavily involved in work for the royal chancellery; hence, we may assume, his frequent absences from the papal commission. The chronicler Jean de Saint Victor refers to him in this period as 'counsellor and master of the Royal Court'. Documentary evidence at this crucial moment of the trial shows him to be engaged in relatively unimportant issues when we might have expected him to devote his full attention to the Templars. On 25 April, a Saturday on which there were no hearings, he was busy adding a clause to an earlier ordinance concerning the beliefs of the Jews of Saintonge and Poitou. Just after this session, on 22 May, he was signing royal documents in Rungis. Yet at the same time he must have been unwilling to give up the ecclesiastical privileges gained by so many years of service to the Church. It was in fact probably as the result of success in the Templar trial – and therefore indirectly of his temporary abandonment of the commission – that the next year he was able to negotiate a solution which, to a certain extent, resolved his broader dilemma. For he was then able to negotiate a straight swap of office with Bernard de Farges, archbishop of Rouen, which allowed him to maintain power in the Church while moving closer to Paris. For the moment, however, his unprecedented action meant that the papal commission was left without its chairman.

The remaining members of the commission, now joined by Jean de

Montlaur, the archdeacon of Maguelonne, were left alone to discuss the new appeal. In what must have been an embarrassing moment for all of them, they too avoided immediate action by postponing any decision. They announced in terms that indicated their uncertainty and hesitancy that the four Templars would receive a reply at the hour of Vespers that same Sunday, but only as far as they were authorised to go. Since Vespers was the sixth canonical hour, just before sunset, that would allow the commissioners the whole afternoon for consultation. Perhaps they planned to discuss the matter in private with Gilles Aicelin, who remained in Paris for the Council; perhaps with the royal lawyers; perhaps even with Philippe de Marigny.

As if they feared such a move, before leaving the commission the Templar procurators presented a further written statement. This time, it was addressed directly to the archbishop of Sens. The terms were much the same as those of the appeal already addressed to the commissioners, but there is an added emphasis on problems of legality concerning the anticipated intervention of the archbishop. The procurators argued that they and their followers wished the hearings to go on '. . . in the best way that they can and should, according to the law'. This slight shift of emphasis is enough to reveal that the Templars feared the introduction of new – and illicit – procedures as their trial fell under more direct control of Philip the Fair.

At Vespers the commissioners met again in St Eloi, where the four Templar procurators were summoned after they had deliberated. Their considered judgment, 150 words that had taken half a day to prepare, was a little masterpiece of evasion and ambiguity: they replied that

> they had rediscussed in their council those facts which the above-mentioned lord archbishop of Sens and his suffragans were discussing, and (had decided that) they were completely different facts, . . . and just as the same lord commissioners had been appointed to the task entrusted to them by the apostolic See, so also the lord of Sens and his suffragans had been appointed with apostolic authority to those things which it was said they discussed in their council; the same lord commissioners had no power towards them or over them, for which reason it did not appear to them at first sight, as they said, that they had any reason to impede the said archbishop of Sens or the other prelates by postponing the trials . . .

In other words: very sorry, but it can't be done.

196

The die was cast. But in spite of the fear which emanates from the twin appeal made by Pierre de Bologna on behalf of the Templars, no one could have forseen the imminent consequences of Philip the Fair's long-smouldering impatience and wrath.

12

THE TERROR: 54 TEMPLARS AT THE STAKE, 12 MAY

On Tuesday 12 May, a semblance of normality veiled the proceedings of the papal commission at Sainte Geneviève. Everyone present knew that the provincial council was now entering its second day under the chairmanship of the archbishop of Sens, just across the Seine at the bishop's palace. The commissioners themselves had conducted their hearings there until a fortnight earlier, so it was easy for them to imagine the scene in the great hall. They must also have been uneasily aware that Gilles Aicelin had now deserted them for the council, perhaps even as a royal observer or representative. Worst of all, the spectre of Philip the Fair was hovering between the two sites.

But at first they attempted to maintain a semblance of normality by meeting before Prime that morning in the chapel of St Eloi. The Bishop of Bayeux was still absent on diocesan business, but the other members were all present. Routine prevailed.

The first prisoner to be brought before them was a fifty-year-old Templar serving-brother named Jean Bertald. He had been received into the Order some eighteen years before, and had seen service in the East. At the time of his arrest, brother Jean had risen to become the preceptor of the Templar house of Bussières which was in the diocese of Paris. He said that he had previously been questioned by Jean de Jamville and the *sénéschal* of Paris. Then, a year later, he had been re-examined by the dean of Paris and a commission of Dominicans and Franciscans – that is, during the episcopal inquiries of early 1309 – and had been reconciled to the Church.

Nevertheless, the commissioners began with painstaking thoroughness to take him through the 127 accusations. It must have seemed to those present another tedious session with ever-diminishing returns. The questions were now asked as if by rote, and the brief and usually negative answers of Jean Bertald were probably barely heard as they were entered in the trial record: 'Item, to articles XIV and XV, concerning the cat, he replied that he neither knew nor had heard anything; Item, to articles XVI–XXIII, he replied that he knew nothing . . .'.

They looked set for a long day's work. So much so, that shortly after beginning the commissioners decided to stop for a break in the proceedings. It was during this break – still before Prime, according to the transcript – that the bombshell exploded: the air of lassitude was electrified by a messenger who came to them with extraordinary news. That same day, they were informed, fifty-four of the Templar prisoners who had come forward offering to defend their Order were to be burned alive.

The cat, in the form of Philip the Fair, had struck again. Just one day of the provincial council had been sufficient to push the issue to this new threshold.

But, it must be said, the commissioners did not accept this stunning news with the fatalism we might expect of them. As though angered by the presumption of the archbishop of Sens to barge into the trial after two and a half years and upset the apple-cart, they demonstrated an unforseen autonomy. In doing so, they also provided evidence of the stubborn attitude and procedural mania which had so frustrated King Philip.

For their answer to the news was to send a message to the archbishop of Sens and his suffragans at the Council. Philippe de Voet, a royal gaoler, and Master Amisius, the archdeacon of Orléans and a royal clerk, bore the message. They were also to report to the archbishop the details of Sunday morning's appeal by Pierre de Bologna and the other three procurators. It appears that doubts sown by Pierre de Bologna and other defenders of the Temple had germinated and taken root in the minds of at least some of the commissioners. They were, in the end, honest men who had been dropped in well out of their depth. For the argument they now put forward to Philippe de Marigny, in an attempt to delay the burnings, was that during questioning they had found that many Templars at the point of death had stated that their Order was pure and that the charges made against them had been totally false. This was to be accepted as important evidence. If the burning went ahead, Philippe de Voet and Master Amisius were to argue, then it would obstruct the work of the papal commission. Many Templar witnesses, it seems, were already terrified at the prospect of this intervention by the royal court.

But the protest was in vain. Politics had now superseded procedure.

Both at Paris and at Senlis, the provincial councils were to push ahead regardless. To have expected otherwise would have been naïve, and it was natural that Philippe de Marigny rejected this last-minute appeal in spite of its provenance.

The new archbishop of Sens had enjoyed at the very least twelve days to prepare for his Council, and perhaps up to a full month. The Council was already in session, and to judge by the speed with which the decision to burn fifty-four recalcitrant Templars had been taken – and the speed of imminent developments – the main resolutions had actually been made at a political level before it opened. There was not even to be the pretence of reviewing evidence during the Council, and no witnesses were to be summoned. Both the Paris and the Senlis councils formed no part of the trial in a procedural sense. They had been summoned to pass judgment on what had already been ascertained.

In fact, unknown to the papal commissioners, the process of judgment was already under way. Templar prisoners in Paris had been divided into three categories, using criteria which were in effect much less harsh than the shock announcement early that Tuesday morning intimated. The chronicler Jean de Saint Victor fills the gap in our knowledge. According to his written account, the first category of prisoners comprised Templars who were prepared to confirm their confessions. In what reads like a generous provision, and nothing like as drastic as some accounts make the trial appear, these prisoners were allowed 'to give up the habit of their Order and dress in secular clothes, to be absolved and to go free'. Many did so, for later in the trial ex-Templars appearing to give evidence are formally entered in the transcript as 'absolved and reconciled'; in other words, they appear as free men. The second category comprised Templars who refused to confess. They were to be kept in perpetual imprisonment which, in the minds of the clerics, meant a kind of limbo pending confession. Again, this was not such a drastic punishment and was in accordance with normal procedures. The full harshness of ecclesiastical law fell on members of the third category of prisoners. These were the Templars who had confessed before the Inquisition, before Pope Clement, before an episcopal commission, or before the papal commission, and who had then retracted their confessions. This was the truly terrible crime, as we have seen in the section on the practices of the Inquisition: for it was perceived as *a relapse into heretical doctrines*. At that point, there was nothing either the Inquisition or the Church could do. The procedure prescribed that such relapsed heretics be 'released to the secular arm', which was a euphemism for burning at the stake.

In other words, Archbishop Philippe de Marigny was simply applying the law to the letter – albeit rather enthusiastically, and under pressure from Philip the Fair. There was nothing illegal in his action, and from a technical point of view *he* was not responsible for the burnings. The experienced inquisitor Bernard Gui recognised this fact: in his chronicle, he observes with scholarly precision that fifty-four Templars condemned to death were given up to the secular arm and 'taken to be burned by secular officials of the royal court'.

Since the news arrived at St Eloi before Prime, it may be supposed that the decision had been taken the previous day. At dawn royal gaolers must have visited the prisons and hostels where the fifty-four were held, slowly assembling the group. Such an unusual movement of royal guards, with their prisoners in chains, cannot have escaped the notice of Parisians as they went about their daily work. The chronicles tell us that a large crowd gathered in the meadow where the burnings took place; we may imagine these people gathering as the procession formed by a four-horse wooden wagon crammed with prisoners, and royal guards in front and behind, drove through the city towards Porte Saint Antoine, near the present place de la Bastille. For the continuator of the chronicle of Guillaume de Nangis informs us in laconic fashion that 'outside the city of Paris, in the meadow near the convent known as Saint Antoine, not far from the city, they were burned to death'.

Saint Antoine des Champs, as we have seen, stood outside the city walls on the road to Meaux (the present rue du faubourg Saint Antoine). It was at that time a huge fortified complex, surrounded with buttressed walls and a moat enclosing agricultural land, orchards and vineyards. After informing us that the burnings took place 'on the Tuesday after the feast day of St Nicholas, in May', the author of the *Grandes chroniques de France* specifies that the exact site was 'towards the mill of Saint Antoine'. This may be taken to mean in the fields between the abbey and a windmill which belonged to the city of Paris.

There was no great ceremony. The Templars were driven through the city presumably still in chains. Once outside Porte Saint Antoine, the procession – with a gathering crowd of citizens following – had to cover a distance of about one-and-a-half kilometres to reach the area where the mill stood. By that time a train of eager citizens would have gathered as word spread through the city, together with the tradesmen, charlatans and pick-pockets who attended public executions in the hope of selling their wares or otherwise taking advantage of the excited crowd. As soon as the prisoners arrived at their destination, the horses which had pulled them were released from their bridles, and fire was applied to the wagons themselves. There was not even the dignity of a stake.

Yet the fifty-four Templars who died there proved in the end to be stalwart defenders of their Order. According to the continuator of Guillaume de Nangis, they bore themselves with dignity before the crowd in the meadow:

> And all of them, without exception, in the end did not recognise any of the crimes imputed to them, but with constancy and perseverance persisted in the collective denial, saying all the time that they were being executed without just cause. Indeed many of the people present were unable to watch without much admiration and vehement astonishment.

Here was powerful confirmation of the doubts expressed by Pierre de Bologna; at the moment of death, truth would out. This 'vehement astonishment' of the populace noted by the chronicler anticipated similar sentiments expressed at the later execution of Jacques de Molay. It did much to instil doubt in contemporaries who observed the proceedings of the trial from outside the privileged vantage-point of the episcopal and papal commissions.

Yet the burnings represented a victory for Philip the Fair. At last, after nearly three years, some of the Templars had been condemned for the heresies he had caused them to be charged with committing. In open fields, beyond the city walls and probably beyond the abbey walls, without the benefit of holy sacraments and with no chance of defending themselves, fifty-four brothers had died.

But who were they?

Not Pierre de Bologna, as might have been expected. In fact, most of them remain anonymous: seven names can be abstracted from the trial record, where later some Templars are referred to as having been 'burned in Paris'. But two of these, Martin de Nice and a certain Gaucerand, never appear elsewhere in the trial transcripts. Nothing can be known of them apart from their names. They, and the other five, may even have been amongst the second batch of five Templars burned later in the month, and not in the meadow near Saint Antoine.

Once again, the royal officials appear to have drawn on secret reserves of Templar prisoners. None of the other five whose names may be extrapolated had played significant roles in the trial, even though some of them had been Templars of long standing and some importance. Two of the five, Raoul de Freynoy and Gautier de Bullens, had been among the 546 Templars who appeared to defend the Order in the bishop's garden the previous March; Raoul, from the diocese of Amiens, was one of the brothers held at the hostel of Penne Vayrie and is mentioned later as having been present at a reception at the house of Oisy in 1284; Gautier, a knight also described as from the diocese of Amiens, sounds even more important, since he was received into the Order by Hugues de Pairaud at the Paris Temple in 1283 after a general chapter. Guy de Nice, who is elsewhere mentioned as being present at a reception ceremony with Hugues de Pairaud, did appear with other prisoners to defend the Order but was not amongst the 546. The last two of this group can be found earlier in the trial, listed – ominously – amongst a group of prisoners from Sens who wished to defend their Order: Laurent de Beaune (also once given as 'de Bretagne') was described later by several witnesses as their receptor, both as preceptor of Mormant in the diocese of Langogne and as preceptor of Colours (Yonne): Henri de Anglesi was a knight, who had been received into the Order in 1304 at the Templar house of Biciis in the diocese of Nevers.

The precise identity of the other Templars must remain a mystery. But we may hazard a conjecture. Given that the message which arrived during the break in the interrogation of Jean Bertald specified that the Templars to be burned were those 'who had come to the defence of the aforesaid order', it seems reasonable to include amongst the fifty-four all those Templars who had appeared amongst the groups of defenders and who now disappear from the evidence: Elias Aymerici, Jean Lozon, Pierre de Landres, Laurent de Provins, Bernard de Saint Paul, Jean de Montréal, Raoul de Thauvenay, Guillaume de Sornay, Raoul de Compendio, Jean de Fontaineville, Nicholas de Romanis, Dominicus de Verdun, Adam de Inferno, Egidius de Parbona, Nicholas Versequin, Guillaume de Fuxo, Bernard Charneri, Jean de Bellafaya, André le Mortoier, Jean de Saint Leonard, and Guillaume de Givry. Together with the seven brothers named above, this conjecture enables us to make a fair guess at the identity of over half of the Templars burned.

For a modern reader the bravery of these fifty-four men at the moment of death might appear as a paradox. According to the *Grande chroniques*, and indeed the remorseless logic of the Inquisition, sucresistance could itself lead to 'the perpetual damnation of their souls'. Since such fortitude could also 'lead the common people into great error' by convincing them in such a display that the Templars were completely innocent, then the condemned men would be considered *fautores* of heresy. It was very much a case of 'heads I win, tails you lose': meek acceptance of the punishment implied guilt, with the consequence being execution; heroic demonstration of innocence was tantamount to heresy.

There was a further gruesome reminder of the heretical aspect of the execution. The chronicles also inform us 'wagons and bones were reduced to dust' after the deaths of the Templars. This had been standard practice during early Christian martyrdoms and was, in the thirteenth century, an aspect of inquisitorial procedure. The reason for this macabre thoroughness was that, in an age when the cult of relics was at a peak, any bones or other surviving pieces of the victims could have been gathered up and used for the creation of a cult of veneration. The example of the systematic destruction of a more illustrious victim, the Bohemian reformer John Hus, who was burned at Constance just over a hundred years later, will illustrate this point: when Hus was already dead, and the flames had died down, his body was torn into pieces, the bones broken, and all these fragments and the viscera were thrown on to a fresh fire and reburned until they were turned to ashes. When this second fire had burnt itself out, the resulting ashes were dispersed in a stream. It is more than likely that the Templar ashes suffered a similar fate. Perhaps they were thrown into the *marais* which surrounded the city, or into the Seine itself – in a perfected example of what is nowadays described as ethnic cleansing.

Neither was this burning at Paris an isolated incident. For at more or less the same time, and perhaps even on the same day, the *Grande chroniques* tell us that the provincial council taking place under Archbishop Robert de Courtenay's supervision made an analogous decision. Nine Templars of unknown identity and rank were burned in similar fashion at Senlis. The stake was an ever-present reminder of the dangers of heresy, and of association with heretics. Any deviation from dogmas and doctrines of the Church was perilous in the context of the late-thirteenth century obsession with heresy. Geoffroi de Paris tells us that those who forget to obey the doctrines of the Church and throw them into doubt in doing so 'commit a kind of heresy':

> . . . en ceste Yglise,
> Nous couvient trestouz la devise
> Tenir du pape et l'ordenance.
> Et celui qui en fet doutance
> Fet une espece d'heresie.

(. . . in this church/it behoves us to observe the doctrines/and the dogmas of the pope./And those who doubt them/commit a kind of heresy.) The people of Paris were constantly reminded of this. Just over two weeks later, on Sunday 30 May, a beguine heretic called Marguerite Porete was paraded on public view in Place de Grève, near the site of the old Temple. Then, the next morning, she too was taken outside the city, and burned at the stake in the same fields near Saint Antoine.

But the mass burning in Paris was in a class of its own. Men and women who had once stood in awe of the red-and-white clad knights, and gazed in wonder at the massive towers which stood sentinel over the *Ville*, must now have watched the wagons trundle past with a new fear in their hearts. If such a great religious order could be toppled and burned, who was absolutely safe from the wrath of King Philip the Fair? For no one present could harbour doubts about the true instigator. From the royal point of view, as an act of intimidation the burning may be acknowledged as a master-stroke. It was a devastating blow to the hopes of the surviving Templar defenders, and to the dignitaries still held in the dungeons of their former headquarters.

No one in Paris can have remained in ignorance of the event. For the shock-waves of terror reverberated through the city's prisons, abbeys and hostels.

This was apparent the following morning, Wednesday 13 May, when the commissioners resumed business in the chapel of St Eloi. The first prisoner to be brought before them was the serving-brother Aimery de Villiers le Duc, from the diocese of Langres. He was fifty years old, and said that he had been received into the Temple some twenty years before; he appeared before the court that morning in secular clothes, wearing neither the cloak nor the habit of the Templars, and had also shaved off his beard. More striking, however, was the sheer terror that emanated from his person. 'And while the lord commissioners', the trial record reports drily, 'explained to him the articles into which they were going to inquire, the said witness, who was pale in the face and very frightened, declared under oath and in fear for his soul . . . that the crimes imputed

205

to the Order were completely false but that he had confessed some of them as a result of the many tortures inflicted upon him by royal knights.' This description of the pale and frightened prisoner is already significant, but further details show that Aimery de Villiers le Duc's words were uttered in a climate of high drama. As he spoke, the transcript goes on, Aimery beat his fists on his chest and sank to the ground on his knees with his arms raised towards the altar. In that truly theatrical position, he swore before the commissioners that if he had lied he would be dragged body and soul down to hell there and then in their presence.

We might be tempted to believe that such behaviour on the day after the burning was mere coincidence, that brother Aimery had been driven to such fear by 'normal' torture and prison conditions. But then, as if to dispel any doubt, he explained the reason in his own words. The day before, 'with his own eyes', he had watched the fifty-four Templars who had refused to confess their crimes led through Paris 'in a four-horse wagon'. Later in the day, he had been informed that they had been burned. Since that moment, he had been reduced to terror for his own life. Trembling, he told the commissioners that 'he himself, doubting that he would be able to resist the suffering of being burned, if interrogated would confess and testify under oath, in fear of death, in the presence of the said lord commissioners and anyone else, that all the crimes imputed to the Order were true, and he would even confess that he would have killed the Lord if it had been required of him'. In conclusion, he begged the commissioners and notaries present that morning not to reveal his words to royal officials or guards. Otherwise, he was convinced, he too would suffer the fate of the fifty-four.

This, then, is how a Templar brother of twenty years standing was reduced by Philip the Fair's tactics: quite literally terror-struck.

Even the usually imperturbable commissioners seem to have been impressed by Aimery de Villiers le Duc's dramatic audience. Seeing that Aimery was 'on the edge of a precipice', and that other prisoners were equally terrorised by what had happened, they decided to suspend the hearing. They obviously needed time to discuss this new problem with their own superiors or with the royal lawyers, and to decide what course to take. Their embarrassment is clear from the words of the transcript. In order to cover themselves, they desired 'and ordered that all this be included by we notaries in the trial record'.

Events of the next few weeks showed that Aimery's fears had been justified. For it is almost as if to legitimate his state of terror that the anonymous author of the *Grandes chroniques* informs us that in Paris on 27 May 1310 five more brothers were burned in the meadow near Saint Antoine: '. . . on the eve of the Ascension of Our Lord Jesus Christ, the other Templars were burned in this same place, and the wagons and bones reduced in ashes.'

With the help of Archbishop Philippe de Marigny, Philip the Fair had dropped the mask of legality and broken the back of Templar resistance. The defence movement was effectively crushed. Protesting innocence to the end, and never having been formally condemned, in the month of May alone sixty-eight Templar brothers had gone to the stake.

PART III
PRESUMED GUILTY

13

FINAL INTERROGATIONS: 18 DECEMBER 1310–26 MAY 1311

Philip the Fair pressed home his attack before the shock waves which followed the burnings had subsided. Given his respect for 'order', the royal lawyers could not overtly move against the Temple as a whole but, with the backing of Philippe de Marigny, it was now possible to strike a blow against the individual Templars.

The first royal targets were the Templar lawyers Pierre de Bologna and Renaud de Provins.

Perhaps in order to ensure that the papal commission enjoyed a degree of political clout equal to that of the provincial council, Gilles Aicelin was brought back into the fold. Or, it might be better to say, the commission was taken back to Gilles Aicelin. For, on the morning of Monday 18 May, the commissioners met again under the archbishop of Narbonne's chairmanship in his own private residence. He was on the line again, and his actions were as ambiguous as ever. Far from resolving his own conflict, his presence created others: that morning a question of conflicting jurisdiction emerged in the case of Renaud de Provins.

Brother Renaud had been expected at the hearing, but he did not turn up since he had been summoned to appear before the provincial council at the same time. The problem was that Philippe de Marigny claimed jurisdiction over the prisoner on the grounds that he came from the diocese of Sens. In effect, two great Metropolitan archbishops contended a single prisoner. Yet both archbishops were, in an important sense, on the same side as supporters of King Philip. So why, we may ask, the conflict? There are two plausible explanations: first, that Gilles Aicelin, in one of those shows of independence which characterised his career, had shifted for a moment to the part of Pope Clement; second, that the archbishop of Narbonne, a long-standing Metropolitan and faithful servant of Philip the Fair, resented the sudden emergence of Philippe de Marigny as the key figure in the Templar trial. On balance, given

Aicelin's recently augmented status as keeper of the seals and now permanent physical proximity to the royal court, the latter explanation seems more plausible. For such a complex and subtle man, the means to achieve his end might have been to feign acting in the interests of Pope Clement. It was the only way available to make a show of resistance to the new power.

In fact his reaction that morning was to dispatch Philippe de Voet and Master Amisius to the provincial council in order to claim Renaud de Provins back from the archbishop of Sens. They were to explain with caution and due respect that Renaud was among 'the brothers of this Order who had come forward to defend it', and should therefore be allowed to appear before the papal commission as had been agreed. But the conflict was not easily resolved. It seems that messages flew thick and fast across Paris between the papal commission and the provincial council all that Monday. Other parties, perhaps King Philip himself or at least members of his intimate court, may have provided mediation and intercession. Certainly, Philippe de Marigny was stubborn all day in his refusal to hand over the Templar procurator. Then, in the evening, he desisted. Renaud de Provins was allowed to return to his original interrogators. This late decision may be seen as a personal victory for the archbishop of Narbonne.

Brother Renaud came after Vespers, together with the knights Bertrand de Sartiges and Guillaume de Chambonnet. The core of the defence team was nearly complete again. Yet the man they all perceived as the key figure, the priest and lawyer Pierre de Bologna, was conspicuously absent. The three procurators protested that they had been separated from him, and said that they did not understand the reason for this. From their point of view, the evening session closed on a hopeful note. For the commissioners, in this case synonymous with Gilles Aicelin himself, ordered the royal gaolers Philippe de Voet and Jean de Jamville to bring Pierre de Bologna before them at St Eloi the next morning.

But brother Pierre never appeared in the trial again. Could that have been Philippe de Marigny's revenge for the loss of face suffered that Monday?

It seems likely. For not only did Pierre de Bologna not appear, he ceased to exist. Literally. References to his name do continue in the pages of the court record for a few days. But then that drops from view as well. There was no clamour, no protest, no explanation. He simply disappeared. In little over a month Pierre de Bologna had risen from relative

212

obscurity to his apotheosis as the leader of the Temple revolt. But his fall had been quicker still.

There can be little doubt that brother Pierre was murdered by the royal guards, or by other officials, because his legal skill and eloquence represented a serious threat to what Philip the Fair perceived as the success of the trial. His death, or at least his disappearance, was the catalyst which brought about the disintegration of the defence movement. News must have spread like wildfire through the prisons and hostels where the remaining Templars were held. It was, after all, only a week since the burnings in the meadow by Saint Antoine, where many of the other leading defenders had probably died. Now the strongest and most respected of all had gone, and a general sense of loss of direction heightened the terror which had paralysed Aimery de Villiers le Duc. Perhaps renewed torture and bribery were also employed to exacerbate this terror.

For on the morning of Tuesday 19 May, when Pierre de Bologna should have appeared to sustain the other three procurators and bolster the defence, the very opposite happened: forty-four Templars who had previously been part of the defence movement now came before the commissioners to announce that they had changed their minds. There could be no clearer evidence of the shock and fear which now predominated. The Templars were again in disarray. But it must be said that the papal commission was little better and, having seen their limited powers overruled by the actions of the archbishop of Sens, they did not know how to proceed. After his brief reappearance as president, Gilles Aicelin had been excused again; it is likely that he had departed for Rungis, just south of Paris, on royal business (as we have seen, he signed official documents there on May 22). In his absence the other commissioners dithered, lacking firm leadership as much as the Templars. They did nothing more than register the arrival of the forty-four dissenters, and listen in silence to their brief statement. Hiccoughing like an engine on its last legs, the commission retreated into the safety of another recess. The hearings were adjourned.

This break in proceedings lasted for eleven days, but even such a long period was insufficient to resolve the impasse. It seem to have been with a sense of hopelessness, frustration and perhaps even desperation that the commissioners met again in St Eloi on Saturday 30 May. The problems were immense, and they could not agree amongst themselves on the correct course to take; this situation was worsened by the fact that Gilles

Aicelin was still away from Paris. Only one element was in their favour: the General Council summoned by Pope Clement two years before, and originally scheduled to begin on 1 October 1310, had been postponed for a year. This provided them with welcome breathing space, as reading between the lines of the papal notaries' formal explanation would seem to indicate. They could not wash their hands of the affair, like Pontius Pilate, as they may well have wished; neither could they simply leave the commission temporarily when an insoluble problem arose, as the archbishop of Narbonne had done. Should they proceed? How should they proceed? Was it worth proceeding at all? The real difficulty was that in the absence of Pope Clement they had no authority to answer such questions.

But they did have the authority to adjourn the hearings. It was the only course open to them. So that day's session ended with the annoucement that the commission was to meet again, in the same chapel of St Eloi in the monastery of Sainte Geneviève, 'on the third day of the coming month of November'. That gave them five full months of respite. Once again, the trial of the Templars in Paris went into abeyance.

During this prolonged summer break four major trials of the Templars outside France were equally unsuccessful: those in Cyprus, the Papal States and the Kingdom of Mallorca came to an end in this period; that in England reached an effective stalemate.

In Cyprus the trial had been formally opened in the cathedral of Nicosia on 12 April 1310. There the conditions of the Templars were quite different from those in France. The governor of the island, Amaury de Lusignan, who was brother to King Henry II of Cyprus, had not only been a good friend to the Templars but was heavily in moral debt to them at the time the *Arrest Order* was issued. The Templars were given advance warning of their arrest, so that the commander in Cyprus, the marshal of the Order, Aymé d'Osilier, had ample time to make preparations. Rather than sudden arrest in a dawn raid, in this case it was more a matter of prolonged negotiation. The Templars had first agreed to give up their arms and their horses, and to have their property and treasure sealed, in exchange for good prison conditions inside the palace of the archbishop of Nicosia. But then they had refused to keep the terms of the agreement. As a consequence, they were eventually captured and, from June 1308, were held prisoner in the castle of Lefkara. Apart from the Marshal, the other senior officials of the Order imprisoned in Cyprus included the turcopolier, the commander of the Turcopoles (troops recruited from the native population), the drapier, the treasurer of the Order, and the commander of Apulia. The high number of thirty-eight knights who appeared amongst the seventy-six Templars interrogated on Cyprus was a sign of the military importance of the new headquarters there after the fall of Acre. But no trace of heresy was found: perhaps because of the great distance from France, and the lack of torture; but also because men of thirty or forty years service in the East were less likely to be trapped by leading questions into confession. One non-Templar witness even asserted that he had begun to suspect the Templars of heresy only *after hearing of the charges.* Aymé de Osilier himself firmly denied all the charges, arguing that the only kiss to be used in the reception ceremony was a simple kiss on the mouth and that 'there were no errors in the said Order'. Unlike in Paris, even the fifty-six non-Templar witnesses who appeared before the court found nothing bad to say about the Order. The only 'crime' which could be attributed to the Order was their sometimes obsessive secrecy, but as we have seen that was pre-scribed by the *Rule.* On the whole, the Templars in Cyprus were perceived by witnesses as good men and honest Christians. This interest-ing but largely negative trial – at least as far as Philip the Fair was concerned – came to an end on 5 June 1310.

At the same time the trial in the Papal States and the Abruzzi was also drawing to a negative conclusion. The inquisitor Pandolfo Savelli, from a prominent Roman family, and his *socius* bishop Jacopo of Sutri, had begun work the previous autumn, travelling out from Rome circumscri-bing a huge loop through the two regions. From the point of view of the trial in Paris, the testimony of a serving-brother from Lanciano named as Ceccus Nicolai Ragonis is one of the most interesting aspects. On 28 April 1310, this brother Ceccus had appeared before the inquisitors in the episcopal palace of Penne, near Pescara. During his testimony he described his own reception ceremony at the Lateran palace in Rome, which seems to have been perfectly orthodox – with no secret rooms or subsidiary ceremonies. This is all the more fascinating because one of the two Templars present at this reception was Pierre de Bologna, a fact which provides confirmation of his presence in Rome as procurator for the Order of the Temple at the curia. It would also tend to establish his innocence, because the ceremony was orthodox.

By June 1310 the itinerant inquisition conducted by Pandolfo Savelli had reached Viterbo where, in the episcopal palace, they heard the evi-dence of one chaplain-brother and two serving-brothers. By that time, the Italian inquisitor must have been as disillusioned as his colleagues in Paris. The birds had flown before his team arrived. In ten months of travel and patient investigation, the team of inquisitors and notaries had obtained fourteen testimonies (of which only seven were actually those of Templars). The last one, at Palombara Sabina, was typical in its distance from the confessions heard in Paris: a serving-brother called Gualtiero Giovanni di Napoli explained that he had been received into the Order in 1300. But he had already left it in 1303, four years before the *Arrest Order*. He did confess to denying Christ, and to spitting *near* the cross, but his principal 'confession' was that he had been ordered not to reveal details of the reception ceremony to non-Templars. With this non-event, the trial in the Papal States and the Abruzzi formally ended on 27 July 1310.

The trial in the Kingdom of Mallorca had also begun late, on Wednesday 14 January 1310, even though the Templars there had been arrested towards the end of 1307. At that time the kingdom possessed lands on the mainland, including the lordship of Montpellier, the county of Cerdagne, and the county of Roussillon. The trial took place in Roussillon, which was part of the diocese of Elne. This meant that the bishop, Ramon Costa, was one of the nine suffragans of the archbishop of Narbonne. Thus it was Gilles Aicelin himself who ordered Ramon Costa to begin his episcopal hearings, in a letter written in May 1309 to accompany the articles of accusation. As a result of this letter, twenty-five Templars were interrogated between January and the summer of 1310. Each was taken painstakingly through the series of accusations as at Paris, and each denied all the charges. But in the absence of torture or harsh prison conditions, no confessions were forthcoming. A typical testimony was that of Pierre Bleda: he had been received into the Order thirteen years earlier in Aragon in a completely orthodox ceremony which he briefly described. He not only denied all the accusations but, when asked about articles 23–31 (including those on absolution by the Grand Master, who was said in Article 31 to have 'confessed this, in the presence of important persons'), brother Pierre replied that if the Grand Master had confessed such things – which Pierre personally did not believe – then he had lied through his teeth. Such, again, was the negative tendency of trials conducted far from the intimidating atmosphere of Paris. The bishop of Elne closed the Roussillon trial formally on 31 August.

In England the situation was perhaps less negative, though hardly encouraging. Two papal inquisitors, Abbot Dieudonné of Lagny and

216

Sicard de Vaursent, were sent to conduct the interrogations there. The long arm of Gilles Aicelin again played its part, because Sicard was a canon of Narbonne and thus directly dependent on the archbishop. The inquisitors arrived in England on 13 September 1309, and immediately encountered difficulties. On English soil they were obliged to comply with laws which forbade the use of torture, and which also required the judgment of local jurors in order to condemn prisoners. Perhaps it was for this reason that the interrogations held by Dieudonné and Sicard in London in the autumn of 1309 produced no confessions among the forty-five Templars involved. More Templars were questioned at Lincoln in April 1310, and at York in May – when a provincial council was held, parallel to those in Paris and Senlis. But again, results were dramatically different beyond the reach of Philip the Fair. No confessions were forthcoming.

The state of stall prevailing in England during the summer of 1310 may be judged from an appeal made by the inquisitors in a letter dated 16 June and addressed to the archbishop of Canterbury. In announcing their desire to give up their duties and return to the Holy See, Dieudonné and Sicard enumerated eight ways in which the trial of the Templars could be brought to a rapid close.

Hostility towards them and disbelief concerning the charges had hampered their activities. To facilitate their work, they argued that confessions obtained elsewhere should be made public in England. This suggests that most people either knew nothing about the charges or refused to believe them. But the real crux for them, a problem which serves to illuminate the flimsy basis on which the machinery of accusation rested, was the prohibition of torture. For the inquisitors expressed their profound discontent with the English gaolers at their disposal, and asserted their belief that other (French?) guards would be better at convincing the prisoners to confess. From their point of view, English prison conditions were far too good. They felt that even moderate forms of torture, such as uncomfortable prisons and a diet of bread one day and water the next, would help the prisoners to speak the truth. To make this easier, they suggested a compromise: that the English Templars should be sent to Ponthieu which, although it belonged to King Edward II, was legally outside England. There, the prisoners could be tortured without any problem. It is likely that the inquisitors repeated these laments to Pope Clement at the same time for, on 6 August, he in turn complained in a letter to King Edward II about the royal unwillingness to allow torture.

217

Shortly after this, on 22 September, a new provincial council met in Canterbury to discuss the matter of the Templars. This council decided that the Templars in London and Lincoln should be separated and questioned again, and that if no confessions were then forthcoming, torture should be used. Even then, however, it was specified that there should be no mutilation, no permanent disablement, and no effusion of blood. In fact the decision of the council made little real difference: the expected flow of confessions never materialised. Nothing much was ever to come of the trials in England. Much later, on 29 July 1311, twenty-four Templars in York abjured heresy, were formally absolved, and went to do penance in various monasteries. But in the autumn of 1310 there was still no progress at all.

In November, therefore, when the hearings of the papal commission eventually resumed at St Eloi, they muddled on in the atmosphere of general failure and apathy which prevailed throughout Europe as far as the success of the trials was concerned. After the spurt in proceedings with the burning of the fifty-four and the death of Pierre de Bologna, the freshly acquired momentum had rapidly fizzled out, even in Paris. The trial had entered a long phase of stall before the imminent Council of Vienne.

In practice, the papal commission feigned working. The bishop of Mende, Matthew of Naples and Jean de Mantua met briefly in St Eloi on 3 November. In the absence of Gilles Aicelin, once again 'busy on royal affairs and holding the seal of the king', that day's session was reduced to a reading of letters of excuse from the other members of the commission. Proceedings were adjourned to an unspecified future date.

More than a month passed before they met again, on 17 December. After hearing the excuse letters of the Bishop of Bayeux and Jean de Montlaur (who wrote from Montpellier claiming such pains and problems in his shin and foot that he was physically unable to make the journey to Paris), the commission turned to Bertrand de Sartiges and Guillaume de Chambonnet, who were present as representatives of the Temple. But they said that they were unwilling to go ahead without the advice and support of Pierre de Bologna and Renaud de Provins. This, they were told, was impossible. Both were unavailable. The official version of Pierre de Bologna's disappearance was now provided: the commissioners said, improbably enough given the courage and strength of character which he had displayed and the severe guard he must have been kept under, that he had 'escaped from prison and fled'. As for Renaud de Provins, there were difficulties. Once again the sway of Philippe de Marigny had proved too much for the defenders – and for Gilles Aicelin, who in this delicate situation could easily be perceived as obstructing the desires of Philip the Fair. The archbishop of Sens had excogitated a technical loophole, as the commissioners now explained to the two shocked Templars: 'The said brother R. could no longer be allowed to defend the Order, since he has been degraded by the provincial council of Sens'.

In effect, brother Renaud had been removed from both the priesthood and the trial as part of the royal strategy. Two down; two to go. That was no doubt how Bertrand de Sartiges and Guillaume de Chambonnet saw things, with the memory of the spring burnings still fresh in their minds. In spite of the fact that they were knights, they had never shown much courage in the courtroom. From their first appearance, like twins, they had always played the role of seconds to the main defenders. Now, as might be expected, they took fright. The commissioners – understanding their men by now – formally offered them the chance to continue their defence of the Order, and also to be present at the hearings. But the two knights replied that they did not wish to go on without the presence and advice of Pierre de Bologna and Renaud de Provins. They must have known that Pierre de Bologna was really dead, and they may have suspected that the same fate had occurred or was about to occur to Renaud de Provins. We may only imagine the exchanges and arguments put forward that day, for the drama lies concealed between the lines of the statement recorded by papal notaries. Rarely can the stalwart defence of a major religious or military order have ended so ignominiously, and have been described in such laconic words: 'And so they left the presence of the lord commissioners'.

In effect, they too disappeared. None of the four leading defenders of the Temple ever appeared again. Neither did twenty-two out of the other twenty-five brothers among the nearly 600 who beyond putting their names forward in a generic context formally stood before the commissioners to defend the Order of the Temple. Each made his brief, brave appearance; and each then vanished. Perhaps, as we have seen, some of them died in the field near Saint Antoine.

Only three of the twenty-five survived the summer of 1310: the serving-brother Robert Vigier (who appeared before the third session of the papal commission on Monday 8 February 1311), the serving-brother Mathieu de Cresson Essart (who appeared on Wednesday 10 February), and Jean de Valbelant (who appeared on Friday 12 February). Yet the evidence of these later appearances suggests that the three had indulged in a kind of plea-bargaining, since all of them had by then been absolved and reconciled to the Church (Vigier and Valbelant by the bishop of Paris, and Cresson Essart by the archbishop of Reims). Robert Vigier provided a faint echo of earlier defences of the Order: he said that he did not believe such errors as were attributed to the Templars could have been kept hidden for so long, and that he believed the Grand Master had been induced to confess by torture or false promises. But he did agree, oddly, that the secrecy of receptions and chapters was an 'error', Mathieu de Cresson Essart went a little further, asserting that at his reception seventeen years earlier he had been asked to kiss his receptor's anus; Jean de Valbelant said that after an orthodox ceremony nineteen years before he had been taken into a separate room, stripped to his shirt and trousers, and received a kiss 'close to his anus'. The insistence of the last-named that he spat near the cross rather than on it also shows that he had been instructed how to present the Order as guilty without inculpating himself – a trick many Templars had learned three years earlier. All in all, however, these confessions, made within a context of general denial and protest, suggest that the three brothers were allowed to avoid death by making the slightest of confessions. Be that as it may, with the death – or supposed escape – of Pierre de Bologna and the unfrocking of Renaud de Provins, the spectre of the stake and the awesome power of Philip the Fair, haunted the Templars who were still held in the hostels or prisons. At the same time, the grand dignitaries of the Order festered powerless in the Temple. To all intents and purposes, the defence of the Order of the Temple had collapsed.

In the absence of the defence movement, the tactics of the papal commission also changed. After Bertrand de Sartiges and Guillaume de Chambonnet had left the court on the morning of 17 December, the commissioners discussed the best and quickest way to go ahead with the proceedings. Their decision was that it would be convenient not to summon witnesses to them in St Eloi, but rather to visit the Templars in 'other colleges' when there were enough of them to justify such a visit. In this way the Templars could not avoid the trial, and the whole process would not be unduly retarded. Clearly, they were concerned to avoid further unnecessary delays: there was still much work to be done, and as they approached the end of another calender year the new date set for the opening of the Council of Vienne must have seemed imminent.

Thus the papal hearing began a second phase of itinerant interrogations, with the difference that this time the entire commission moved from place to place rather than the information-gathering notaries. In the next few months they heard witnesses in four different places. From a theological point of view, these interrogations – or perhaps more precisely interviews – were quite different from those in earlier sessions. The majority of the Templars appearing now had in fact already been absolved of any crimes imputed to them, and reconciled to the Church. Rather than appearing on trial, they were now witnesses providing evidence for the eventual condemnation of the Order of the Temple. They had nothing to fear from the court. In a sense, the real trial was over.

But some of the most interesting evidence was yet to come.

The Templars were brought before the commissioners in groups, many of which appear to have been chosen according to the diocese in which they had been tried, absolved and reconciled. Here again the impact of the royal strategy is evident: of the 191 Templars described in the trial record as having received absolution, 124 had been absolved within the metropolitan areas controlled by Archbishop Philippe de Marigny and Archbishop Robert de Courtenay. Fifteen are said to have been absolved directly by the Council of Paris, while de Marigny's suffragans in Orléans, Paris and Chartres had absolved twenty-nine, thirty-five and five respectively; thirty had been absolved directly by the Council of Senlis, and de Courtenay's suffragans at Amiens and Soissons had absolved seven and three respectively. Thus a high percentage of the 212 Templar witnesses in this third and last session of the papal commission, probably around fifty per cent, had been present at the provincial councils of Paris and Senlis in May 1310. Their relief at not having been chosen among the sixty-eight brothers to be burned may only be imagined. The problem is that their testimony was unlikely to be in favour of the Order of the Temple.

Neither was that of the other witnesses. For a further sixty-seven of them had been absolved by bishops beyond the two main metropolitan areas concerned: in the dioceses of Limoges, Tours, Poitou, Clermont, Saintes and Rouergue. Only about twenty of the Templar witnesses are recorded as not yet absolved and reconciled.

This, then, was the human material on which the commissioners were to work for the next six months.

They decided that the first session would be held in the residence of the abbot of Fécamp, known as 'de la Serpent', which was in the parish of St Andrée des Arts. This 'college' was on a site between the present rue Serpente, running west from boulevard St Michel parallel to boulevard St Germain, and rue Hautefeuille; the turreted building at number 5 of the latter street still bears the name 'Hôtel des Abbés de Fécamp'. Interrogations were held there for twenty-four days, from Friday 18 December to Friday 22 January. The only breaks in this period were for the Sundays, plus six days for Christmas and a day each for the Circumcision, Epiphany and the Conversion of St Paul.

On Tuesday 26 January, after an adjournment for the feast day of the Conversion of St Paul, the commission transferred briefly to the house of the abbot of Meulins-sur-Allier a few paces away, next to the church of St Cosmos and St Damian. This church, built around 1211 and demolished in 1836, used to stand on the corner of rue Racine where it meets the present boulevard Saint Michel. The commission only met there for three days, the Tuesday, Wednesday and Thursday of that week.

On Friday morning they moved just along the street to the monastery of the Franciscans or, more precisely, as the transcript tells us, 'to that part of the monastery right next to the residence of the Bishop of Laon'. The Franciscans, who were always known in Paris as the 'cordeliers' from the cord they wore, arrived in the city around 1216 or 1217. But they had no permanent base until their principal convent was founded in 1230 by St Louis, with what was until its destruction by fire in 1580 one of the biggest churches in Paris. The vast convent stood on the area comprised between the present rue Racine, rue Monsieur le Prince, and rue de l'Ecole de Médécine right up to the Odéon station of the Métro. It included the areas where the Lycée St Louis and the Faculty of Médicine now stand. The nineteenth-century Ecole Practique was built on the same land after the demolition of the monastery, and today it is the site of the Université Paris VI, which maintains a hint of these distant origins in its designation 'Cordeliers'. At this monastery the hearings continued throughout February and most of March, except for the two feast days of the Purification of the Virgin (2 February) and St Matthew the Apostle (24 February), and two days which appear to have been skipped. In all, the commission met in the monastery for forty days of intensive work.

Then, on Monday 22 March, they transferred for the last time. This move was to the residence of Pierre de Savoie, archbishop of Lyon, which was situated opposite the monastery. There the hearings maintained their rhythm until Easter, with a single feast day for the Annunciation on 25

March. Finally, as if the commissioners themselves had lost interest and were trying to bring their hearings to an end, all regularity in the proceedings was thrown to the wind. They met once after Easter, on 19 April, and immediately adjourned until Friday 7 May; then followed five more days of hearings, and another break for six days; they met anew on Wednesday 19 May, and then adjourned for Ascension the day after; then they had two consecutive days of hearings on Friday and Saturday, followed by yet another break. The last session, during which three Templar witnesses were heard, was held on Wednesday 26 May in the residence of the archbishop of Lyon.

Altogether, in the months between December 1310 and the end of the third session of the papal hearings in June 1311, as many as 212 Templars appeared before the commission. All but a handful of these confessed to some of the charges, including as many as eighty-four of the eighty-seven of those who had previously come forward to defend the Order. Such was their loyalty when placed under threat! There were also three non-Templar witnesses: one Franciscan friar, one Dominican, and one Italian apostolic notary. Evidence flowed as it had done during the inquisitorial hearings of autumn 1307. But while from the point of view of the trial proper, testimony gathered in this period represented little more than the death throes of the proceedings, from that of the subsequent history of the Templars, Templarism, and the legends attributed to the Templars, it produced some of the most significant evidence.

In this sense the most interesting feature of this third session is the number of detailed testimonies concerning the existence of an idol or head which the Templars were said to worship.

Now the story of the idol was an essential part of the whole trial, and in fact appeared on the very first day of the inquisitorial hearing carried out by Guillaume de Paris. On that morning, 19 October 1307, after the initial testimony of Jean de Foilliaco, a serving-brother from the diocese of Sens called Jean de Larchant had been interrogated. This man had been received into the Order at Beauvoir (Gastines) by the Treasurer of the Temple, Jean de Tour, in 1281. He claimed, as we have seen, to have observed a head which the Templars adored as many as 'twelve times in twelve chapters' including once in the Temple in Paris. 'Asked what it was,' the inquisitorial record states, 'he said it was a certain bearded head which they adored, kissed and called their Saviour.' Although Jean de Larchant himself later revoked his confession and stated in an appearance before the third session of the papal commission on 27 January 1310

223

that his reception ceremony had been perfectly orthodox, the original story held. No amount of denial could ever erase such a story once it had purchase on the popular imagination. Fourteen of the articles of accusation elaborated on the basis of the first interrogations concern this idol of the Templars, which it was claimed could not only 'save them' but 'has given them all the wealth of the order' and 'makes trees flourish and the land fruitful'.

The first and most important of the new confessions concerning the idol was that of the serving-brother Raoul de Gizy, once described as preceptor of Lagny-le-Sec (Oise) and Sommereux, and elsewhere as preceptor of Champagne. He had already made one of the most curious statements before Guillaume de Paris on 9 November 1307, while describing his reception into the Order around 1285 by Hugues de Pairaud. Asked then about the head, he replied that he had seen it seven times at chapters held by Hugues, and swore under oath that 'when it was shown all those present threw themselves on the ground, removed their cowls, and worshipped it'. The inquisitor had then asked him what this head was like. Raoul was unable to describe it, simply stating that it was a frightening face such as would be expected of a demon. He used the French word *maufé* to describe it, and added that he was so struck with terror whenever it appeared that his entire body shook and he could hardly stand looking at it. One further detail is worth noting in view of later events: on being asked who were the other brothers who worshipped this head, Raoul named Gérard de Villiers, the preceptor of France.

Now, on Friday 15 January 1311, in the abbot of Fécamp's house, the same Raoul de Gizy provided further details concerning his reception. He, too, seems to have indulged in plea-bargaining; indeed, he had never appeared among the defenders of the Order, whether in the bishop of Paris' garden or in the other groups who announced their desire to defend it. Now he had relinquished the Templar habit, and been absolved and reconciled to the Church by the provincial council of Sens 'like many others'. So he was describing the errors of the Temple as if from the outside. After going through the orthodox ceremony in terms similar to those used in the *Rule*, he adopted the common tactic of claiming that he had denied Christ only in his mouth but not in his heart. Also, that he had spat near, rather than on, the cross. Then the commissioners asked him about the idol. Raoul said that nine or ten years ago he had been at a chapter-general held by Gérard de Villiers at the Temple in Paris, in the week after the feast of St Peter and St Paul. At the end of

224

the chapter a serving-brother called Hugues de Bisuncio brought a certain head of an idol and placed it on the bench next to Gérard de Villiers: 'and the witness, on seeing this head, was so terrified that he hardly knew where he was', and so left the chapter at once. As a result of this haste, he was unable to describe the head with any kind of detail. But in answer to another question he declared that he believed it to be evil.

The repeated link with Gérard de Villiers is important. For, as we have seen, of all the senior Templar officials he was the only one to escape from Paris before the arrests: according to the witness Jean de Chalons, who testified before the pope at Poitiers, de Villiers had managed to escape with fifty horses and it was also rumoured that he had managed to leave France with eighteen Templar galleys. The secret of this getaway was kept until Jean de Chalons' testimony, which was recorded in the summer of 1308. But it almost immediately became the kingpin of an entire category of Templar legend. The fact that the head, or idol, whatever form it may be thought to have assumed, is linked with the mass escape is at the root of many of the suppositions and theories which derived from the downfall of the Templars. Those referred to in the Preface, and elaborated in books like Baigent and Leigh's *The Temple and the Lodge* or Currer-Briggs' *The Shroud and the Grail*, will suffice as examples. For the dramatic story of the escape of Gérard de Villiers provides a hypothesis concerning the way in which this idol, if indeed it existed, was safely removed from Paris – and from the grasp of the royal searchers who rummaged meticulously through all the Templar houses, and then made an inventory of their property. Thence it could have been transported to Lirey, Templecombe, or wherever.

But what was this idol, or 'maufé', which the transcript mentioned? And how was it used? This was the period of the trial in which most of the information we possess concerning the idol came to light. The evidence was sometimes surprising, and often at variance with that gleaned from earlier testimony. For instance, the serving-brother Guillaume d'Arbley, who had been the preceptor of the Templar house at Soissy in the diocese of Meaux, had already appeared before Guillaume de Paris on 22 October 1307, just after the arrest of the Templars. On that occasion, he had testified that Hugues de Pairaud had twice brought a gilded head made of wood and silver into Templar chapters at which he was present; when pressed for more details about this idol, he had sworn under oath that it was bearded. Now, on Friday 10 February 1310, he provided a more elaborate description which may indicate how much the memory of his perceptions had been adjusted as the result of four years of imprisonment. On the other hand, this second testimony, which was provided after the prisoner's absolution and reconciliation, may be much closer to the truth: that the 'bearded man' was an element originally insinuated by means of torture or leading questions. If that is the case, then many of the theories concerning the Baphomet figure look weaker after this more plausible account of the idol, since it is hard to dismiss these changes as tricks of memory. Certainly the variation in brother Guillaume's testimony was dramatic: the once bearded idol had metamorphosed into the figure of a woman.

Guillaume d'Arbley now claimed that in general chapters he had often seen a silver head placed on the altar, and added that he had believed it to be a representation of 'one of the 11,000 virgins'. At first sight, this might seem a foolish assertion, unworthy of serious consideration. But it is a reference to the Christian legend about a group of Breton or Cornish noblewomen who had travelled to Rome with St Ursula in the fifth century; on their way to England from Rome, so the story goes, they had been murdered by Huns beneath the walls of Cologne while seeking to protect their chastity. The problem was that in the atmosphere of the inquisitorial hearings, brother Guillaume had been influenced by the force of suggestion: he states in his own words that he had come to understand from the charges made public during the trial that this silver head must be the idol mentioned in the articles of accusation; for this reason, he had no longer recalled it as a virgin, but as a two-faced Janus-like figure of frightening appearance with a silver beard. This confession provides a damning criticism of the procedures of the Inquisition, and indicates clearly how much of the 'evidence' of the trial was virtually spoon-fed.

Further unravelling of this new testimony leads to a fascinating and plausible explanation of the Templar idol, or at least one of the idols – since it is possible that they venerated more than one. First of all, brother Guillaume says that the silver idol was only seen by leading officers of the Order on certain feast days. Furthermore, according to the transcript, this statue bore a number: 'Head LVIII' (*capud LVIII*). This may be taken to suggest that there was an original, or master-copy, of the idol (originally in Jerusalem?), and that copies were made for use in chapters in other Templar houses. Secondly, Guillaume had been received into the Order by the Treasurer Jean de Tour – in this case twenty-seven years earlier in the Templar house at Furchis, in the diocese of Sens. This is pertinent because it is the repeated association with two high-ranking officials of the Temple in Paris, the Treasurer and the preceptor for France, which lends credence to the confessions concerning the idol.

Now the curious thing about this story was that a silver head did actually exist amongst the Templar belongings. Following this fresh testimony of Guillaume d'Arbley, the commissioners ordered the royal official charged with administering Templar property during the trial, a certain Guillaume Pidoye, to search the Temple for any wooden or metal heads which might fit the new description. He and his two associates eventually succeeded in finding such a head, although the time lapse suggests that it had been well hidden. Finally, on Tuesday 11 May – two full months later – Guillaume Pidoye appeared before the commissioners bearing a silver-gilt head which was 'shaped like that of a woman'. This head, the only one to be found in the Temple according to the royal custodian, seems to have been fashioned as a container, for inside were the bones of a real head stitched into white linen which was in turn covered by red muslin ('syndone' in the Latin original, the same word used for the Turin Shroud). He observed that some people believed this head to be that of one of the 11,000 virgins.

Authors of books on the Templars have not investigated the story of this head, or that of the 11,000 virgins, in the context of the trial. Yet the legend of St Ursula is pertinent, and the possession of such a head was perfectly reasonable in an age when holy relics were such an important part of religious life. That there was a cult of veneration of St Ursula in Templar houses is significant, because it provides us with at least one annual occasion on which a head was effectively 'adored'.

The feast day of 'St Ursula and Companions' was, until the reforms of Pope Paul VI in 1969, celebrated on 21 October, the anniversary of the date in 451 when they were thought to have suffered martyrdom. According to the legend, Ursula was a Breton (or possibly Cornish) princess of extraordinary beauty and deep religious faith who was betrothed to Conon, the son of King Agrippus of England. She had made it a condition of her forthcoming marriage that she should first be allowed to go on pilgrimage for three years, to visit the shrines of the Christian saints. She set out with ten noble virgins, each of whom had a thousand handmaidens, and another thousand virgins as her own servants (the ludicrous number is thought to derive from the name of one of the ten noblewomen, Undecimilla, which was misread many centuries ago by some absent-minded scribe as 'undecim millia', meaning 11,000). The martyrdom took place at Cologne after they had made their pilgrimage to Rome, where the major pilgrim goals were the tombs of the founders of the Christian church, St Peter and St Paul. It is worth recalling the original function of the Temple, to protect pilgrims. For St Ursula possessed a series of qualities which would make her an attractive figure to the Templars: she was devout, a pilgrim, a martyr, and possibly French. In the twelfth and thirteenth centuries, nothing could have been more natural than for them to conserve a cult dedicated to a legendary martyr who had died while fulfilling her obligations of pilgrimage. Perhaps the bones of one of St Ursula's virgins had been acquired as the Templars emulated such great model-collectors of relics as St Louis?

The iconographical tradition offers another fascinating link. In pictorial representations of scenes from St Ursula's life, she is usually shown holding a pilgrim's staff which bears a white banner with a red cross that is strikingly similar to the Templar baucent, the battle standard. This may be seen in the fifteenth-century Florentine painter Benozzo Gozzoli's painting of St Ursula now in the National Gallery in Washington, in Hans Memlinc's *Shrine of St Ursula* in the St John's Hospital Museum in Bruges, or in the magnificent, recently restored fourteenth-century fresco cycle of the life of the saint by Tomaso da Modena in Treviso (painted in the church of Santa Margherita, but now detached and remounted in Santa Caterina). Hence, we may assume, the red and white cloths which the trial transcript records mention as being used to wrap the silver head within its reliquary stem from this. It was a symbolism which the Templars could hardly miss, and which provided at the very least a sympathetic association with St Ursula and her virgins.

So the silver casket, far from being an idol employed in heretical rituals, was probably a legitimate relic – and one of many statues and relics which a great religious order might be expected to have accumulated. It is likely that other witnesses who referred to silver, gold or copper heads, had in mind this casket or copies of it; one witness in particular, the serving-brother Gerald de Mursac, described a golden picture in which he thought he had seen the figure of a woman. It was also quite normal that this silver casket in the form of a head should be seen on the feast day of St Peter and St Paul (i.e. 29 June), as Raoul de Gizy had specified. In #74 of the Templar *Rule*, St Peter and St Paul is given precedence over all the other feast days 'that all the brothers should celebrate and observe'. On such a grand occasion, the members of a religious house would be proud to exhibit the holy relics in their possession.

Thus one mystery can be laid to rest. But the problem is that more sinister stories emerged during this phase of the trial, concerning other idols or heads used by the Templars.

On Monday 1 March a non-Templar witness called Antonio Sicci, an apostolic notary from Vercelli in northern Italy, appeared before the commission while it was sitting in the Franciscan monastery. To the standard confessions Sicci added a remarkable tale concerning necrophilia, which emerged during a rambling statement covering the forty-year period in which he claimed he had worked for the Templars in the Holy Land. When the commissioners questioned him on the articles of accusation about the adoration of idols, he told the story of a love affair between the lord of Sidon and an Armenian noblewoman. Apparently, this affair was never consummated in her lifetime, but on the night of her death the lord of Sidon had secretly entered her tomb and made love to her dead body. Afterwards, a voice had told him that he should return to the tomb nine months later when the corpse would give birth, and that he would find a head which would be his child. When the time had elapsed he did go back, and discovered a head in human form resting between the legs of the woman. While he was in the tomb on this second occasion, the voice returned: 'Guard this head', it had ordered, 'since it will bring you good fortune'.

In his book *The Trial of the Templars*, Malcolm Barber has shown that this account taps in to a long series of similar stories which ultimately derive from the legends of Perseus and Medusa. In medieval times, something similar first appeared in the chronicle of Walter Map just over a century before the arrest of the Templars. Around 1300 there were many variants in existence, so a learned man such as an apostolic and imperial notary could easily have read them or heard of them. The interesting point here is that the compilers of articles of accusation may themselves have drawn on this tradition. Just as the sinister head would bring good fortune to the lord of Sidon, so Articles 55 to 59 state that the Templars believed their idol would bring them great riches, make 'the trees flower' and the 'land germinate'.

While this may sound absurd to us, to a contemporary observer it would have been the Armenian background of the noblewoman involved which rendered the story at once plausible and dangerous. The association was potent to any learned theologian because the Paulician sect of the Armenian Church was one of the sources (together with the Bogomils and Patarenes) of the doctrines of Catharism. They too were divided into

229

the 'Perfect' and the 'Hearers', rejected the veneration of the Virgin Mary, and held both a nocturnal Eucharist and a love feast known as the 'Agape'. A man like Antonio Sicci would have heard of the Paulicians and their doctrines during his residence in the East, and such a link would certainly not be lost on the bishops who made up the papal commission. Necrophilia was and is one of the more unpleasant aspects of heresy and witchcraft, but around 1310 many were prepared to believe in the powers it could confer. In Germany just thirty years later a necromancer convinced the people of Turrenburen that he was capable of turning ordinary objects into gold. Thus such stories had a certain credibility, and the expert rumour-mongers at the royal court would have known this. Was Antonio Sicci just one more well-prepared witness, adding damning testimony to the gathering evidence in exchange for payment, like Raoul de Presles? Or had the story really been current in Sidon, and associated with the Templars there? These are questions which must be left unanswered. But, as so often in this prolonged trial, the important thing was to sow the seed of doubt. In this sense, Sicci's tale certainly functioned.

On Wednesday 19 April a sixty-year-old Templar knight called Bartholomew Bochier appeared before the commission in the house of the archbishop of Lyon. He described an orthodox reception ceremony in the Temple at Paris forty-one years earlier. At first this had been carried out according to 'the good customs which then prevailed in the Order', after which brother Bartholomew was taken into the small chapel of the Temple where a head had been placed on the altar near the other relics of the Order. He had been obliged to worship this head, which he described as having a long grey beard and wearing a hat – although, when pressed, he was uncertain whether it had been made of metal, wood, bone, or had been a human head. This, although the ceremony had taken place in Paris, was almost certainly not the silver head of the virgin which the royal officers managed to find. Unfortunately, although Brother Bartholomew had spent some time in the Holy Land, at Castle Pilgrim, he had not witnessed any reception ceremonies there. Even in the twelve ceremonies at which he did claim to have been present, he said that he had seen nothing illicit. Once again, then, the focus was on the French capital: the fact that he had seen the head only once and in Paris suggests either that there was some truth in his statement that it was used at the Temple there, or that he had been well instructed before entering the archbishop's house to testify.

The idea that witnesses were again being fed with carefully prepared information is bolstered by a cluster of interesting statements which emerged in the last ten days of the hearings of the papal commission. It was as though someone were trying to cram in as much damning testimony as possible in the short time available. Several of them provide further information about the head or idol; two testimonies of particular interest in terms of future developments concern the Grand Masters of the Temple and their contacts with Islam.

The first was that of the serving-brother Guillaume Audenbon, from the diocese of Périgord, who appeared on Saturday 8 May in the house of the archbishop of Lyon. He was a young man, around thirty, and a recent recruit, having been received into the Order only a year before the arrests. Now he had been absolved and reconciled by the bishop of Saintes. He had been received into the Order at the Templar house of Syourac, also in the diocese of Saintes, in the presence of the local preceptor Hugues Rainaud. But the interesting fact is that the ceremony was carried out by Geoffroi de Gonneville, who was the preceptor of Aquitaine and Poitou and one of the senior officials of the Order. Following an orthodox reception, brother Guillaume narrated, the postulant was ordered to deny Christ and to spit on the cross, after which Geoffroi de Gonneville produced a copper idol. 'Next the above-mentioned receptor, who held something wrapped up in paper in his lap, something that was in any case made of copper, was seen to desire that the same witness adored it and kissed it; this nevertheless the same receptor did not explicitly say, but it was clear that it was his meaning.' This was the only evidence that ever appeared against the preceptor of Aquitaine and Poitou, a man who in the previous March had described himself as 'illiterate and unable to defend the Order', but who had held one of the highest offices of the Temple.

Further important testimony was provided on Wednesday 19 May by a serving-brother called Hugues de Narsac. This Templar had been the Preceptor of Espansès, and was a Templar of long-standing since he was recorded by other witnesses as having been present at three reception ceremonies dating back to 1290. Now he too had confessed, and had been absolved and reconciled by the bishop of Saintes. He himself had been received into the Order at Dempuho four years earlier than the above ceremony, during the Mastership of Guillaume de Beaujeu. His evidence exhibits considerable rancour towards both that Grand Master and Jacques de Molay.

The imprisoned Grand Master was the subject of special venom. Brother Hugues claimed 'that he had often heard from many brothers returning from beyond the sea, although he could not recall their names, that Brother Jacques the Grand Master of the Order when living beyond the sea committed the crime of sodomy with a certain personal valet called George whom he loved very much'. He believed that the practice of sodomy had been normal among the high officials of the Order when they were in the Holy Land, and adds that he knew of reception ceremonies in which Jacques de Molay had kissed postulants 'not only on the mouth but even on the navel and on bare skin at the base of the spine'. We can almost sense the pleasure in his words when he observes that George the valet had drowned unexpectedly in the presence of Jacques de Molay and others. This, he suggests, was the result of divine vengeance. The story is not confirmed elsewhere, but the details of the valet's name and the authentic-sounding detail that he was then drowned do make it sound plausible. If all witnesses' words were to be taken at face value, then this too would be damning testimony.

More serious still are the allegations which Hugues de Narsac made against Guillaume de Beaujeu, especially because they were exactly what the royal lawyers were seeking in 1311 and what speculative authors of works on the Templars have sought ever since. It is worth quoting his remarks in full:

> He believes that the above-mentioned errors have been in the Order for a long time, and that they originated beyond the sea, where they frequently had occasion to speak with the Saracens; and the brother knight Mathieu le Sauvage developed a close friendship with the Sultan and the Saracens, and the above-mentioned brother Guillaume had several Saracens in his pay when he wished; and they said that they did this for their greater safety, though others said that this was untrue.

Here an explicit link is made between the accusations and their putative Saracen source. Not only did the witness offer circumstantial evidence concerning the close relations which must have been usual in such a geographically limited and overlapping context; he claimed that Muslims had often been in the pay of the Templars.

This allegation was not new to the trial. It had first been made by no less a person than Geoffroi de Gonneville, in the evidence he gave to the inquisitorial hearing of 15 November 1307. Referring to his own reception by Robert Torteville, Master of the Temple in England, which had taken place in London in 1279, he had provided a curious explanation of the need to deny Christ. This practice, Robert Torteville had told him, had been introduced into the Order after 'a certain evil Master' had promised 'a certain Sultan' that in the future all Templars would be required to deny Christ as part of their reception ceremony in order to obtain his own release from the sultan's prison. Since that time, he had said, this custom had always been observed.

Now, on the same session of Wednesday 19 May, the preceptor's story received confirmation from the Dominican witness Pierre de la Palud, who came from the diocese of Lyon and was graced with the title of Bachelor of Theology. After having had the articles read to him and given his opinion on the guilt of the Order, he said that he had been present at the interrogation of 'many Templars' and had heard many stories about them both then and at other times. As a Dominican, with all the necessary credentials to be an inquisitor, it was likely that he had been present during the first interrogations carried out by the inquisitor-general in November 1307. For he now repeated the testimony of Geoffroi de Gonneville in a more detailed fashion and with some elaboration. He reported that he had heard it said, though he did not recall by whom, that

> in former times a Master of the Order of the Temple who had suffered for a long time in the prisons of the Sultan was released after having promised to introduce to the above-mentioned Order all of the errors or at least some of them contained in the said articles, and on this condition the Sultan promised that he and his successors would keep the Order under their protection and that they would provide material assistance to the said Templars and their Order.

In truth, Pierre de la Palud concluded with an untypical display of honesty, he did not know whether this story was true or false. The fact was, however, that with his testimony it entered the trial record with new emphasis.

Pierre de la Palud never named the Grand Master. When Geoffroi de Gonneville had been pressed by the inquisitors in 1307, he said that some attributed the introduction of 'errors' into the Order to the then Master Roncelin, while others said it had been the Grand Master Thomas Berard (1256–73). In other testimony, the next long-term Grand Master

233

Guillaume de Beaujeu (1273–91), who presided over the decline of the Templars, was also named. The real point is that once again, as in the case of the virgin's head, there was at least some truth in these garbled stories of links between the leaders of the Templars and their putative enemies. For intimate cohabitation of restricted spaces had since the conquest of the Latin Kingdom of Jerusalem generated strange alliances.

It also entailed a certain tolerance of alien customs. A example of this may be seen in the account by the Muslim chronicler Usama ibn Munqidh (1095–1188), who was the emir of Shaizar, of a visit to his 'friends the Templars' at their headquarters in what had previously been the Al-Aqsa mosque in Jerusalem. The emir began his prayers facing Mecca, which is approximately south-south-east of Jerusalem. While he was doing so, someone rushed at him and forced him to turn towards the East, shouting at him: 'That's how you pray!' Some of his Templar friends took the intruder away, and Usama was able to continue with his prayers. But as soon as the Templars had turned away, the man persisted. He grabbed Usama, and again forced him to face the East. Once more the Templars came to his aid, and removed the nuisance. The comment they then made to the Muslim is a fascinating example of the tolerance of the Templars, and of their understanding that provision had to be made for differences in a multi-cultural society. 'He's a newcomer,' they explained in apology, 'arrived only a few days ago from the land of the Franks. He's never seen anybody pray other than with their face to the East.'

Peaceful cohabitation made unexpected bedfellows. In their years in the Holy Land the Templars had come to own Bedouin pasture rights which were paid to them in horses, camels and sheep. At one stage, they even collected an annual tribute of 2,000 gold bezants from the sect of the Assassins. The chronicler William of Tyre tells the story of how Rashid al-Din Sinan, leader of the Syrian Assassins and known to westerners as the 'Old Man of the Mountains', once sent an envoy called Muhammad to King Amalric I of Jerusalem offering to convert his followers to Christianity if the Templars would forsake their tribute. The authenticity of the episode has been put in doubt by modern scholars, and in any case nothing came of the embassy since the Templars murdered Muhammad. Yet the very fact that the archbishop of Tyre recounted it provides an insight into the alliances necessitated by the new conditions of life which permanent settlers found in the Holy Land. The Templars too were forced to adapt.

No one did so more than Guillaume de Beaujeu, who commanded the

Templars when they were fighting what amounted to a rearguard action aimed at saving the Kingdom. In the last year of his mastership, when little more than the stronghold of Acre was left to the crusaders, he was forced by circumstances to enter into a peace treaty with the Mameluke Sultan al-Malik al-Mansur, known as Qalawun (1279–90). The Muslim chronicler Ibn 'Abd Az-Zahir (1233–92), secretary to Qalawan and possibly the man who drew up the treaty, recorded that 'the peace must last for ten full, continuous and consecutive years, and ten months, beginning from Wednesday the 5 of Muharram of the year 681 from the hegira of the Prophet Muhammad' (i.e. 15 April 1282). On the Muslim side, the treaty included the whole of Egypt and Syria, the provinces of Hims and Aleppo, and the castles of the Assassins; on the Templar side, it included Tortosa and all remaining Templar lands – thirty-seven districts were mentioned in the treaty. It also made provisions of safe-conduct for passengers from shipwrecks, and specified that there should be no rebuilding of castles, forts or any other military installations within the territory of Tortosa.

This brief account is sufficient to illustrate the truth of allegations that Guillaume de Beaujeu dealt with and was perhaps acquainted with the sultan. From the operational point of view, nothing could have been more natural for the Templars; for years they had dealt with the Muslims on many levels. On a day-to-day basis, and in a predominantly monetary economy, they bought provisions from local traders and farmers. They trained specialised brothers such as interpreters to facilitate negotiations, and employed local people both for military and for non-military functions. The notary Antonio Sicci, mentioned above, claimed that the preceptor in Sidon, a certain Matthew known as 'le Sarmage', a native of Picardy, had even become a blood-brother of the then sultan. The problem was that Christians living within an entirely Christian environment such as Paris were unable to grasp these everyday realities of life in the Holy Land, and could only view such relations with misgivings or contempt. It needed little manipulation for skilled propagandists to convert these legitimate dealings into suspicions of heretical discourse and malign influence, especially in an age when Islam was portrayed as the source of all evil – and of the heresies which plagued the Roman Church.

When subtle associations were tuned in to deep-rooted prejudice, they could distort a few basic facts into a fabric of hideous dimensions. And this was to be the last chance to complete the construction. As things turned out, the fresh and regurgitated examples provided by Hugues de Narsac and Pierre de la Palud provided the decisive insinuation.

235

The last session of the papal commission took place exactly a week after the Dominican friar had given his evidence, on Wednesday 16 May 1311. After hearing three witnesses that morning, the commissioners expressed their desire to bring their inquisition to an end. To this effect, they wrote a letter to their fellow member the bishop of Bayeux, Guillaume Bonnet, who was then in Avignon on royal business, requesting him to present their case to Pope Clement. For the commission was nominally a papal one, and they therefore required formal papal consent to close the proceedings. When this had been gained, Guillaume Bonnet showed his true colours by at once travelling north to the *parlement* which Philip the Fair was then holding at Pontoise – where the commission president Gilles Aicelin was also to be found.

The commission was papal only in name. It was at the request of King Philip the Fair, *not* of Pope Clement, that the four other commissioners who had stayed the course – Renaud de la Porte, bishop of Limoges; Guillaume Durant, bishop of Mende; the apostolic notary Matthew of Naples; and Jean de Mantua, the archdeacon of Trent – closed the third session of the papal hearings in Paris. They too then travelled to Pontoise with the notaries who had worked for them for nearly two years. In a strange but significant sense Pontoise was the ideal place to conclude the hearings. For the same intense piety which seems at least partly to have instigated King Philip's struggle against the Templars also made Pontoise – with its profound links to his grandfather, St Louis – one of the emotional centres of his being. If the trial of the Templars may be intepreted as the personal crusade of Philip the Fair, then this crusade began and ended in Pontoise: it was from the abbey of Saint Martin that the letter from Guillaume de Paris ordering inquisitions into the Templars had been sent on 22 September 1307; now, in the presence of King Philip, the hearings of the papal commission were formally terminated on Saturday 5 June 1311.

It was also at Pontoise, no doubt in a climate of immense relief that the trial was at last over, that the king and his counsellors began to elaborate their strategy for the final act of the drama of the Templars.

236

14

THE COUNCIL OF VIENNE AND ABOLITION: 1311–12

In the winter of 1311–12 the leading participants of the trial of the Templars came together at Vienne, which stands over the River Rhône. It was at that time part of the Dauphiné, whose name in fact derived from a twelfth-century count, dauphin of Vienne.

In the mind of Clement V, Vienne must have seemed a shrewd choice of location for the Church Council. The Dauphiné was then a part of the Kingdom of Arles and therefore fell under the jurisdiction of the Holy Roman Emperor Henry VII (it only became a fief of France in 1349, under King Philip VI of Valois, and shortly afterwards the apanage of the heir to the throne). Pope Clement had in fact wished to be crowned there, perhaps because two great predecessors, Innocent IV and Gregory X had both sojourned in the city, but Philip the Fair had insisted on nearby Lyon (significantly, in view of the attempt to bring the Church under royal control, Clement had been crowned in the church of Saint-Just – which was *inside* the royal domain – rather than in the cathedral). In 1311 Vienne was governed by archbishop Briand de Lagnieu, who exercised both sovereign rights and a half share in those of the count of Vienne, which he divided with the dauphin, Jean II. Vienne was a city with ancient traditions of ecclesiastical power. Since its foundation around AD 250 it had been one of the sixteen bishoprics of Roman Gaul, and from around 450 it was one of the twelve metropolitan dioceses of France. Only in 1790 did it lose this status, when the archbishopric was suppressed as part of a new ecclesiastical division of France. This may be seen as a single event in a long and relentless historical process of erosion of commercial importance and status of the city by nearby Lyon. Today, Vienne is in every sense overshadowed by its large neighbour. But in the early fourteenth century it was a proudly independent city, with an enviable position on the fastest route from Paris and northern France to the south and Italy (which in the south was essentially a river journey:

237

along the River Saône from Chalons to Lyon, and then down the Rhône). In 1312 the archbishop of Vienne controlled the suffragans of Aosta, Geneva, Grenoble, St Jean de Maurienne, Tarentaise and Valence. Thus his extensive power also straddled the Alps, and the main overland route south into Italy via the Mont Cenis pass.

From a political and geographical point of view Vienne was therefore an ideal choice for an international council, with delegates expected from England, Germany, Spain and Italy. It stood at the centre of Christian Europe, yet – unlike neighbouring Lyon – it possessed the added advantage of being just beyond the realms of Philip the Fair.

From a practical point of view, however, it was far from perfect. Vienne was a small, walled city of between six and seven thousand inhabitants, lacking sufficient hostels and rooms to house the large number of delegates. During the Council the Bishop of Valencia complained in a letter to King Jaimé of Aragon that the city was cold, bad for his health and hopelessly overcrowded. It was necessary, he observed, 'to endure it with patience'. In fact many of the delegates fell seriously ill during the winter they spent in Vienne, and Cardinal Etienne de Suisy died there. To the cold and discomfort were added soaring prices for everyday goods and food which we tend to think of as a modern phenomenon at such great events. The English procurator to the Roman curia, Henry Ffykeis, complained that he could buy more provisions in Avignon for a single black *denarius*, or shilling, than he could for a sterling in Vienne. Moreover, the cathedral of St Maurice in which the formal sessions of the Council were to be held had not been completed. Rebuilding of the old cathedral had been started by a previous archbishop, and the new church consecrated by Pope Innocent IV during a visit in 1251. But the vast Gothic structure, ninety metres long with three naves and two ranges of side-chapels, still lacked four bays, two towers, and the façade. Building work was only terminated in the fifteenth century.

Evidently, political considerations outweighed these disadvantages in the mind of Pope Clement.

Preparations for the Council had been meticulous. Invitations were sent out in good time to prelates, kings, and secular princes throughout Christendom. Then in the summer of 1311 the pope had set up a special commission at Malaucène in the Vaucluse, east of Orange at the western foot of Mount Ventoux. This might sound a remote place for such proceedings, but Pope Clement was fond of the Malaucène area. He found the cool summer climate, the pure water, and the countryside suitable for

238

his perpetual ill-health. He built a house for himself in the village, as well as the still-surviving church with its fine façade and machicolations. The commission which met there was to make summaries of the episcopal inquiries to facilitate the work of delegates at the Council, who would otherwise have had to read the hundreds of pages of often repetitive trial records. In addition to these summaries, some members of the clergy had prepared what might be described as personal position papers stating their opinions on Templar guilt or innocence. Pope Clement himself spent this period at the Benedictine monastery of Grozeau, less than a mile south-east of Malaucène, together with his personal curia and some of the cardinals. He was near enough to maintain constant contact with the commission while in the monastery, which regularly served as his summer residence. From the Council of Vienne to his death in 1314, the pope spent more time at Grozeau than in Avignon. Today the monastery has disappeared: only the simple chapel, known as Notre-Dame-de-Grozeau, still survives.

It was from Grozeau that the pope departed to reach Vienne when the opening date of his council drew near. Leaving on 15 September, he first travelled overland to Donzère on the banks of the Rhône; then he took a boat upriver to Vienne, where he arrived on 30 September. After the customary three-day fast which preceded such events, Pope Clement formally opened the Council of Vienne in the cathedral of Saint Maurice on Saturday 16 October 1311.

The ceremony was performed with suitable grandeur in spite of the absence of the kings who had been invited. Philip the Fair was represented by a modest delegation comprising Guillaume de Plaisians, a chaplain and two secretaries. Other kings sent ambassadors. It was very much an ecclesiastical matter, but did not lack the pomp associated with such occasions. First, mass was celebrated for the participants gathered in the cathedral. Then Pope Clement took his place on the papal throne, which was set on a raised dais at the entrance of the choir facing the main nave. To one side of him, on the same dais but slightly lower, sat the only secular prince to be present that day, the dauphin Jean II; on the other side were two cardinal-deacons, and the cardinal-chamberlain Arnaud d'Auch. In front of them, in the nave, the other participants were seated in three large semi-circles facing the papal throne. This formal arrangement was made strictly according to the hierarchy of the Church: the twenty cardinals and twenty-nine archbishops thought to have been present were seated in the front row; the seventy-nine bishops were in the second row; then, in the third row, sat the

Patriarchs of Antioch, Alexandria, Aquilea and Grado, the abbots who had come to attend the Council, and other lesser members of the clergy.

Once the opening ceremony and other formalities had been completed, Pope Clement announced the business of the Council. There were three main items on the agenda: the matter of the Templar trial, the problem of the Holy Land (and the possibility of launching a new crusade), and general reforms of the Church. The primary purpose was to resolve the affair of the Templars, but Pope Clement realized that it would be 'difficult, and nearly impossible' to deal with such an intractable issue in full council. Even with the transcripts and other documents reduced to the summaries which had been prepared the previous summer, there would still be too much material for an open discussion. For this reason, he set up a special commission of between forty and fifty bishops, abbots and procurators, who would study the papers in plenary meetings and then submit their conclusions to the Council. This new commission was to meet in the cathedral each day to hear readings of the evidence that had been accumulated against the Templars. When this initial process had been completed, a smaller commission of archbishops and bishops would be formed under the chairmanship of Ottobono Razzi, the Patriarch of Aquileia, north-east Italy, to discuss the accumulated material in detail.

As always in the story of the trial of the Templars, however, things did not go that smoothly. Perhaps in their hearts even the commissioners themselves half-expected some dramatic turn of events. It certainly came.

We may picture the group of fifty prelates gathered without much enthusiasm in the Gothic cathedral on those chill October mornings to hear the mostly monotonous evidence against the Temple. A cleric at a lectern recited to them facts which they must already have known, at the very least by hearsay. Many of them, as we shall see, had travelled to Vienne unconvinced of the truth of the confessions which they were now obliged to hear. Imagine their surprise when, as if in a dream, one morning towards the end of October, seven Templars dressed in the full regalia of white mantle and red cross suddenly entered the great doors of the nave while the commission was in session. To the shock of the prelates, these seven announced that there were as many as two thousand Templar brothers in the countryside around Lyon ready to sustain them in a defence of their Order. As if to confirm what they had said, two more Templars turned up. The commission was in a quandary. The gelid air was charged with an eery tension. Suppose, they must have thought, there really were 2,000 armed men prepared to ride into Vienne?

240

Pope Clement called the bluff. Formally, representatives of the Templars were to have been allowed to appear at Vienne to defend the Order, as Pierre de Bologna had asked before his disappearance two years ago. But that measure had not been intended to condone the arrival of mounted knights in the Templar habit. In fact both the provenance of these nine Templars and their names are a mystery. Their moment of glory was brief, and their reasons for riding into Vienne from apparent freedom remain enigmatic. They were imprisoned on papal orders, and nothing was heard of them again. Yet their apparition had injected at least a momentary tension into the hearings in the cathedral.

There were other hiccups to come.

In December, after two months of hearing and sifting evidence, many of the delegates seemed to be in favour of allowing the Templars to defend themselves. Some were as openly critical as they dared to be. Abbot Jacques de Thérines, for instance, was one man present who expressed his scepticism and doubts concerning the guilt of the Templars. He was a Cistercian theologian, trained as a scholar and as a philosopher. He had been born around 1270 at Thérines, near Songeons in the department of l'Oise. The first step in his ecclesiastical career was to enter the monastery of Chaalis, in the diocese of Senlis, as a young man. Like his contemporaries Guillaume de Paris and Raoul de Presles, he must have displayed exceptional gifts for, in 1308, Jacques de Thérines had been one of the fourteen masters of theology of the University of Paris called upon to give an opinion on the trial of the Templars. This meant that he possessed detailed knowledge of the earlier stages of the trial as well as a solid grounding in canon law. By 1312 he had become the abbot of Chaalis, and a professor of theology (later he was to be appointed abbot of the important abbey of Pontigny, near Auxerre). As we have seen in several cases, clerics of this stature could afford to be critical of King Philip's actions. Abbot Jacques was very much an independent spirit, well outside the royal sphere of influence. The doubts and uneasiness which he expressed during the Council of Vienne may be taken as representative of other dignitaries of the Church who were present. But in his case we are fortunate that he put down his thoughts in written form, in a polemical theological tract entitled *Contra Impugnatores Exemptiorum* which he wrote while the Council was still in progress. While the main purpose of this work was to refute an earlier pamphlet, in passing, Abbot Jacques advanced thoughts and arguments which it is likely he first aired during the open sessions of the Council.

A cool, rational and independent mind can be detected behind his words, which display a healthy dose of scepticism. Phrases like 'if what is said is true' and 'if it is true' pepper the passage concerning the Templars, which begins in the following terms:

> The deeds ascribed to the Templars, and which many of them within the kingdom and elsewhere – notably the leaders of the Order – have publicly confessed, are certainly loathsome. They must inspire horror in every Christian. If what is said is true, these men had fallen into a shameful and wicked error both from the point of view of the faith and from that of natural morality . . .

How was it possible, Abbot Jacques goes on to ask, that so many men of varying background, race and language, men who had been brought up in good families within the Christian faith, could have invited such shameful darkness upon themselves? Is it possible that they had entered the Order with the noble motivation of defending or recovering the Holy Land and fighting the enemies of the faith, but then once in the Order fell under the spell of the Prince of Darkness – who possessed them 'in such an unfortunate and prodigious manner'? He argues that only the presence of such a figure as the Devil himself could explain how the Grand Master and other leaders had been able to confess such horrendous crimes before the scholars of the University of Paris, and again before Pope Clement. After these considerations he adds with renewed scepticism, as if recalling the astonishment of the Parisian crowd in the meadow near Saint Antoine:

> . . . if this is true, and if it is true for all of them, how is it that in the provincial councils of Sens and Reims (i.e. Paris and Senlis) many Templars allowed themselves to be burned, retracting their previous confessions, when they could have escaped this punishment by simply renewing these confessions?

This is a convincing line of argument with which many of those present at Vienne must have sympathised.

Then the abbot moves towards his conclusion, revealing himself as a perceptive, pious and honest man who looks – as befits a man of his position – to God for assistance in a case in which he finds no certainty one way or the other. In these comments he also reveals his presence as a theologian during the hearings of the commission set up by Clement V at Vienne, although unfortunately he does not provide details of the contradictions which he noticed in the trial summaries:

242

Another thing: after the opening of the general council, the results of the inquiries made in the different kingdoms have been read publicly in the cathedral of Vienne; now, on many points there are contradictions. Therefore let He who knows all hearts and from whom no secret escapes, the Spouse of the Church, Jesus Christ, deign to reveal the whole and pure truth on this matter before the closing of this council, so that the Church may be glorified, purified and pacified. That once the truth is known, the pure and ardent zeal of the king procures a result in conformation with reason . . .

Here is a rational mind at work, albeit within the limitations of the medieval Church. If the other prelates had possessed the independence of mind and clarity of thought of Jacques de Thérines, the outcome both of the Council of Vienne and of the trial might have been quite different.

But there was also a strong anti-Templar sentiment in the air, represented by an old guard which might be described as conservative or reactionary. That sentiment was represented by Guillaume le Maire, bishop of Angers from 1291 to 1317, who expressed his opinions in language redolent of scriptural and classical learning. The passage concerning the Templars occurs in the work known as the *Liber Guillelmi Majoris*, which is an important source both for information on the Templar trial and for the texts of papal bulls concerning the Order. Quoting the works of Ezekiel and St Matthew, and of the Fathers of the Church St Jerome and St Augustine, the bishop works himself up into a fine rhetorical fervour in contrast to the cool tone used by Jacques de Thérines. His manner is peremptory rather than rational. Instead of wasting further time by allowing the Templars the possibility of defending themselves, he argues, the Order should be destroyed 'without delay'. This phrase recurs four times in the brief passage in which Guillaume le Maire discusses events at the Council of Vienne. Since the evidence accumulated in the episcopal and papal hearings was overwhelmingly against the Templars, he felt, and the whole matter damaging to the reputation of the Church, there was no need to listen to any further attempts at defence. The Order, he asserted with vehemence, should be suppressed at once by papal authority.

The bishop illustrates the fear of further contamination of the Church by the Templar error by means of recourse to a striking metaphor:

And again I repeat: without delay, in case as a consequence of delay a capricious spark from this error bursts into flames which would

243

devour the whole world and bring the Catholic faith into no little disrepute . . .

Then, to reinforce his point, he introduces a parallel between the 'heresy' of the Templars and that of Arius, the fourth-century priest of Alexandria, who was responsible for the most pernicious of all early Christian heresies. Arianism shook the early Church, survived for 400 years, and was introduced into Europe by the invading Goths, Vandals and Lombards. It represented the first great threat to Christendom in Western Europe, while the second was the wave of heresies such as those of the Bogomils and Cathars which swept through France and Italy from the middle of the twelfth century. This makes bishop le Maire's parallel particularly insidious at a Council where the participants were well aware of the effects of Arianism. Developing the metaphor of fire, he goes on to argue with the authority of a Father of the Church that: 'As St Jerome said, Arius was a simple spark in Alexandria, but because he was not destroyed his flame devastated the entire world'. Thus, by none too subtle implication, the Christian Church would suffer if an Order like that of the Templars which had brought about so much disrepute were allowed to exist any longer. He concluded this argument by quoting a pertinent passage from the Gospel of St Matthew (5,29):

> If your right eye causes you to sin, pluck it out and throw it away;
> it is better that you lose one of your members than that your whole
> body be thrown into hell.

Such vehemence could not be further from the rational assessment of Jacques de Thérines. Yet it represents a position close to that of Philip the Fair, the royal lawyers, and the French archbishops at the Council who were close to the throne.

Uneasy at the eloquent protests of the sceptical, but at the same time awed by the determination of the dogmatists (and the spectre of King Philip hovering over the Rhône), Pope Clement summoned a secret meeting to assess progress so far. His intention was to decide once and for all whether a Templar defence should be allowed. At this meeting, which took place at the beginning of December, the pope posed four thorny questions to the prelates chosen to attend: first, should the Templars be allowed the right to present a defence of their Order; second, if so, should this right be conceded to the nine Templars now held in Vienne; third, if not, should the Templars now dispersed throughout Europe be allowed to appoint procurators to appear in their defence; and fourth, if this procedure were too complex in practical terms, should the pope himself appoint a defence lawyer? The prelates were to provide a written reply to these questions.

Most of those present responded positively to the first question. Ptolemy of Lucca, the bishop of Torcello (an island in the lagoon of Venice), committed his impressions to writing in the following words:

> Meanwhile, between the two first sessions, the bishops and cardinals were convoked to discuss the matter of the Templars and read the summaries. The pope then questioned them individually. They were unanimous in saying that the Order should be allowed to present a defence. All the Italian bishops except one were won over to this opinion, together with all the Spanish, German, Swedish, English, Scottish, and Irish bishops, and the French too with the exception of the metropolitan archbishops of Reims, Sens and Rouen.

This shows how close the party of Jacques de Thérines had come to winning over the pope to its cause. For the most striking fact in Bishop Ptolemy's account is that most of the French archbishops and bishops appear to have been in the camp with the 'sceptics'. Yet the ominous truth lurking amidst this formal majority was the fact that the small number of three 'dogmatists', who appear almost anonymously here as 'Reims, Sens, and Rouen', comprised Robert de Courtenay, Philippe de Marigny and Gilles Aicelin. Their collective power was awesome.

Pope Clement himself might have been willing to go with the majority, and to allow the Templars a fresh opportunity to present a defence. But the determined opposition of the three archbishops was enough to tilt the balance, since everybody knew that behind them loomed the spectre of Philip the Fair. On 12 December, the Aragonese ambassadors wrote to King Jaimé II in the following terms: 'No one dares to make any decision without the king knowing, so in the end we do what he desires. Business is carried out more and more under the impulse of the prelates who are loyal to him and follow his advice.' The Englishman Henry Ffykeis was even more explicit about the almost tangible presence of King Philip: 'The pope is annoyed with the prelates. The king of France even more so. He is about to arrive with many men and in a great fury. We fear his anger and dread his arrival.'

The prelates shivered in Vienne, waiting for the cat to pounce again as he had in Poitiers and Paris.

Two days before the end of 1311, the first distant rumble portending a royal initiative reached the anxious ears in St Maurice. Philip the Fair announced that an Estates General was to be held at Lyon, beginning on 10 February 1312. Both the declared object of this Estates General and the site chosen left no margin for doubt. Many hearts must have tremored at the news. For the king with his barons and lords was to encroach on the territory of the prelates by discussing the defence of the faith, which in the words of his announcement was 'threatened by the crimes and heresies of the Order of the Temple'. He could hardly have been more explicit. Furthermore, this news signified an an imminent royal arrival in the area, since Vienne was less than a day's downstream journey from Lyon. The fears of such as Henry Ffykeis were now justified.

Under the gloomy foreshadow of this imminent arrival, however, the Council of Vienne proceeded with other business. In the new year the main object of discussion at the Council was the idea of a new crusade, an argument which entailed resolving the problem of redistribution of Templar property. Most of the prelates now seemed to desire the creation of a new crusading order, to be stationed in the East and founded on the basis of surviving Templar property and wealth. This new order, which would have been in substance a variant of the united order that Jacques de Molay and his predecessors had so firmly rejected, could then be the focus of a crusade. Such a solution would have resolved two of the main items on the agenda of the Council, killing two birds with one stone. But many of the other prelates did not agree: some, including Pope Clement, believed that Templar property should be passed to the Hospital of St John; others thought that it should be distributed amongst the bishops themselves, to be employed in unspecified ways for the support of the Holy Land. It was only in February that some discussion of the fate of the Templars on trial took place.

As the new month opened, however, thoughts must have been turned towards Lyon as the participants of the Council anxiously awaited the opening of King Philip's Estates-General. But Philip the Fair himself remained almost ostentatiously in the north of France. Keen as ever to keep the opposition on tenterhooks, he had in the meantime – perhaps on the advice of the royal lawyers – decided on a new strategy.

For the moment, the feared royal arrival was postponed. Instead, on 17 February 1312, a secret royal embassy arrived in Vienne to *negotiate* the end of the trial of the Templars rather than to force the issue by the physical intimidation implicit in an armed royal presence. The embassy was led by three prominent noblemen: the king's half-brother Louis, count of Evreux (Philip III's son by his second wife, Mary of Brabant), together with the count of Boulogne and the count of Saint-Pol. But the real negotiators were presumably the royal counsellors who were by now 'old hands' in the Templar trial. The royal chamberlain, Enguerrand de Marigny, whose role in this matter had perhaps been enhanced now that his brother had played such a crucial part, seems to have been the chief negotiator. But the back-up team was no less eminent, consisting as it did of the instigator of the arrests, Guillaume de Nogaret, and his right-hand man Guillaume de Plaisians. After a long period in the background while Gilles Aicelin and his commission had taken centre stage, the two lawyers who had initiated the proceedings now returned as if for the final kill.

When they arrived in Vienne, Pope Clement appointed his own team of five cardinals to meet the royal representatives across the negotiating table. These were cardinals Arnaud de Canteloup, Arnaud de Pellegrue, Bérengar Frédol, Nicolas de Fréauville, and Arnaud de Nouvel. The stage was set for an evenly balanced discussion. But, as so often during the trial of the Templars, all was not as it seemed. For a more detailed analysis of the papal negotiating team than is usually made reveals an almost hopeless bias in favour of King Philip.

The first two cardinals were Gascons and relatives of the pope who had been elevated after Pope Clement's election in 1305. But if their initial rise to power might be subject to criticism, their comportment during the intervening years had been impeccable. Arnaud de Canteloup, who was perhaps a nephew of Pope Clement, was the papal Chamberlain – a key position as head of papal finances, the controller of official acts, and private confidant to the pope. Equal power within the curia had been assumed by the pope's cousin Arnaud de Pellegrue, who had come to this position of prestige with no particular qualifications for the job. His strong point was that he enjoyed the special trust of his cousin. This was enough to guarantee him boundless authority. To those who visited the curia in this period he appeared to be all-powerful, the man who could obtain papal favours and whose judgment Pope Clement publicly praised. In short, these cardinals owed everything to the pope. They could be expected to operate in his favour during the negotiations.

But the remaining three cardinals were a different kettle of fish, and very much royal men. The most senior, Cardinal Bérenger Frédol, who was the chairman of the negotiating team, was a nobleman from

Laverune near Montpellier. He was a renowned jurist whose career had begun modestly in 1285 as precentor in Béziers, and who had then become a chaplain to Pope Honorius IV. It was perhaps with papal patronage that he had studied canon law at the prestigious University of Bologna. From this moment, promotion was rapid: he taught for a while at the University of Paris; then in 1289 his career entered the mainstream of events leading towards the Templar trial when he was appointed a canon of Narbonne. For the next year Gilles Aicelin became the archbishop and seems to have taken the young canon on as a personal protégé. Four years later, in fact, Bérenger Frédol became one of the archbishop's suffragans when he was created bishop of Béziers; one of his first tasks was to emulate his archbishop by rebuilding his own cathedral. At the same time he had become as well considered in the royal court as in the curia, and began to travel on royal business with his patron Aicelin. At the court he met and presumably liked Guillaume de Nogaret for, in 1304, he gave a rent to the royal lawyer after de Nogaret's return from the notorious visit to Anagni. By then Bérenger was a rising star of both Court and Church, still closely linked to Gilles Aicelin. When Pope Clement was elevated to the Holy See the next year, he was one of the first new cardinals to be appointed. With one foot in both camps, Cardinal Frédol became a key figure in the trial of the Templars. On 5 November 1306, he was sent together with Cardinal Etienne de Suisy on a mission to Philip the Fair. It has been suggested that this was the occasion on which secret advance preparations for the arrest of the Templars were made. His later involvement confirms this to be a reasonable hypothesis: after the arrests had been made, he again travelled to the royal court with de Suisy to claim the Templars as papal prisoners; then, in 1308, he was president of the papal commission which interrogated the Templars in Poitiers. Now, in 1312, as Grand Penitencier in the curia, confessor to princes and personal representative of the pope, Bérenger Frédol was virtually the number three man in the papal hierarchy (after the Pope and the Chamberlain). He was noted for his zeal in the name of the Church, but was at the same time considered a royal man by the king himself; others perceived him as someone always willing to sell his services to the highest bidder. In conclusion, this cardinal was a lawyer and theologian of vast experience and knowledge as far as the trial of the Templars was concerned but, like his own sponsor Gilles Aicelin, he was a man of ambiguous loyalty in the affair.

The last two cardinals in the negotiating team were less experienced than Bérenger Frédol, but just as much royal men. Cardinal Nicolas de Fréauville was a Norman by birth. As a young man he had entered the Dominican Order, and then he too had studied theology at the University of Paris; it is likely that he also worked as an inquisitor for some years. So far, his story was that of many other anonymous clerics. But Nicolas too had his patron, and a remarkable one considering the task he was about to embark on, for he was cousin to Enguerrand de Marigny, chief negotiator for Philip the Fair. It was as the result of his cousin's influence and patronage that he had become a private confessor to the king, like his confrère Guillaume de Paris. Once again, the status of a key figure in the trial was at the very least dubious.

On the face of things, the last of the five, Cardinal Arnaud de Nouvel, was a different matter. He was a Cistercian who had studied canon law at the University of Toulouse and had also taught there. Later, he had become abbot of the great Cistercian abbey of Fontfroide. Recalling Abbot Jacques de Thérines' scepticism, it would be reasonable to imagine him as equally objective in his assessment of the Templar affair. But, from that point of view, there was a serious blemish in his record. Not much is known of Arnaud de Nouvel's life and character. But two negative facts emerge from the documents: first, that he was considered a 'friend' by Philip the Fair; and, second, that in June 1311, as preparations were being made for the Council of Vienne, he had received as a royal gift an annual rent of 50 *livres tournois* – thus placing himself on a similar plane to that of Raoul de Presles.

These, then, were the men who sat across the table supposedly negotiating in the interest of Pope Clement and *against* those of King Philip.

For twelve days, assuming the meetings began on Thursday 17 February, the two negotiating teams met nearly every day in secret at Vienne. No details of their discussions emerged, and no decisions were taken. For the main purpose of these talks was to prepare the ground for the arrival of Philip the Fair. The king was now poised at Macon, whence a short downstream journey could take him to Vienne. But he wished the preliminary problems concerning the future of the Order of the Temple to be ironed out before making any further move. Then he would be able to descend on the papal court with no fear of losing face. But despite the strong royal faction amongst the eleven negotiators, no simple resolution was forthcoming. On Tuesday 29 February the royal envoys departed from Vienne without having clinched the deal. They arrived in Macon the same evening.

Wednesday was spent in private consultation between Philip the Fair and his counsellors. Then, on Thursday 2 March, Philip signed a letter to Pope Clement composed by his counsellors which made the royal position explicit. A week later Enguerrand de Marigny returned to Vienne alone to discuss the contents of the royal letter (he may even have delivered it in person), which provide some idea of the problems which had been discussed by the envoys during the twelve-day period of talks.

Although it began with effusions of formal courtesy, and declarations of willingness to kiss the papal feet, the letter was typically blunt. In language reminiscent of the *Arrest Order*, which suggests the hand of Guillaume de Nogaret in its composition, the royal message drove straight to the crux of the issue:

> Your Holiness knows that it has been given to us to understand by persons worthy of faith that it appears or follows from what has emerged from the inquiries made against the brothers and the Order of the Knighthood of the Temple, into such and so many heresies and other crimes so horrible and detestable committed by them, that it is just that the Order *should be suppressed*.

At this stage, Philip the Fair wanted no more dithering or talk of procurators for the defence. He hovered at Macon awaiting papal approval in respect for 'order', but at the same time was issuing what amounted to commands to Pope Clement. For the royal proposals for the use of Templar wealth and property were also made explicit:

> Wherefore, burning with zeal for the orthodox faith and so that such a great wrong to Christ should not go unpunished, we beg Your Holiness affectionately, devotedly and humbly to suppress the aforesaid Order and create a new military order and grant it – together with the rights, honours and duties – the property which the aforesaid Order had and possessed at the time of the arrest of the Master of the Order, the Preceptors of France, the Holy Land, Normandy, and Poitou and Aquitaine, and many other brothers of the aforesaid Order . . . or allow them to be transferred to another of the established military orders, such as your holy caution will judge expedient for the honour of God and the good of the Holy Land.

In this, King Philip was perfectly aligned with the majority of prelates at the Council of Vienne, and apparently willing to follow Pope Clement in any decision he made.

250

This letter is of enormous interest in any analysis of Philip the Fair's motivation in attacking the Order of the Temple, since it appears to discredit those – both contemporaries and later authors – who believe that he destroyed Templars in order to gain its wealth for his personal coffers. Such a desire was never made explicit before or during the trial, and is here negated in the clearest terms. This could mean two things: either King Philip had never planned to obtain the wealth of the Templars; or he had done so in the beginning, but later changed his mind. An alternative view is that his original desire had been for a united crusading order with one of his sons as its master. But that itself could have been perceived as removing a religious order from its ecclesiastical context. Perhaps Enguerrand de Marigny had reported the reluctance of Pope Clement and the prelates at Vienne to allow the property to be transferred to secular ownership? Yet papal reluctance, or even blunt refusal, had never stopped King Philip before. This was the man who had attacked Pope Boniface in his home territory, who had held the papacy virtually hostage over the Templar affair for seven years, and who had taken the trial into his own hands with the burnings of May 1310. Would such a man, once he had decided to obtain the property of the Temple at all cost, then change his mind? Could it be that the cupidity which contemporaries imputed to him was not the real reason for the arrest of the Templars, and that Philip the Fair fully believed in the accusations he had caused to be made against the Templars?

If so, then the letter which Pope Clement wrote in reply on the day after Enguerrand de Marigny's arrival, Wednesday 8 February, must have infuriated him yet again. For there is no trace of papal weakness; nor of the slightest desire to capitulate. From its strange, almost distant tone, a reader would never imagine the struggles and drama of the previous seven years. It sounds like a vague, friendly letter which wholly ignores King Philip's desires and strength. In a sense, it may be considered the swan-song of papal resistance. Accepting the pope's words at face value, it must have seemed to the royal recipient that even the suppression of the Order of the Temple was far from a foregone conclusion. 'In consideration of your devotion to Our Lord,' Pope Clement replied, 'we both grant and desire that *if* the Order of the Temple should be dissolved, its property with rights and duties should be preserved for the defence of the Holy Land . . .' The conditional was bound to anger Philip the Fair, but nothing in these subtle exchanges of position was entirely casual. It may have been inserted as a bargaining counter to be used in negotiations on the last details of the suppression of the Temple.

Enguerrand de Marigny stayed in Vienne for about a week, meeting and conferring with Pope Clement and the five cardinals every day. Even though the condemnation of the Templars now appeared to be imminent, in spite of the show of papal resistance, it was still necessary for the Council to decide who would inherit their wealth. On this matter, Pope Clement found himself under pressure from all sides. As we have seen, a majority of the prelates favoured using the wealth to found a new order. But there were powerful objections. King Jaimé of Aragon wrote to the pope reminding him that property given to the Templars in Spain had been donated with the aim of bolstering Spanish defences against Islam – especially during the *reconquista*. In that case, he argued, if the Temple were to be suppressed, then its property should be devolved on the Order of Calatrava. Philip the Fair's position was stated by Enguerrand de Marigny, who expressed himself in favour of passing all Templar property to the Hospital. An assiduous lobby was at work for the rival order in Vienne: dignitaries of the Hospital pressed their case in person with clergy and royal counsellors alike, supporting their arguments with expensive gifts (for example, a gold cloth was given to King Philip). Then there was the camp of Pope Clement himself and his familiars in the curia. They must at least have been tempted to assert the right of the Holy See to retain Templar property for its own use: men with their eyes constantly scanning the horizon for the main chance cannot have overlooked such a possibility. The sale of some of the grander fiefs would have enabled the pope to build a new and worthy seat at Avignon – or elsewhere, for as yet little had been done to create a permanent base there for the Holy See.

In the meantime, unknown to the curia, the menace of Philip the Fair was drawing closer. After an earlier postponement, the announced Estates General was probably held in Lyon on or around Wednesday 15 March. It seems certain that King Philip was present in that city two days later, on Friday, when Enguerrand de Marigny sailed upriver from Vienne once again to report to his master.

Easter fell early that year, and Holy Week began on Monday 20 March. But it is unlikely that Pope Clement looked forward to the coming celebrations with pleasure. He was now isolated, trapped in a net suspended between three conflicting points of view: that of Philip the Fair, that of Jaimé II, and that of the majority of delegates to the Council. *He* had to decide, but, to borrow a term from chess, he found himself in a situation of zugzwang where his natural bent for prevarication undermined his authority. That same Monday he wrote that he did not know whether or not the Order of the Temple should be suppressed.

The proceedings were stalled once again.

Once again it was Philip the Fair who resolved the impasse. Just as in Poitiers in July 1308, and in Paris in May 1310, when his patience passed beyond an almost tangible threshold, he struck. On Monday evening, while the ink of Pope Clement's indecision had barely dried, the French king entered Vienne in force. His imposing entourage included his brother Charles of Valois, whose son became Philip VI and initiated the Valois dynasty, his half-brother Louis the count of Evreux, and the three sons who were to succeed him briefly in turn, Louis, Philip, and Charles. In the summer of 1308 he had homed in on Poitiers with the barons and knights who had attended the Estates General at Tours; now he repeated the manoeuvre with those who had been at Lyon. Using this strategy of first gathering his nobles for a great public assembly, King Philip contrived to call up what amounted to a ready-made army at low cost.

The arrival of so many members of the nobility, with their accompanying servants and horses, suffocated all free space and opinion in an already overcrowded city. Ambassadors, diplomatic niceties and polite exchanges of letters were suddenly superfluous. On Tuesday morning, Pope Clement negotiated directly with Philip the Fair. While their discussions took place, the royal counsellors exercised their formidable influence. On a conscious level, this influence was exerted by means of persuasion of the French delegates to the Council; subtle bribes or blunt threats were employed as necessary. At a deeper level, the very presence of such a large body of armed men in a small enclosed space was in itself a deterrent to opposition.

No time was lost. After years of minimal forward motion, the proceedings accelerated as the emanations of Philip the Fair's wrath permeated both cathedral and city. Members of the commission which had heard the evidence against the Templars were summoned to a secret consistory with Pope Clement on the morning of Wednesday 22 March. The pope presented his dilemma to the commissioners in the form of a simple choice: either we allow the brothers of the Order of the Temple to present a formal defence, or the Holy See will declare the dissolution of the Order. This would not be done by means of a judicial sentence, he explained, but by decree and statute. All the pretence of proceeding according to canon law was now thrown to the wind. The formal care taken in drawing up the *Arrest Order*, the

253

expense of long-term imprisonment, and the meticulous interrogations, were all suddenly irrelevant; inquisitors, bishops, notaries and scribes may just as well have stayed at home for the past five years. For the Templars were not to be judged on the basis of their 'crimes' at all. There would be no formal sentence, and no formal condemnation.

Pope Clement's ultimate dilemma was to be resolved by a vote. Each of the fifty or so prelates in the secret consistory must have been aware of the presence of Philip the Fair. The king was not permitted to attend the consistory in the cathedral personally. But he was certainly waiting nearby, perhaps in the palace of the Dauphin Jean II. This time the vote *was* a foregone conclusion. It is impossible to guess what King Philip's reaction would have been if the vote had gone against his wishes, but the archbishops and bishops inside the cathedral must have indulged in speculation as they decided, albeit within the privacy of their own minds. In the event, the commission voted overwhelmingly for suppression, with a fourth-fifths majority. The papal bull of suppression, *Vox in excelso*, was not in fact promulgated until twelve days later. But it was dated 22 March 1312, and had probably been drafted in the consistory that morning. Once that task was completed, Pope Clement – no doubt with a huge sigh of relief – adjourned the meetings of the Council of Vienne until after Easter, now just four days away.

The official promulgation of the bull of suppression was made at the second formal session of the Council of Vienne. This was held in the cathedral of St Maurice on Monday 3 April 1312, and was a much grander occasion than that of the previous October. The papal throne was once again placed on a dais at the beginning of the choir, so that Pope Clement faced the potentates of the Church ranged according to degree in a semi-circle in front of him. But this time the lay presence was more impressive. To the pope's right, a little lower but on the same dais, sat King Philip the Fair with his youngest son Charles and the count of Saint-Pol at his feet; to the pope's left was Philip's eldest son and heir King Louis of Navarre, a kingdom he had inherited through his mother, Joan; Peter the son of King Frederick of Sicily (i.e. Frederick I of Aragon, king of Sicily 1296–1337 since Sicily had been given to Peter III of Aragon after the Sicilian revolt against the French); the duke of Burgundy, and other nobles. With the cardinals, archbishops, bishops, kings and nobles in resplendent clothes worthy of the occasion, the choir and nave of the cathedral must have been a magnificent sight. Yet the grandeur was tempered by awe and nervousness which charged the vaults above them. For everyone present knew that the sole function of this magnificence was the abolition of the Order of the Temple and, in their own minds, many were not convinced that the Order should be suppressed. The authorities were aware of this undercurrent of silent protest and unease, and evidently feared that it could easily be provoked into something more dangerous. For this reason, an announcement had been made before proceedings began that *no one would be allowed to speak without express permission from Pope Clement.* Just in case some obstreperous cleric should be tempted to ignore this order, it was also announced that failure to obey would be punished by excommunication.

No one was to suffer the delusion that this was an open session of the Council of Vienne: in all but name, it was closer in spirit to a summary execution.

The proceedings opened with prayers and litanies, after which the cardinal-deacon chanted the Gospel 'Vos estes sol terre ...'. Then the entire congregation in the cathedral sang the *Veni Creator*. When these ritual preliminaries were over, Pope Clement himself preached the sermon on a text which was clearly chosen for its implicit reference to the Templars and their 'errors'. For the words were taken from Psalm 1 (v.5): 'Therefore the wicked will not stand in the judgment, nor sinners in the congregation of the righteous'. Unfortunately the surviving accounts of the session do not give details of the sermon but, when it was finished, the pope went on to provide a brief summary of the 'errors' of the Knights Templar and the main events of the long trial. He then announced the suppression of the Order by apostolic decree, and the bull *Vox in excelso* was read out to the congregation in the cathedral. Since the terrible crimes of which the Templars had been accused could not go unpunished without inflicting damage on God, the argument ran, and bearing in mind the severity of the sins of apostasy, idolatry and sodomy which the brothers of the Order of the Temple had committed, there was really no choice but to abolish the Order by apostolic decree. Moreover, other religious orders had been abolished in similar fashion in the past, so Pope Clement would not be setting a precedent. After five tormented years, the concluding words brought home the reality of Philip the Fair's action – and now his victory – with a punch:

> After long and mature reflection, having before our eyes only God
> and bearing in mind only the interests of the Holy Land ... we
> abolish by perpetual sanction and with the approval of the Holy

Council the aforesaid Order of the Temple, its *Rule*, its habit and its name, strictly forbidding anyone to enter into the said Order, to receive or wear its habit, or to act as if he were a Templar.

If there were by some remote chance a last nucleus of Templars lurking in wait near Lyon, or even elsewhere in Europe, to present a defence of their Order, a clause tacked onto the bull was designed to crush their hopes. 'Anyone who violates this decree', it specified, 'will by that very fact incur a sentence of excommunication.' This really was the end of the road. The only remaining matters to be decided were provisions for the distribution of Templar property, and the fate of the remaining Templar prisoners. Both were to be reserved exclusively for papal judgment.

Philip the Fair must have walked out of St Maurice with a huge sense of relief, like a plaintiff emerging from a major court action at the Old Bailey. Five years of legal and diplomatic struggle were enough to mark any man for life, even when it is mostly carried out by proxy. Once he had dreamed of creating a new crusading order, along the lines of the visions of Ramon Lull and Pierre Dubois, with one of his sons as its Grand Master; perhaps he had schemed in order to acquire the vast Templar properties in France for his own kingdom. Now both dreams had been renounced. But he must have been pleased to come out of the lengthy trial relatively unscathed. His physical proximity to Vienne was no longer a matter of urgency, and he was free to return to the complex everyday business of running his kingdom without the need to have one ear permanently cocked in the direction of the trial. The next day, Tuesday, he was still in Vienne. But he departed within a matter of days. Documents issued by the royal chancery place King Philip in Lyon on 12 April, and back in Paris by Thursday 27 April.

In these weeks Pope Clement worked on the bull which concerned the provisions for Templar property, presumably along lines agreed with King Philip or his lawyers before their departure. This bull was promulgated as *Ad providam Christi Vicarii* on Tuesday 2 May 1312. In it the pope argued that since property owned by the Templars had originally been donated or acquired for the purpose of sustaining the crusading effort in the Holy Land, it should continue to be used for the same purpose. Thus all lands and property which the Knights Templar had possessed at the moment of the arrests in October 1307 were to be transferred to the Order of the Hospital of St John. The only exception to this *diktat* concerned the Iberian peninsula. This was a major success for

King Jaimé II and the Aragonese ambassadors, who had also acted in the interests of King Ferdinand IV of Castille (1296–1312), King Diniz of Portugal (1279–1325), and King Sancho of Majorca (1311–24). Templar property in those kingdoms was to be transferred to local crusading orders (although in fact the negotiations were protracted beyond the death of Pope Clement in 1314, and the matter only finally resolved in 1317).

The transfer was no simpler elsewhere. This was mainly a consequence of the huge extent of Templar property, but also because the system of tenures under which they were held was so complex. In many cases this situation was made worse by the fact that the Hospital could not obtain the necessary deeds and charters to establish ownership: in England these were not acquired for at least a decade after *Ad providam*.

In fact the situation in England illustrates the general difficulties. King Edward II had begun to employ Templar resources almost immediately after the arrests, and now blocked any attempt by the prior of the Hospital to claim the property which the papal bull granted to his Order. The king had sold Templar wool, used their stores of grain for his wars against Scotland, felled trees on their land for timber, and used Templar funds to pays arrears to his clerks and give alms to religious houses. For a king come to the throne at a moment of severe financial shortages, news of the arrest of the Templars had come like a manna: he had even drawn on Templar reserves of meat and fish for his coronation feast on 25 February 1308. Later, when it must have seemed evident that the trial would drag on for years, moveable property such as horses, livestock and kitchen equipment had been stripped from Templar houses. Whereas Philip the Fair needed finance for his wars, Edward II ran an extravagant court and indulged in lavish clothes and feasts: over £4,000 of the £10,000 spent by the royal household during 1311–12 was for wine alone; gifts to royal favourites such as Piers Gaveston also required huge sums of money. Templar property contributed to this expenditure. In short, by the summer of 1312 there was not much left.

When King Edward did give up the possession or use of Templar property, the situation was no better from the point of view of the Hospitallers. In the words of Clarence Perkins, a historian of the Templars in England: 'The removal of the royal keepers seems to have been the signal for a scramble in which the lords of the fees and the king were in a much better position to succeed than the small number of Hospitallers'. Without deeds or other documents, and in the general confusion, it was easy for neighbouring landowners to absorb Templar property. Perkins described the consequences of formal suppression of the Templars throughout Europe as 'a wild orgy of plunder which quickly passed beyond papal control'.

In some cases, even when they succeeded in claiming their inheritance, it took the Hospitallers as long as twenty years to come into effective possession of property granted by Pope Clement's bull. Much of it simply disappeared, and the financial burdens resulting from the bull also created problems. Philip the Fair had relinquished any ideas he may have had of acquiring the Templar property for himself but, on 24 August 1312, we find him writing to the pope yet again. He and his ministers had been doing their sums. In this letter he formally accepted the idea of transferring Templar property to the Hospital, but at the same time he argued that all the expenses incurred in his kingdom for custody and administration of Templar property should be deducted from the total value before any transfer took place. The following spring an agreement on these expenses was made, and the Hospital paid 200,000 *livres tournois* to King Philip over the next three years – a sum which represented a notable drain on Hospital cash reserves.

In the end, no one seems to have benefited at once from the suppression of the Order of the Temple. The post-abolition phase was characterised more by fragmentation of the property than by pacific and integral transfer to other orders.

The last step in the process was to decide the fate of Templars still in custody. This may have been less urgent than the transfer of property, but was no less complex. Once again it required negotiations with the envoys of both Philip the Fair and Jaimé II. Pope Clement's decision was announced on 6 May 1312 at the third and final formal session of the full Council of Vienne, much reduced in the absence of King Philip and his court. It came in the form of the papal constitution *Considerantes dudum*. The essence of this constitution was that the pope only reserved for his personal judgment the leading dignitaries of the Order of the Temple imprisoned in Paris: in particular Jacques de Molay, Hugues de Pairaud, and Geoffroi de Charney. At the same time, he effectively relinquished his powers over the many Templars still held throughout Europe. They were all to be judged by provincial councils and, as far as can be ascertained from the terms used, in a humane manner. The worst of the storm had passed. In fact the constitution specifies that those Templars who had been absolved and reconciled to the Church were to be treated leniently. They would be allowed to continue to live on Templar properties, and even to receive pensions deriving from the income on those properties.

One example will suffice. In 1313, the archbishop of Tarragona declared Ramon Sa Guardia, the preceptor of the Templar house of Mas Dieu in Roussillon who had earlier been interrogated by Gilles Aicelin's suffragon bishop Ramon Costa, to be both innocent of all charges and absolved. He then assigned the ex-preceptor a pension of 350 livres a year, and also provided smaller pensions for the other Templars there. Neither were these short-term measures. There were fifteen ex-Templars drawing pensions at Mas Dieu in 1319, and ten years later in 1329. Remarkably, in 1350 there was still one ex-Templar knight, Berengar de Collo, living in the old preceptory and regularly collecting his pension – *forty-three years* after the original arrests. According to the evidence he gave before the episcopal commission on 16 February 1310, Berengar had been received into the Order nine years earlier. Assuming he was in his early twenties at the time, in 1350 he must have been around seventy years old. There had been many other new entrants in the Order at the time of the arrests, so a good half-century was necessary before the last of them died.

But how many of the 14 or 15,000 Templars of all ranks, to accept our earlier estimate, were given their freedom after Pope Clement's 1312 constitution? How many had survived Philip the Fair's onslaught? The answer must be most of them. Thousands. Retellings of the legend often give the impression that *all* members of the Order of the Temple died between 1307 and 1312, or were at least imprisoned for life. The truth was quite different, as we have seen. Ironically, there is no need to fabricate stories of dramatic escapes or local survivals in order to sustain continuation myths. There really were a lot of ex-Templars around: some repentant, some camouflaged, and some still proud of their own and the Order's past – like many old soldiers.

For in the years following the trial of the Templars many knights throughout Europe, just like Berengar de Collo, continued to reside on Templar property. Serving-brothers, rural brothers (*frères casaliers*), and servant brothers (*frères de métier*), who probably had no where else to go, just carried on their everyday routines – unlike their companions in Paris who were driven to begging. There is evidence that they were left in relative freedom, as long as they remembered their monastic vows and conducted a life devoted to prayer. Moreover, since their individual vows remained valid, other religious orders seemed more than willing to accept ex-Templars. A few years later, in 1318, Pope John XXII *ordered* the Franciscans and Dominicans of Naples to support ex-Templars still living in that kingdom, while in Compostella the Templars who had been arrested were mostly acquitted of all charges and allowed to become anchorites. Absolution and reconciliation were unnecessary. Part of the problem in generalising about the Templars is that there was no universal practice, just as there had been no common reaction to the original arrests outside the kingdom of France. In fact the surviving military orders also accepted ex-Templars, and in Germany the 1317 Conference of Frankfurt even granted permission for German ex-Templars to join the Hospital of St John. The pressures of the Aragonese ambassadors allowed Templars in that kingdom to merge into existing military orders. In Portugal, King Diniz rewarded Templar assistance in the past against the Saracens by transferring both the ex-knights and their land to his newly-founded Order of Jesus Christ, which received papal approval in 1318. In effect, the Order of the Temple survived there under a new name.

The Council of Vienne was closed on the morning of Saturday 6 May 1312. The Order of the Temple had been formally suppressed, though neither found guilty nor condemned. Its property had been divided, at least in theory, between the rival Order of the Hospital of St John and the Iberian crusading orders; its former brothers had transferred into other crusading orders, merged into conventional monastic orders, continued to live on Templar property, or had simply disappeared into the cities and forests of Europe.

All, that is, except Jacques de Molay, Hugues de Pairaud, Geoffroi de Gonneville and Geoffroi de Charney, who had been reserved for papal judgment. Those former dignitaries still lay chained to the walls of the dungeon-tower of the Temple in Paris.

15

JACQUES DE MOLAY AT THE STAKE: MARCH 1314

For eighteen months after the suppression of the Temple, the trial, in the broadest sense of the term, entered another phase of abeyance. Jacques de Molay and his fellow prisoners continued to languish in the dungeon of the Temple. When the royal pressure diminished, urgency evaporated.

The year 1313 was in fact a tempestuous one for Philip the Fair and his family. Compared to the celebrations and scandals associated with the French throne that summer, the events which excite royal watchers today are tame affairs. On Whit Sunday there were great celebrations in Paris as the three sons of King Philip, Louis, Philip and Charles, were formally inducted into the order of knighthood. The festivities which followed, and which engaged the entire population of Paris for a week, were such as to astonish even a notoriously extravagant guest like King Edward II – whose wife, Isabelle, was sister to the three new knights. That summer the capital buzzed with news of plans for a new crusade, and for a military campaign against Flanders. The royal administration, in particular the Treasury, was at the same time undergoing a drastic reorganisation.

But the outstanding event that sumnmer was the scandal of the adultery of Philip the Fair's daughters-in-law: Marguerite de Bourgogne, who had married Louis – then king of Navarre – in 1305; Jeanne d'Othon, wife of Philip, count of Poitiers, since 1307; and Jeanne's sister Blanche d'Othon, wife of Charles, Count of La Marche, since 1308. Rumours circulating at court prompted King Philip – presumably following information provided by 'persons worthy of faith' – to order an enquiry. Evidence was found and all three were accused of committing adultery with two young squires, the brothers Philippe and Gautier d'Aunay. In the eyes of such a severe and upright monarch, it was a scandal which threatened the very future of the Capetian dynasty; in a sense, too, it did literally break the line by rendering the birth of future heirs impossible.

Neither was the adultery a mere question of morality or marital infidelity. According to feudal law the two brothers were guilty of high treason, exacerbated by *lèse-majesté*, and the prescribed punishment for this double crime was death. The daughters-in-law were arrested and thrown into prison while their lovers were brutally tortured – just as the Templars had been – until royal officials obtained confessions. Philippe confessed to committing adultery with Marguerite over a period of more than two years, and Gautier with Blanche for the same time. Jeanne was absolved of this charge, though not the charge of having been an accessory to the facts. The three women were kept in prison until the death of Philip the Fair, when Jeanne alone was released; when her husband ascended the throne as Philip V in 1316 she became the Queen of France. Marguerite died in prison, while her sister Blanche died in 1326 in the convent at Maubuisson. But that was nothing compared to the atrocious fate of the two squires. Geoffroi de Paris relates in his verse chronicle how they were first flayed alive in view of their erstwhile mistresses; then, when their 'nature' had been cut off and thrown to dogs and other animals, they were decapitated and their corpses hanged from a gibbet for all to see. So the Paris gossip-mill had plenty of news to grind in 1313 without the Templars; probably the people had been inured to their long-drawn-out story. In short, the Templars were no longer front-page news.

Pope Clement, too, had his problems. These were mainly of ill-health, a supposed cancer of the bowel which was gradually devouring him. He spent several months of 1312 and 1313 at Grozeau, by then in an almost permanent state of convalescence. We may imagine that he too had little interest in the ex-knights in Paris now that their Order had been abolished. Eventually, in December 1313, he did appoint a commission of three cardinals which was to decide the fate of the Templar leaders still in prison. But such was the soporific rhythm of events by this stage that nothing happened for a further period of three months. It was not until March 18 1314, on 'the Monday after the Feast of St Gregory', almost exactly two years since the suppression of the Temple, that the cardinals summoned a council in Paris to deal with the matter.

When they did meet, yet again the dice were heavily loaded against the Templars. Two members of the commission could be considered royal men: the senior cardinal in terms of service was Nicholas de Fréauville, the Dominican scholar and ex-royal confessor who had negotiated with the royal embassy in Vienne. Recently, he had been the representative of the Church who handed the cross of pilgrims to Philip the Fair as the king announced a forthcoming crusade (an idea which soon evaporated). The second cardinal was Arnaud de Nouvel, a canonist and friend of Philip the Fair, who was also in the commission at Vienne and, as we have been seen, who enjoyed privileges and rents granted by the king. Only the third member of this special commission seems to have enjoyed independence from King Philip. But he too was an old hand in the trial of the Templars, and may not have been well disposed towards them. For Cardinal Arnaud d'Auch, papal chamberlain since 1312 and therefore the highest-ranking member of the commission, was the same Arnaud – a fellow Gascon, a papal relative, and an intimate of Bertrand de Got since childhood – who as bishop of Poitiers had provided hospitality to Pope Clement and the papal commission in the summer of 1308.

On that Monday morning early in 1314 the business of the special council must have appeared to the participants a straightforward matter. It may be assumed that this council also met at first in the palace of the bishop of Paris. Cardinal Nicholas de Fréauville presided over a gathering which included Archbishop Philippe de Marigny – who acted as the king's alter ego – and scholars of canon law and theology from the University of Paris. Yet there was no real legal or theological problem to discuss, and most of those present must have viewed the council as no more than a formal occasion to announce the prescribed punishment. Jacques de Molay and the other dignitaries of the Temple had made public and repeated confessions of the crimes with which they had been charged. From the theological point of view they were therefore confessed and repentant heretics. Pope Gregory IX's 1231 bull *Excommunicamus* had established that the standard sentence for repentant heretics was life imprisonment. Unlike a modern life sentence, imprisonment was usually perpetual; nourishment, in Bernard Gui's eloquent phrase, was 'the bread of suffering and the water of tribulation'. The only variation within this sentence concerned the type of imprisonment, which could be either the *murus largus* or the *murus strictus* ('wide walls' or 'narrow walls'). In the former, prisoners were allowed to mingle with other prisoners and to take exercise, while relatives could make gifts of food, drink and clothing in the latter, prisoners were chained at least by their feet and often by the hands too, and were placed in smaller, darker cells. While the prison conditions in the abbeys and hostels during the Templar trial sound closer to the *murus largus*, those of the dignitaries in the Temple itself were likely to have been the *murus strictus*. Thus even the harshest of

263

sentences would make little tangible difference to their present plight. Jacques de Molay was now about seventy, Geoffroi de Charney in his mid-sixties, Hugues de Pairaud also in his sixties, while Geoffroi de Gonneville was probably a little younger, in his fifties. They must have been reduced to such physical wrecks after seven years of torture and prison that to be condemned to *perpetual* imprisonment would be something of an ironic joke.

How did *they* view the council? What could have been going through their minds that morning as guards accompanied them from the Temple to appear before the three cardinals?

It is quite possible that Jacques de Molay perceived the event as a liberation. According to the trial record he had been in prison, and in solitary confinement, continuously since his last appearance before the papal commission on 2 March 1310 – just over four years to add to three previous years of torture and harsh treatment. There is no evidence of his leaving the Temple dungeon in those four years (save a mention on Geoffroi de Paris' chronicle which suggests that he may have been for some time imprisoned in Gisors), or of any other prisoners communicating with him. To come into the open air, to see comrades-in-arms he had known and fought with for decades, must have been something of an exhilarating experience – if his aged body was still strong enough to allow even momentary pleasure. To a man who had spent nearly thirty years of his life as a knight and commander in the brilliant sunlight and open spaces of the deserts and coastal plains in the Holy Land, the *murus strictus* would have been a terrible restriction. We may imagine his emotions that morning as something akin to those evoked by Beethoven's moving chorus in *Fidelio*, when Leonora gains permission for the prisoners to come out into the courtyard for light and fresh air: 'Oh, what joy . . .'.

Subsequent events suggest that this is no exaggeration. It may have been the sheer joy of temporary release, or perhaps the terror of being taken back to his dungeon. But something generated in the Grand Master a sudden burst of life, a last explosive scintilla of that pride for which the Templars were renowned.

From the bishop's palace the three cardinals and the archbishop of Sens walked a few paces to the square in front of the main façade of Notre Dame, the ancient square known as the Parvis. Today the denomination 'place du Parvis Notre Dame' covers a vast area, but until the nineteenth century and Baron Haussmann's rebuilding of the city, it was a fraction of its present size: just a small public space in front of the cathedral. This site was chosen because, as in inquisitorial proceedings, the leaders of the Temple were to be required to repeat their previously private confessions in public – a traditional function of the Parvis. The normal practice in a situation like this was for final judgment to be passed before a mixed court of senior religious figures, inquisitors, secular clerks and lawyers. Then a public sermon, or *sermo generalis* would be preached to the people of the town in which the trial had taken place, followed by public announcement of the sentences imposed (this procedure was the progenitor of the great ceremonies of *auto de fé* in the Plaza Mayor of Madrid in later centuries).

Six contemporary chroniclers describe the scenes of that day in Paris: three who provide greater detail write as though they were eyewitnesses, namely the continuator of the Latin *Chronicle* of Guillaume de Nangis, Giovanni Villani in his *Chroniche*, and Geoffroi de Paris in his verse chronicle; the other three, the anonymous author of the *Grandes Chroniques de France*, Bernard Gui in his *E Floribus Chronicorum*, and the Benedictine monk Jean de St Victor provide only brief, though fascinating, mentions.

The most informative and vivid of these sources is the verse chronicle which has been attributed to Geoffroi de Paris. Little is known about the author except that he was a Parisian and probably of bourgeois origins; the poem is in fact anonymous, and no external evidence exists to reveal the identity of the poet. But whoever he was, the author was extremely well informed about the royal court and about political issues of the day, and he nurtured strong critical sentiments against King Philip and Enguerrand de Marigny. He was also a learned man and a skilled poet. These facts have led the modern editor of the chronicle to suggest that the author may have been a clerk or notary in the royal chancellery or *parlement*. Such a position would provide a plausible explanation for his presence at the execution of Jacques de Molay. Certainly he was a shrewd and observant eyewitness of the events of that dramatic Monday.

The Florentine chronicler Giovanni Villani informs us that 'pulpits', or temporary platforms erected on scaffolding, were set up in front of Notre Dame for the Council to conduct its business in public. The number is not specified, but it may be assumed that there were at least two: perhaps one for the cardinals, the archbishop of Sens, and their respective entourages; and another for the Templar leaders and their guards. They were simple wooden platforms erected on timbers which were

265

lashed together, with steps leading up on the cathedral side. A large crowd of Parisians had gathered in the square beneath these platforms to watch the final act of the Templar tragedy; the whole drama had been so protracted that there must by then have existed a new generation of adolescent spectators who barely recalled the original arrests.

The whole procedure was solemn and formal, with the rank of those present sufficient to guarantee respect and silence. Many present in the crowd recalled the ferocity of royal executioners in the summer of 1310, for which the presence of Philippe de Marigny on the platform was a tangible reminder. That moment had occurred no more than a stone's throw from where they now stood. When the prisoners had been brought out and placed on their platform, the full list of charges which had been made against them was read out once again. It was emphasised before the public that the Templar dignitaries had already confessed to the charges. Then, according to Geoffroi de Paris, it was Cardinal Nicholas de Fréauville in person who preached the required short sermon. Following this, the cardinals and other members of the Council made at least a show of discussion and deliberation of the matter in hand. Last of all, to use the words of the continuator of Guillaume de Nangis, the Templars 'were sentenced to be thrown into harsh and perpetual imprisonment' (although, in a significant variation, Villani's account makes it sound as though final sentence had not yet been passed).

That, it must have seemed to those present, was that. The multitude gathered in place de Parvis beneath the platforms was probably on the move already, just as the spectators of a major sporting event begin to trickle out of the stadium when no further change of score seems likely. In the eery hush which surrounded the now-condemned Templars, the sigh of relief that it was all over could almost have been heard in the royal palace. At that point, even the cardinals themselves 'believed that they had imposed an end to the trial'.

But the trial of the Templars had always proceeded by fits and starts, an alternating sequence of dithering lethargy on the one hand, and dramatic events on the other. And the surprises were not yet over. For that morning, to the astonishment of all present, the same Grand Master who had meekly confessed, who had refused to defend the Order which he once commanded, and who had cowered in obstinate silence in the background for the seven years of the trial, seems to have been shot through by an unexpected tremor of pride.

Jacques de Molay began to shout and demand that he be heard by the members of the Council. Soon he was joined in this protest by Geoffroi de Charney, the preceptor of Normandy. The murmuring crowd was shocked into silence again. With a force of personality which stunned those present, they both launched into a stubborn defence of the Order in what amounted to an attack against Cardinal Nicholas de Fréauville and Archbishop Philippe de Marigny. They not only made a vociferous denial of the validity of their earlier confessions, but denied every detail of them. From the continuator of Guilllaume de Nangis' terse comment that they 'showed little reverence or admiration' for the ecclesiastical dignitaries opposite them, we may postulate a fierce harangue with no holds barred. Jacques de Molay argued that he had never committed the heresies and sins of which he was accused, and that the Order of the Temple was holy and just in its devotion to the Roman Catholic Church. He deserved to die now, he shouted for all to hear, but at the same time he wished to suffer with his soul in peace.

The shock of the people below echoed that of the crowds in the meadow by Saint Antoine in 1310. A universal sense of surprise reinforced doubt in the sceptics. In the words of Bernard Gui:

> One more thing was worthy of astonishment, that both together and as individuals one by one they retracted completely the confessions which they had earlier made in the trial and which they had made after having sworn to state the truth, saying that in their confessions they had made false statements and had lied both about themselves and about others, advancing no other reason for this but that of the violence or the terror of torture . . .

This from a man who knew something about torture! In effect, Jacques de Molay was simply adhering to the line of defence established by Pierre de Bologna and Renaud de Provins exactly four years earlier.

Yet the effect of such an unexpected and public denial by the Grand Master of the Temple was such that the cardinals were left both speechless and uncertain what to do. 'And the sermon having been interrupted,' Villani wrote with only a slight contradiction, 'and not having pronounced the sentence, the cardinals and other prelates left that place.' For the time being the prisoners were given over to the provost of Paris. The provost, who just *happened to be there at the time*, according to the chronicler, was clearly representing the royal interests in the Council; no legal presence had been deemed necessary since the conclusion had seemed foregone. The idea of having the prisoners taken away,

267

the continuator of Guillaume de Nangis explains, was for them to be held until a fuller discussion of the matter could be held the next day. In other words, Nicholas de Fréauville and Philippe de Marigny needed time to confer with Philip the Fair and the royal lawyers.

News of this upset must have reached Philip the Fair within minutes, for he was in residence at his newly completed palace just 300 metres away on the Ile de la Cité. We learn in fact that the king discussed the matter almost immediately 'with the prudent men of his council'. Since the continuator of Guillaume de Nangis explicitly states that he 'did not call upon the clergy', we may assume that among these 'prudent men' were Enguerrand de Marigny and Guillaume de Plaisians. The original architect of the trial, Guillaume de Nogaret, could not be present because he had died in 1313. It may however, in spite of this testimony, have been the case that Philippe de Marigny and Nicholas de Fréauville were also present, since the former was the brother and the latter the cousin of the man who now dominated the royal court.

In a sense, however, it no longer mattered who was present. There was not really much to discuss. For no lawyer or inquisitor in the early fourteenth century would have had the slightest doubt about the consequences of that morning's outburst. In retracting their confessions after having listened to the *sermo generalis*, and after having heard the sentence (or while it was being read, according to which version of the events we accept), Jacques de Molay and Geoffroi de Charney had placed themselves beyond all dispute in the category of relapsed heretics. The irrevocable sentence for this, the most appalling of crimes for the Church because it meant there was nothing more to be done, was consignment to the secular arm for public burning at the stake, just like the fifty-four Templars in 1310. At this point the Grand Master was at last a direct prisoner of the King of France. All ecclesiastical jurisdiction, and any lingering papal protection, had been effectively renounced by his own denial – as he must have known. As might have been expected – it was, after all, a moment he must have dreamed of for years – Philip the Fair showed no hesitation: he ordered that Jacques de Molay and Geoffroi de Charney be burned that very evening at the hour of Vespers.

The site chosen for the executions was a small island in the Seine 'between the royal garden and the chapel of the hermit brothers of St Augustine'.

The unembanked downstream tip of the Ile de la Cité then broke up into three small islands which have since been formed into the regular ship's bow which leads to the point at Square du Vert Galant. In 1314 King Philip's palace, on whose site the present Palais du Justice stands, overlooked the royal gardens which covered place Dauphine until the line of the Pont Neuf. At this point on the Left Bank stood the monastery of the Augustinian canons, whose kitchen-gardens were split into two when rue Dauphine was built in 1607 to provide access to the then new Pont Neuf. St Louis had founded a convent named Notre-Dame-de-la-Rive for the Frères Sachets on that site in 1261, but the Augustinians took possession of it in 1293. During Philip the Fair's reign the old chapel and cloister had been enlarged, and the Augustinians became special chaplains of the Sainte Chapelle just across the river. In 1313, the quai des Grands Augustins was constructed (and still exists in name between Pont Neuf and Pont St Michel). At the time of the Templar trial the lands of the Augustinians stretched from the present rue des Grands Augustins downstream almost to the Tour de Nesle, the river bastion of the walls of Philippe Augustus (between the site of the present Hôtel des Monnaies and the Institut de France). Like many of the monasteries and churches which appear in the story of the Templar trial, this one was later demolished – in 1797. But its location allows us to pinpoint the site of the execution of Jacques de Molay and Geoffroi de Charney.

For there has been some confusion about the exact point. The chronicle of Guillaume de Nangis does not name the island, but merely describes it as 'a certain small island'; the modern editor of this chronicle states in a footnote that the island was called the Ile aux Juifs. Jean de St Victor simply says 'on a small island under the chapel'; Villani refers as vaguely as might be expected of a foreigner to 'the island of Paris in front of the royal palace'; and the Grandes Chroniques refer to 'the island in front of the Augustinians'. Geoffroi de Paris says it was the Ile-des-Javiaux, and has been followed by many later authors. But the Ile-des-Javiaux was further upstream, beyond the Ile St Louis, and was later incorporated into the right bank as the area between boulevard Morland and quai Henri IV. Taken together, however, the contemporary chronicles evidently refer to one of the three islands beyond the royal palace, which other documents refer to as the islands of Buci, Patriarches and Gourdaine. Plans of medieval Paris drawn by Louis Halphen (1909), and by Anne Lombard-Jourdan (1976), clearly show the three islands: a larger one to the left of the royal palace looking downstream, one smaller one slightly beyond it, and another facing the Right Bank. Now the second of these islands, still clearly visible on the 1572 map of Paris by

269

Georges Braun, stands exactly opposite the Augustinian monastery, and is probably the island in question. On the 1690 map of Paris by Nicolas de Fer it is obvious how part of this island had provided a solid base for the northern foundations of the first arch of the Pont Neuf, which seems to have jumped the Seine over the two furthest islands like a stone skipping across water (the Ile-des-Javiaux then being the only remaining small island at this point on the Seine).

In short, while Hugues de Pairaud and Geoffroi de Gonneville were sent back to perpetual imprisonment in the Temple as unrepentant heretics, Jacques de Molay and Geoffroi de Charney were burned at the stake near the point at which the Pont Neuf joins the Ile de la Cité from the Left Bank.

They were brought out towards the hour of Vespers, in front of an even bigger crowd of Parisians who had gathered for the scene – drawn out after the morning's surprises by their curiosity to see how the Grand Master faced his death. Some of them must have had clear recollections of the brave deaths of the fifty-four, and wanted to see here too whether there would be a last-minute change of heart. In fact, as Geoffroi de Paris recounts the scene, Jacques de Molay was every bit as courageous and steadfast as his predecessors had been. Relief at ending his long ordeal was transformed into an apparent eagerness to die:

> Le Mestre, qui vit le feu prest,
> S'est despoillié sanz nul arrest.

(The Master, on seeing the fire near/Cast off his clothes without restraint.) Then, dressed only in his shirt, his face was filled with joy as he allowed the guards to tie him to the stake. His only complaint must have been perceived by both guards and the audience below as provoked by extreme piety. For while he was willing to be tied to the stake, the Grand Master wished to have his hands free so that he could pray:

> Seingnors, au mains,
> Lessiez moi joindre un po mes mains,
> Et vers Dieu fere m'oroison,
> Car or en est temps et seison.

(Sirs, at least/Let me join together my hands/And say my prayers to God,/Since this is the time and season.) For soon, he argued, he was to die and only God could be the judge who decided whether such a death was just.

270

This sense of the Grand Master preparing for his execution in a strikingly calm state of mind is confirmed by the continuator of Guillaume de Nangis, who speaks of the 'readiness of mind and will' with which Jacques de Molay and Geoffroi de Charney were seen to sustain the flames as they began to lick at their feet.

In the midst of this public resignation, extreme courage, and piety, Jacques de Molay allowed himself one last gesture of defiance which reflected the anger which had built up inside him during years of harsh imprisonment. He made a final appeal to God, but this time in the name of vengeance:

> S'en vendra en brief temps meschié
> Sus celz qui nous dampnent a tort:
> Diex en vengera nostre mort.

(Let evil swiftly befall/Those who have wrongly condemned us;/God will avenge our death.) This was the famous 'curse of Jacques de Molay', which was both to have an imminent consequence and to resound down the centuries to the French Revolution. He went further than the papal bull which had condemned the Order of the Temple, in making a precise reference to Philip the Fair and Pope Clement, and to their role in the downfall of the Temple. Anyone who had in the slightest way opposed the Temple, or had believed in the articles of accusation, was branded in similar fashion:

> Seignors, dist il, sachiez, sanz tere,
> Que touz celz qui nous sont contrere
> Por nous en aront a souffrir.

(Sirs, he said, know, without any doubt,/That all those who are against us/For us will have to suffer.) In a time of superstition and belief in such prophecies, and given the status of the pronouncer, these words must have struck fear into the listeners. Yet he did not continue in this vein.

As if pleased to have got the 'curse' off his chest, the Grand Master returned to pious sentiments. In yet another striking gesture which makes of his death such a magnificent moment, he begged the royal executioners to turn his body on the stake so that he could gaze on to the nearby façade of Notre Dame at the moment of death:

> En ceste foy veil je mourir.
> Vez ci ma foy; et je vous prie

271

> Que devers la Vierge Marie,
> Dont Nostre Seignor Crist fust nez,
> Mon visage vous me tornez.

(In this faith I wish to die./Witness my faith; and I pray you/That towards the Virgin Mary,/In whom Our Lord Christ was born,/You turn my face.) His request was granted, and so it was serenely and in prayer that the Grand Master of the Temple died. This calm and beautiful end – 'so gently did he accept his death', the poet said – not only astonished those present in the crowd but inspired Geoffroi de Charney to similar heroism. If God wills it, he announced to those beneath, I shall follow my Master and die like him:

> Seignors, sanz doute,
> De mon mestre ensivré la route.
> Comme martyr occis l'avez;
> Ce que fet avez ne savez.
> Et ce Dex plest, a cest jor d'ui
> En l'ordre morrai comme lui.

(Lords, without doubt,/I shall follow the way of my master/As a martyr you have killed him/This you have done and know not/God willing, on this day,/I shall die in the Order like him.) Geoffroi de Paris echoes a general air of uncertainty which prevailed that evening in Paris. The second death reinforced the impression generated by the Grand Master's gesture. The contradiction between the heinous crimes ascribed to Jacques de Molay and his comportment that spring evening, between his evasion and incompetence during seven years of imprisonment and his pious certainty in God at the stake, was enough to generate centuries of doubt about his personal guilt. Perhaps the only man to be utterly convinced was Philip the Fair, who may have watched the executions from a window of his palace.

Thus the Grand Master in the end died a noble death, creating 'much admiration and astonishment' in onlookers by his courage and serenity. A further clue to his unexpected decision and this last-minute bravery may be found in Villani's comment on the deaths of the other two leaders of the Temple, Hugues de Pairaud and Geoffroi de Gonneville. It was in 'fear of martyrdom', he asserts, that they confessed and confirmed everything they had said in earlier hearings. In this way they avoided being burned at the stake. Instead, and this is his telling comment, they '*died miserably*' in their cells.

272

Jacques de Molay, on the other hand, by a single gesture of pride on a single day of a seven-year trial for which he must at least in part be held responsible, died the death of a hero such as he had seen at Acre over twenty years before. For while the author of the *Grandes chroniques de France* simply notes that as in the earlier burning at Saint Antoine 'their bones were reduced to powder'. Villani hints at the future fame of Jacques de Molay. 'And note', he says, 'that the night after the said master and his companion were martyred, friars and other religious gathered up their remains and bones as relics, and took them away to holy places.' The very verb he uses ('*martorizzati*') suggests future developments, and the rapid consequences of the curse Jacques de Molay uttered at the stake did much to enhance the general credence that he was indeed the bearer of strange and secret powers. Thirty-three days later, on 20 April, as if in answer to the Grand Master's plea for God's justice, Pope Clement died; eight months later, on 29 November, Philip the Fair also died.

But the Order of the Temple had already ceased to exist. 'In this way,' Villani concludes his brief account, 'the wealthy and powerful house of the temple of Jerusalem was destroyed and reduced to nothing.'

No better conclusion could be written to the story of the trial of the Knights Templar than that of Geoffroi de Paris, who witnessed the execution of Jacques de Molay in person nearly 700 years ago. His observation on the impossibility of deceiving God suggests the way the Grand Master himself may have seen things; his ironic concluding observation that whoever wishes may add further comment ('Qui voudra die le seurplus') was very much to the point. For much 'seurplus' has been uttered in the intervening centuries. Here, then, are the words of Geoffroi:

> One can easily deceive the Church,
> But one can never in any way
> Deceive God. I shall say nothing else.
> Whosoever desires may add more.

273

BIBLIOGRAPHY

ALBON, Marquis d', *Cartulaire de l'Ordre du Temple*, Paris: Champion, 1913.

ANGLO, Sydney (Ed), *The Damned Art: Essays in the Literature of Witchcraft*, London: Routledge & Kegan Paul, 1977.

ATIYA, Aziz Suryal, *The Crusade in the Later Middle Ages*, London: Methuen, 1938.

— *Crusade, Commerce and Culture*, Bloomington & London: Indiana University Press, 1962.

BAIGENT, M., LEIGH, R., LINCOLN, H., *The Holy Blood and the Holy Grail*, London: Jonathan Cape, 1982.

BARBER, Malcolm, 'The Origins of the Order of the Temple', *Studia Monastica*, XII (1970), pp. 219–40.

— 'James of Molay, the Last Grand Master of the Temple', *Studia Monastica*, XIV (1972), pp. 91–124.

— 'Propaganda in the Middle Ages: the Charges Against the Templars', *Nottingham Medieval Studies*, XVII (1973), pp. 42–57.

— *The Trial of the Templars*, Cambridge: Cambridge UP, 1978.

— 'The World Picture of Philip the Fair', *Journal of Medieval History*, Vol. 8, No. 1 (March 1982), pp. 13–43.

— *The New Knighthood: A History of the Order of the Temple*, Cambridge: Cambridge UP, 1993.

BENTON, J.F., & BISSON, T.H. (Eds), *Medieval Statecraft and the Perspectives of History: Essays by Joseph R. Strayer*, Princeton: Princeton UP, 1971.

BENVENISTI, Meron, *The Crusaders in the Holy Land*, Jerusalem: Israel Universities Press, 1970.

BERGERON, Louis, *Parigi*, Bari: Laterza, 1989.

BERNARD OF CLAIRVAUX, *Liber Ad Milites Templi De Laude Militiae*, in *Sancti Bernardi Opera Omnia*, Ed. J. Mabillon, Paris: Apud Gaume Fratres, Bibliopolas, 1839, Vol.1, pp. 1252–78.

BINI, Telesforo, *Dei Tempieri e del loro Processo in Toscana*, Lucca: La Reale Accademia Lucchese, 1845.

BIVER, Paul & Marie-Louise, *Abbayes, Monastères et Couvents de Paris: des Origines a la fin du XVIIIe Siècle*, Paris: Nouvelles Editions Latines, 1970.

— *Abbayes, Monastères, Couvents de Femmes, à Paris des Origines a la Fin du XVIIIe Siècle*, Paris: Presses Universitaires de France, 1975.

BLANCARD, L., 'Documents relatifs au procès des Templiers en Angleterre', *Revue des Sociétés Savantes*, 4e Ser., VI (Octobre 1867), pp. 414–23.

BORDONOVE, Georges, *La vie quotidienne des Templiers au XIIIe Siècle*, Paris: Hachette, 1975.

— *Les Rois qui ont fait la France: Philippe de Bel, Roi de fer*, Paris: Pygmalion/Gérard Watelet, 1984.

BOUTARIC, Edgard, *La France sous Philippe de Bel: Etude sur les Institutions politiques et administratives du Moyen Age*, Paris: Henri Plon, 1861.

— 'Clément V, Philippe le Bel, et les Templiers', *Revue des Questions Historique*, X (1871), pp. 301–42; XI (1872), pp. 5–40.

BOUVIER, Abbé H., *Histoire de l'Église et de l'Ancien Archidiocèse de Sens, Vol II: De 1122 a 1519*, Amiens: Imprimerie Yvert et Tellier, 1911.

BROOKE, Christopher, 'Heresy and Religious Sentiment: 1000–1250', *Medieval Church and Society: Collected Essays*, London: Sidgwick and Jackson, 1972, pp. 139–61.

BULST-THIELE, Marie Luise, *Sacrae Domus Militiae Templi Hierosolymitani Magistri: Untersuchungen zur Geschichte des Templeordens 1118/9–1314*, Göttingen: Vandenhoeck & Ruprecht (Abhandlungen der Akademie Der Wissenschaften in Göttingen), 1974.

CAUZONS, Th. de, *Histoire de L'Inquisition en France*, Paris: Bloud, 1909, 2 vols.

CHENEY, C.R., 'The Downfall of the Templars and a Letter in their Defence', in *Medieval Texts and Studies*, Oxford: Clarendon Press, 1973, pp. 314–27.

CHRISTIE-MURRAY, David, *A History of Heresy*, London: New English Library, 1976.

CLARK, S., 'Inversion, Misrule and the Meaning of Witchcraft', *Past & Present*, No. 87 (1980), pp. 98–127.

COHN, Norman, *Europe's Inner Demons*, London: Paladin, 1976.

CURRER-BRIGGS, Noel, *The Shroud and the Grail: a Modern Quest for the True Grail*, London: Weidenfeld and Nicolson, 1987.

CURZON, Henri de (Ed), *La Règle du Temple*, Paris: Librairie Renouard, 1886.

— *La Maison du Temple de Paris: Histoire et Description*, Paris: Librairie Hachette, 1888.

DANIEL, Norman, *Islam and the West: The Making of an Image*, Edinburgh: Edinburgh UP, 1960.

— *The Arabs and Medieval Europe*, London: Longman, 1975.

DANIEL-ROPS, H., *Cathedral and Crusade: Studies of the Medieval Church 1050–1350*, London: Dent, 1957.

DELAFORGE, Gaetan, *The Templar Tradition in the Age of Aquarius*, Vermont: Threshold Books, 1987.

DELAVILLE LE ROULX, J., *Documents concernant les Templiers, extraits des Archives de Malte*, Paris: Plon, 1882.

— 'La suppression des Templiers', *Revue des Questions Historiques*, XLVIII (1890), pp. 29–61.

DELISLE, Léopold, *Mémoire sur les Opérations Financières des Templiers* (Mémoires de l'Institut National de France, Académie des Inscriptions et Belles-Lettres, Vol. 33, Part 2), Paris: Imprimerie Nationale, 1888.

— 'Gilles Aicelin, Archevêque de Narbonne et de Rouen', in *Histoire Littéraire de la France*, Vol. XXXII, Paris: Imprimerie Nationale, 1897, pp. 474–502.

DESSUBRÉ, M., *Bibliographie de l'ordre des Templiers*, Paris: Librairie Critique Emile Nourry, 1928.

DIVERRÈS, Armel (Ed.), *La Chronique Métrique Attribuée a Geffroy de Paris*, Strasbourg: Publications de la Faculté des Lettres de l'Université de Strasbourg, 1956.

DOUAIS, C., *L'Inquisition: Ses Origines – Sa Procédure*, Paris: Librairie Plon, 1906.

DUBOIS, Pierre, *De Recuperatione Terre Sancte: Traite de Politique Générale* (Ed. Ch-V. Langlois), Paris: Alphonse Picard, 1891.

EDWARDS, John, 'The Templars in Scotland in the Thirteenth Century', *The Scottish Historical Review*, Vol. 5 (1908), pp. 13–25.

FAVIER, Jean, *Un conseiller de Philippe le Bel: Enguerrand de Marigny*, Paris: Presses Universitaires de France, 1963.

— *Philippe le Bel*, Paris: Fayard, 1978.

FAVREAU, Robert (Ed), *Histoire de Poitiers*, Toulouse: Privat, 1985.

FAWTIER, Robert, *The Capetian Kings of France: Monarchy and Nation 987–1328*, London: Macmillan, 1983.

FERRIS, Eleanor, 'The Financial Relations of the Knights Templar to the English Crown', *American Historical Review*, VIII (October 1902), pp. 1–17.

FIDENZIO OF PADUA, *Liber Recuperationis Terrae Sanctae*, in Bio-Bibliografia della Terra Sancta, Ed. G. Golubovich, Vol 2., Florence: Quaracchi, 1913.

FLICHE, A., Thouzellier, C., Azais, Y., *Histoire de l'Eglise, Vol. X: La Chrétienté romaine (1198–1274)*, Paris: Bloud & Gay, 1950.

FOREY, A.J., *The Templars in the Corona of Aragon*, London: Oxford UP, 1973.

— 'The Military Orders in the Crusading Proposals of the Late-Thirteenth and Early-Fourteenth Centuries', *Traditio*, Vol.36 (1980), pp. 317–45.

— 'Women and the Military Orders in the Twelfth and Thirteenth Centuries', *Studia Monastica*, 1987, pp. 63–92.

GABRIELI, Francesco (Ed), *Storici arabi delle Crociate*, Turin: Einaudi, 1987.

GATTO, Ludovico, *La Francia di Filippo IV Il Bello (1284–1314)*, Rome: Bulzoni, 1973.

GÉRAUD, H., *Paris sous Philippe le Bel, D'Après des Documents Originaux*, Paris: De L'Imprimerie de Crapelet, 1837.

— (Ed), *Chronique Latine de Guillaume de Nangis de 1113 a 1300, avec le Continuations de cette Chronique de 1300 a 1368*, Paris: Jules Renouard, 1843, 2 vols.

GILMOUR-BRYSON, Anne, *The Trial of the Templars in the Papal State and the Abruzzi*, Città del Vaticano: Biblioteca Apostolica Vaticana, 1982.

GRANSDEN, Antonia (Ed), *The Chronicle of Bury St Edmunds (1212–1301)*, London: Nelson, 1964.

GROUSSET, René, *Histoires des Croisades du Royaume Franc de Jérusalem*, Paris: Plon, 1934–6, 3 vols.

GUERRIERI, Giovanni, *I Cavalieri Templari nel Regno di Sicilia*, Trani: Vecchi, 1909.

GUI, Bernard, 'E Floribus Chronicorum, se catalogo Romanorum pontificium, Necnon et Chronico Regum Francorum', in *Recueil des Historiens des Gaules et de France*, Vol. 21, Paris: Imprimerie Impériale, 1855, pp. 690–734.

— *Practica Inquisitionis Heretice Pravitatis*, Ed. C. Douais, Paris: A Picard, 1886.

— *Manuel de l'Inquisiteur*, Ed. G. Mollat, Paris: Librairie Ancienne Honoré Champion, 1906, 2 vols.

GUIGNIAUT & DE WAILLY (Eds), 'Philippi Quarti Mansiones et itinera', in *Recueil des Historiens des Gaules et de France*, Vol. 21, Paris: Imprimerie Impériale, 1855, pp. 430–64.

GUILLEMAIN, Bernard, *La Cour Pontificale D'Avignon 1309–1376: Etude d'une Société*, Paris: Editions E. De Boccard, 1966.

BIBLIOGRAPHY

HAMILTON, Bernard, *The Medieval Inquisition*, London: Edward Arnold, 1980.

HAMMER-PURGSTALL, Joseph von, 'Mysterium Baphometis revelatum', *Fundgruben des Orients*, VI (1818), pp. 1–120; pp. 445–99.

— *The History of the Assassins, derived from oriental sources*, New York: Burt Franklin, 1968 (Reprint of 1835 edition).

HANCOCK, Graham, *The Sign and the Seal: A Quest for the Lost Ark of the Covenant*, London: Heinemann, 1992.

HAUREAU, Barthéemy, 'Guillaume de Baufet, Evêque de Paris', in *Histoire Littéraire de la France*, Vol. XXXII, Paris: Imprimerie Nationale, 1897, pp. 469–74.

HEFELE, Charles-Joseph, 'Les trois sessions du Concile de Vienne, 1311–12', in *Histoire des Conciles, d'après les Documents Originaux*, Vol I, Part 2: *Quinzième Concile Oecuménique à Vienne, 1311–12* (trs. into French by H. Leclercq), Paris: Letouzey et Ané, 1915, pp. 643–661.

HILL, Sir George, *A History of Cyprus*, Cambridge: Cambridge UP, 1948–52, 4 vols.

HILL, Rosalind (Ed), *Gesta Francorum: The Deeds of the Franks and other Pilgrims to Jerusalem*, Oxford: Clarendon Press, 1972.

HILLGARTH, J.N., *Ramon Lull and Lullism in Fourteenth Century France*, Oxford: Clarendon Press, 1971.

— *The Spanish Kingdoms 1250–1516*, Oxford: Clarendon Press, 1976, 2 vols.

HODGSON, Marshall G.C., *The Order of the Assassins: The Struggle of the Early Nizari Isma'ilis against the Islamic World*, The Hague: Mouton, 1955.

HORNE, Alexander, *King Solomon's Temple in Masonic Tradition*, Wellingborough: Aquarian Press, 1972.

HOUSLEY, N., *The Avignon Papacy and the Crusades 1305–1378*, Oxford: Oxford UP, 1986.

— *The Later Crusades, 1274–1580: from Lyons to Alcazar*, Oxford: Oxford UP, 1992.

HUFGARD, M. Kilian, 'Saint Bernard of Clairvaux', in *Medieval Studies*, Vol. II, Edwin Mellen Press, 1989.

IBN-ALATYR, 'Extrait de la Chronique intitulée Kamel-Altevarykh', *Recueil des Historiens des Croisades: Historiens Orientaux*, Vol. I, Paris: Imprimerie Nationale, 1872, pp. 187–744.

JEAN DE SAINT-VICTOR, 'Excerpta e Memoriali Historiarum', in *Recueil des Historiens des Gaules et de France*, Vol. 21, Paris: Imprimerie Impériale, 1855, pp. 630–76.

JONES, W.R., 'Political Uses of Sorcery in Medieval Europe', *The Historian*, XXIV (1972), pp. 670–87.

KEEN, Maurice, *Chivalry*, New Haven & London: Yale UP, 1984.

KIECKHEFER, Richard, *European Witch Trials: Their Foundation in Popular and Learned Culture, 1300–1500*, London: Routledge & Kegan Paul, 1976.

— *Magic in the Middle Ages*, Cambridge: Cambridge UP, 1989.

KORS, A.C. & PETERS, E. (Eds), *Witchcraft in Europe, 1100–1700: A Documentary History*, London: Dent, 1973.

LADNER, Gerhart B., 'Homo Viator: Medieval Views on Alienation and Order', *Speculum*, XLII (1967), pp. 233–59.

LAJARD, Félix, 'Guillaume de Paris, Dominicain', in *Histoire Littéraire de la France*, Vol. XXVII, Paris: Imprimerie Nationale, 1877, pp. 140–74.

LAMBERT, Malcolm, *Medieval Heresy: Popular movements from the Gregorian Reform to the Reformation*, Oxford: Blackwell, 1992.

LA MONTE, John L., *Feudal Monarchy in the Latin Kingdom of Jerusalem*, Cambridge, Mass: The Medieval Academy of America, 1932.

LANGLOIS, Ch.-V., 'Les Procès des Templiers d'après des documents nouveaux', *Revue des Deux Mondes*, CIII (1891), pp. 382–421.

— 'Doléances du clergé de France au temps de Philippe le Bel', *Revue Bleue*, 5th ser., IV (1905), pp. 329–33; pp. 486–90.

LEA, Henry Charles, *Superstition and Force*, Philadelphia: Lea Brothers, 1892.

— 'The absolution formula of the Templars', Papers of the American Society of Church History, 5 (1893), pp. 35–8.

— *The History of the Inquisition in the Middle Ages*, New York: Macmillan, 1908, 3 vols.

LECLER, Joseph, *Vienne (Histoire des Conciles Oecuméniques*, Vol 8), Paris: Éditions de l'Orante, 1964.

LEES, Beatrice, *Records of the Templars in England in the Twelfth Century: the Inquest of 1185 with illustrative charters and documents*, London: Oxford UP, 1935.

LEFF, Gordon, *Medieval Thought*, Harmondsworth: Pelican, 1958.

— 'Heresy and the Decline of the Medieval Church', *Past & Present*, No. 20 (November 1961), pp. 26–51.

— *Heresy in the Later Middle Ages*, Manchester: Manchester UP, 1967, 2 vols.

LEGMAN, G., *The Guilt of the Templars*, New York: Basic Books, 1966.

LÉONARD, E.G., *Introduction au Cartulaire Manuscrit du Temple (1150–1317), Constitué par le Marquis D'Albon*, Paris: Edouard Champion, 1930.

LERNER, Robert E., 'Medieval Prophecy and Religious Dissent', *Past & Present*, No. 72 (August 1976), pp. 3–24.

LEWIS, Bernard, *The Assassins: A Radical Sect in Islam*, London: Weidenfeld & Nicholson, 1967.

LEYS, A.M., 'The Forfeiture of the Lands of the Templars in England', in F.M. Powicke (Ed), *Oxford Essays in Medieval History Presented to H.E. Salter*, Oxford: 1934, pp. 155–63.

LITTLE, Lester K., *Religious Poverty and the Profit Economy in Medieval Europe*, London: Elek, 1978.

LIZERAND, Georges, *Clément V et Philippe le Bel*, Paris: Hachette, 1910.

— (Ed.), *Le Dossier de L'Affaire des Templiers, Edité et Traduit*, Paris: Honoré Champion, 1923.

LOMBARD-JOURDAN, Anne, *Paris – Genèse de la Ville: La Rive Droite de la Seine des Origines à 1223*, Paris: Editions du Centre National de la Recherche Scientifique, 1976.

— *Aux Origines de Paris: La Genèse de la Rive Droite Jusqu'en 1223*, Paris: Éditions du Centre National de la Recherche Scientifique, 1985.

MAALOUF, Amin, *The Crusades Through Arab Eyes*, London: Al Saqi Books, 1984.

MACDONELL, Sir John, *Historical Trials*, Oxford: Clarendon Press, 1927.

MACKENZIE, Kenneth, *The Royal Masonic Cyclopaedia*, Wellingborough: Aquarian Press, 1987 (1st Ed. 1877).

MAILLARD de CHAMBURE, Charles Hippolyte, *Règles et Statuts Secrets des Templiers*, Paris: Brockhaus & Avenarius, 1840.

MANSELLI, Raoul, *L'Eresia del Male*, Naples: Morano, 1963.

— 'De la "persuasio" à la "coercitio"', *Le Crédo, la Morale et l'Inquisition*, (*Cahiers de Fanjeaux*, 6), Toulouse (1971), pp. 175–9

— *I Fenomeni di Devianza nel Medio Evo: Le Devianze nella Società Ecclesiastica*, Turin: G. Giappichelli, 1972.

MARSHALL, Christopher, *Warfare in the Latin East 1192–1291*, Cambridge: Cambridge UP, 1992.

MARTIN, Edward J., *The Trial of the Templars*, London: George Allen and Unwin, 1928.

MELVILLE, Marion, *La Vie des Templiers*, Paris: Gallimard, 1951.

MICHAEL the Syrian, *Chronique de Michel le Syrien*, Vol. III, ed. J.B. Chabot, Paris: Ernest Leroux, 1905.

MICHELET, Jules (Ed.), *Le Procès des Templiers*, Paris: Imprimerie Royale (Collection de Documents Inédits sur l'Histoire de France), 1841 and 1851, 2 vols (Reprint, Paris: Les Editions du C.T.H.S., 1987).

MIROT, L. & A., *Manuel de géographie historique de la France*, Paris: Picard, 1980.

MOLLAT, G., *Les Papes d'Avignon (1305–1378)*, Paris: Letouzey & Ané, 1949.

MONTER, E. William (Ed), *European Witchcraft*, New York: John Wiley, 1969.

— *Ritual, Myth and Magic in Early Modern Europe*, Brighton: The Harvester Press, 1983.

MOORE, R.I., 'The Origins of Medieval Heresy', *History*, Vol. 55 (1970), pp. 21–36.

MORGHEN, Raffaello, *Medioevo cristiano*, Bari: Laterza, 1978.

MÜLLER, Ewald, *Das Konzil von Vienne 1311–1312: seine Quellen und seine Geschichte*, Münster in Westfalen: Aschendorff, 1934.

MURRAY, Alexander, 'Piety and Impiety in Thirteenth-Century Italy', *Studies in Church History, 8: Popular Belief and Practice*, Cambridge: Cambridge UP, 1972, pp. 83–106.

NEU, H., *Bibliografie des Templer-Ordens 1927–1965*, Bonn: Wissenschaftliches Archiv GMBH, 1965.

PANOFSKY, Erwin, 'Abbot Suger of St-Denis', in *Meaning in the Visual Arts*, Harmondsworth: Peregrine, 1970, pp. 137–80.

PARTNER, Peter, *The Murdered Magicians: The Templars and their Myth*, Oxford: Oxford UP, 1982.

PEGUES, Franklin J., *The Lawyers of the Last Capetians*, Princeton: Princeton UP, 1962.

PERKINS, Clarence, 'The Trial of the Knights Templars in England', *English Historical Review*, XCV (July 1909), pp. 432–47.

— 'The Wealth of the Knights Templar in England, and the Disposition of it after their Dissolution', *American Historical Review*, XV (1910), pp. 252–63.

— 'The Knights Templars in the British Isles', *English Historical Review*, XCVIII (April 1910), pp. 209–30.

PICOT, J. (Ed), *Documents relatifs aux États Généraux et Assemblées réunis sous Philippe le Bel*, Paris: 1901.

PLONGERON, Bernard, *Le Diocèse de Paris: Vol I, Des Origines à la Révolution*, Paris: Beauchesne (*Histoire des Diocèses de France*, Vol. 20), 1987.

PORT, Célestin (Ed), 'Liber Guillelmi Majoris', in *Mélanges Historiques: Choix de Documents*, Paris: Imprimerie Nationale (Collection de Documents Inédits sur l'Histoire de France), 1877, Vol. 2, pp. 203–537.

POWICKE, Sir Maurice, *The Thirteenth Century: 1216–1307*, Oxford: Clarendon Press, 1955.

PRAWER, Joshua, *The Latin Kingdom of Jerusalem: European Colonisation in the Middle Ages*, London: Weidenfeld & Nicholson, 1972.

— *Crusader Institutions*, Oxford: Clarendon, 1980.

PROBST-BIRABEN, J.-H., *Les Mystères des Templiers*, Paris: 1947.

PRUTZ, Hans, *Entwicklung und Untergang des Tempelherrenordens, mit Benutzung Bisher Ungedruckter Materialen*, Berlin: Grote, 1888.

PURCELL, Maureen, 'Changing Views of Crusade in the Thirteenth Century', *The Journal of Religious History*, Vol. 7, No. 1 (June 1972), pp. 3–19.

RAYNOUARD, M., *Monumens Historiques Relatifs à la Condamnation des Chevaliers du Temple, et l'Abolition de leur Ordre*, Paris: Adrien Égron, 1813

REINACH, Salomon, 'La Tête magique des Templiers', *Revue de l'Histoire des Religions*, LXIII (1911), pp. 25–39.

RENAN, E., 'Bertrand de Got, pape sous le nom Clément V', Histoire littéraire de France, XXVIII (1880), pp. 278–314.

RILEY-SMITH, Jonathan, *The Knights of St John in Jerusalem and Cyprus c. 1050–1310*, London: Macmillan, 1967.

— 'Crusading as an Act of Love', *History*, Vol. 65 (1980), pp. 177–92.

ROBERTS, J.M., *The Mythologies of the Secret Societies*, London: 1972.

ROBINSON, John J., *Born in Blood*, London: Century, 1990.

ROULEAU, Bernard, *Le Trace des Rues de Paris*, Paris: Presses du CNRS, 1988.

RUNCIMAN, Steven, *A History of the Crusades*, Harmondsworth: Penguin, 1978, 3 vols.

— *The Medieval Manichee: A Study of the Christian Dualist Heresy*, Cambridge: Cambridge UP, 1982.

RUSSELL, Jeffrey Burton, *Witchcraft in the Middle Ages*, Ithaca and London: Cornell UP, 1972.

SCHLUMBERGER, Gustave, *Prise de Saint-Jean-d'Acre en l'an 1291 par l'armée du Soudan d'Egypte*, Paris: Plon, 1914.

SCHOTTMÜLLER, Konrad, *Der Untergang des Templer-Ordens, mit Urkundlichen und Kritischen Beitragen*, Berlin: Ernst Siegfried Mittler, 1887, 2 vols.

SETTON, Kenneth M., (General Editor), *A History of the Crusades*, Madison, Milwaukee & London: Wisconsin UP, 1969–75, Vol I: *The First Hundred Years*, and Vol II: *The Later Crusades 1189–1311*.

SEWARD, Desmond, *The Monks of War: The Military Religious Orders*, London: Eyre Methuen, 1972.

SMAIL, R.C., *Crusading Warfare (1097–1193)*, Cambridge: Cambridge UP, 1956.

SOUTHERN, R.W., *Western Society and the Church in the Middle Ages*, Harmondsworth: Penguin, 1970.

— *Western Views of Islam in the Middle Ages*, Cambridge, Mass.: Harvard UP, 1962.

STEVENSON, David, *The Origins of Freemasonry*, Cambridge: Cambridge UP, 1990.

STRAYER, Joseph R., *The Reign of Philip the Fair*, Princeton: Princeton UP, 1980.

THEODERICH: *Theoderich's Description of the Holy Place* (circa AD 1172) trs. & ed. Aubrey Stewart), London: Palestine Pilgrim's Text Society, V, 1896.

TIERNEY, Brian, *The Origin of Papal Infallibility 1150–1350*, Leiden: E.J. Brill, 1972.

ULLMANN, Walter, 'The Defence of the Accused in the Medieval Inquisition', *Irish Ecclesiastical Record*, LXXIII (1950), pp. 481–9.

— *The Individual and Society in the Middle Ages*, Baltimore: Johns Hopkins UP, 1966.

UPTON-WARD, J.M., (Trs.), *The Rule of the Templars: The French Text of the Rule of the Order of the Knights Templar*, Woodbridge: Boydell & Brewer Press, 1992.

VACANDARD, E., *Étude Historique and Critique sur la Pourvoir Coercitif de l'Église*, Paris: Bloud, 1912.

BIBLIOGRAPHY

VALOIS, Noël, 'Jacques de Thérines, Cistercien', in *Histoire Littéraire de la France*, Vol. XXXIV, Paris: Imprimerie Nationale, 1895, pp. 179–219.

VIARD, Jules, 'Le Concile de Paris de Mai 1310', in *Revue des Questions Historiques*, 3° serie. Vol. XIX (1931), pp. 358–61.

— (Ed), *Les Grandes Chroniques de France*, Vol. 8: *Philippe III le Hardi, Philip IV le Bel, Louis X Hutin, Philippe V le Long*, Paris: Librairie Ancienne Honoré Champion, 1934.

VILLANI, Giovanni, *Croniche di Giovanni, Matteo e Filippo Villani, secondo le Migliori Stampe e corredate di Note Filologiche e Storiche*, Trieste: Sezione Letterario-Artistica del Lloyd Austriaco, 1857, 2 vols.

VIOLLET, Paul, 'Bérenger Frédol, canoniste', in *Histoire Littéraire de la France*, Vol. XXXIV, Paris: Imprimerie Nationale, 1895, pp. 62–178.

— 'Les interrogatoires de Jacques de Molai, grand maitre du Temple, conjectures', *Académie des inscriptions et belles lettres*, XXXVIII (Part 2 (1911), pp. 121–36).

VITRY, Jacques de, *History of Jerusalem* (Trs. Aubrey Stewart), London: Palestine Pilgrims' Text Society, XI, 1896.

WAKEFIELD, W.L., *Heresy, Crusade and Inquisition in Southern France, 1100–1250*, London: George Allen & Unwin, 1974.

WATT, W.M., *The Influence of Islam on Medieval Europe*, Edinburgh: Edinburgh UP, 1972.

WILLIAM OF TYRE, *A History of Deeds done beyond the Sea* (trs. and annotated by Emily Atwater Babcock & A.C. Krey), New York: Octagon Books, 1976, 2 vols.

WILSON, Ian, *The Turin Shroud*, Harmondsworth: Penguin, 1979.

WOOD, Herbert, 'The Templars in Ireland', *Proceedings of the Royal Irish Academy*, Vol. XXVI, Section C, No.14, pp. 371–5.

INDEX

Abelard Peter, 105
Abu'l-Fida, chronicler, 31
Abu L-Mahasin, chronicler, 33
Acre, 16, 28, 29, 124, 168
  fall of, 19, 31–3, 40
Adam de Inferno, Templar, 150, 152, 203
Adam of Wedale, 131
Agarni, Jean, provost, 83
Aicelin, Gilles, archbishop of Narbonne,
  41, 44, 45–7, 48, 53, 55, 83, 85, 88,
  111, 132, 133, 134, 135, 157, 160, 168,
  170, 173, 188, 189, 190, 192–3, 194–5,
  216, 219, 236, 245, 248
  absences from court, 113–14, 186, 191,
  198
  hearings at his private residence,
  211–12
  leaves court whilst in session, 194–5
Aicelin, Jean, abbot of Bourges &
  Clermont, 46
Aicelin, Hughes, cardinal Archbishop of
  Ostia, 46
Aimery de Villiers le Duc, 205–7, 212
Al-Ashraf, Sultan, 29, 32, 40
Albert I of Hapsburg, Holy Roman
  Emperor, 75
Albertus Magnus, 96
Alcantara, order of, 18
Alexander III, pope, 27
Amanieu de Fargues, nephew of Clement
  V, 56
Amalric I, king of Jerusalem, 27, 234
Amaury de la Roche, Templar Master of
  France, 64

Amaury de Lusignan, governor of
  Cyprus, 214
Amiens, bishop of, his residence in Paris,
  140
Amisuis, Master, archdeacon of Orléans,
  199, 212
André de Montbard, Templar, 20
André le Mortoier, Templar, 155, 161,
  203
Anjou, Charles I of, 4
Antioch, 16, 17
Anudei, Robert, 108, 150, 152
Aquinas, St Thomas, 96
Arius, priest of Alexander, 244
Arnaud, brother to Clement V, 56
Arnaud d'Auch, bishop of Poitiers, later
  cardinal, 74, 262, 239
Arnaud de Canteloup, cardinal, 247
Arnaud de Nouvel, cardinal, 247, 263
Arnaud de Pellegrue, cardinal, 247
Artois, count Robert of, 4, 29, 30
Assassins, the, xi, 234, 235
  as Ismailis, 27
Audebon, Guillaume, Templar, 231
Avignon, 56–7
Aymé d'Osilier, Templar Marshall, 214,
  215
Aymerici, Elias, Templar, 15, 115, 149,
  161, 193, 203
  his defence testimony, 142–3
Aymo de Pratim, Templar, 151

Baigent, Michael, ix, x, xiii, 225
Baldwin II, king of Jerusalem, 19, 20, 22

282

Coulours, 203, Dempuho, 231,
Espancès, 231, Etampes, 64, Gard,
11, Langy-le-Sec, 224, Mas Deu, 25,
259, Mont Ferrand, 143, Mormant,
182, Oisy, 203, Orléans, 133,
Oysimont, 173 Payen, 63, Payns, 10,
Soissy, 225, Sommereaux, 224,
Syourac, 231, Toulouse, 179
Rule, their, 16, 19, 20–22, 122–9, 131,
166–7, 228
 Absolution in, 127–8
 Reception ceremonies in, 125–6,
 163–4
 Secrecy in, 128–9
Scotland, in, x
Trials outside Paris,
 Cyprus, 234–5
 England, 216–18
 Florence and Lucca, 60
 Mallorca, 216
 Papal States, 59, 139, 215–16
 Scotland, 131
Temple, London, 98, 100, 101
Theoderich, pilgrim, 18
Tiron, abbot of, his residence in Paris,
107, 156
Tomaso da Modena, 228
Torteville, Robert, Templar Master in
London, 233
Tortosa, 16, 28–9
Tripoli, 16
Turin Shroud, 12–13, 64, 123
Tyler, Wat, xi
Tyre, 29

Ursula, St, 226–8
Usuma ibn Munqidh, emir of Shaizar and
chronicler, 234

Vernondus de Santoni, Templar, 17
Versequi (or Versequin), Nicholas,
Templar, 116, 152, 203
Vigier, Robert, Templar, 143, 149, 161,
219, 220
Villani, Giovanni, chronicler, xiii, 10–11,
49, 78, 265, 266, 269, 272

Vitale, sister to Clement V, 56

Wilde, Oscar, 124
William de la More, Templar Master in
London, 13
William of Tyre, archbishop, 23, 26, 130,
234
Wilson, Ian, xii
Witchcraft, 65–6
Wycliff, John, xi

Zengi, Imad ed-din, sultan, 26